Dr. Julio Gonzalez

The Federalist Pages

Dr. Julio Gonzalez is an attorney, orthopaedic surgeon, and published author residing in Venice, Florida. He also serves in the Florida House of Representatives for District 74.

Born in Miami, Florida, after his parents fled Cuba's communist regime in 1961, Dr. Gonzalez obtained his medical degree from the University of Miami School of Medicine and his law degree from Stetson University College of Law where he graduated with honors. He served as a flight surgeon with the United States Navy from 1990 through 1995, deploying twice aboard the U.S.S. America to the Mediterranean Sea, the Persian Gulf, Yugoslavia, and Somalia. He has published a book on health care reform and is a member of the Florida Bar.

He is married to Dr. Gina Arabitg, a gynecologist, with whom he has two daughters, Monica and Jessica.

Dr. Gonzalez is available for speaking engagements and may be contacted at *gonzopod@gmail.com*.

Learn more at *www.thefederalistpages.com*.

To Mary Anne
my favorite author!
Best wishes.
26 Nov 17

THE FEDERALIST PAGES

A Constitutional Path to Restoring America's Greatness

Bardolf & Company

The Federal Pages
A Constitutional Path to Restoring America's Greatness

ISBN 978-1-938842-31-3

Published by Bardolf & Company
5430 Colewood Pl.
Sarasota, FL 34232
941-232-0113
www.bardolfandcompany.com

Cover design by Shaw Creative
www.shawcreativegroup.com

**To my wife, Dr. Gina Arabitg,
the love of my life,**

and

**to our daughters, Jessica and Monica,
the objects of every bit of our efforts.**

The FEDERALIST Pages

A Constitutional Path to Restoring America's Greatness

Julio Gonzalez, M.D., J.D.

Bardolf & Company
Sarasota, Florida

Contents

Acknowledgments

No man is an island, and no great venture can be undertaken alone. This work is the culmination of the efforts of many who have supported me and encouraged me to bring *The Federalist Pages* to its fruition. Of course, for me there is no possible success without the selfless support of my wife, Dr. Gina Arabitg, who somehow has found it fitting to believe in my abilities to persevere and achieve when I did not. My two daughters, Monica and Jessica Gonzalez, have been incredibly patient in their resolve to see me through this. You two are the best!

A special mention goes to Jessica, the burgeoning editor who slaved through a substantial part of her summer to make sure that she approved of every word and every punctuation in her dad's work. Thank you!

I also send my greatest appreciations to Rod Thomson. I am unworthy of your trust, but incredibly grateful and lucky to have gotten it.

A special thank you goes to Chris Angermann who produced this book despite tight deadlines and a hurried schedule. We had no time to spare in our efforts to deliver our message to the public, and Chris wasted none of it.

To Mac Stevenson, my consultant, and Vickie Brill and Amy Miller, my assistants, a special thanks to you for all your concerns and worry. Really. . . it'll be fine because I know in my heart these are the right things to say.

To my medical office staff, who worked furiously to make sure I got out of the office in time so I could get through law school and later so I could add more characters to this file, I thank you for your patience and resilience.

To my mom and dad, who fled tyranny so the mere concept of me could have a chance in life. I can never even come close to repaying you for the privilege of being your son.

And most of all, I thank God for all the innumerable blessings He has given me; certainly not the least of which is the privilege of being born on American soil, and for granting me the opportunity to defend and promote this, the greatest form of government ever created by man.

Preface

Growing up, I saw, first hand, America's greatness and the miracle that is the freedom laid out by the Founders of our great country. For my family, the wonder of political freedom and liberty was a palpable part of their daily existence and a gift to be celebrated and revered. My parents had seen the destruction of a democratic system of government. Residents of Havana, Cuba, my parents saw the claws of oppression descend upon their home in the form of a communist regime aiming to suppress any semblance of dissension against the Revolution.

My father was a young clerk working for the American embassy when President Dwight D. Eisenhower, incensed at the increasing hostilities from communist Cuba, found it necessary to close the American embassy. Swiftly, the American government offered passage to embassy employees and their immediate families.

The son of a furniture maker, my father acted quickly to escape the embattled island with his parents and sister. Within weeks, they were in the United States with little more than the shirts on their backs. Regardless of how trying their existence may have been in foreign soil with no money and no job, they thanked God daily for the opportunity this great country had afforded them as they heard of the tragic and sometimes fatal fates of their friends and loved ones back home.

My mother, in the meantime, was the teenaged daughter of a seamstress. On the day Eisenhower closed the American embassy in Cuba, and while my father was getting instructions from his superiors at the embassy, my mother and her best friend were directed to remain outside the embassy gates so they could run inside and beg for asylum should the embassy reopen. Obediently, my mother slept that night on a concrete slab, knowing that she was the best hope for her mother and her to escape for freedom.

Her plan never came to fruition as the embassy, some 55 years later, has not yet reopened. Instead, she was "declared" by my uncle who had managed to find safe passage to Miami. Despite the close proximity to my father on that fateful day, her chance encounter with my dad would have to wait for another day and another country.

For my parents, the conversation was always one of admiration for America, but always with the fear that the same process that destroyed their country would take place in their newly adopted home.

As a kid, I certainly did not know the meaning of these concepts or concerns. But as I came to understand their plight, it became evident just how important their vision for our future was and the reasons why they so unabashedly treasured the freedoms enjoyed by this nation's citizens.

Now that I appreciate our liberties, I have come to guard them just as zealously as my parents do theirs because I have seen what losing those freedoms does to a person's soul.

Decades ago, I was commissioned an ensign in the United States Naval Reserve and took an oath to support and defend the Constitution of the United States. This work is a direct consequence of that oath, not only because I dearly love this country that so graciously opened its doors to my parents so they may be free, but because I honestly believe that a robust and strong Constitution is the only guarantee we Americans have at continued freedom, continued prosperity, and at continued happiness. It is for its protection and promotion that I submit this volume.

Please forgive the title: *The Federalist Pages.* As the reader knows, this is a shameless bastardization of *The Federalist Papers*, that historic compilation of essays delivered by Alexander Hamilton, James Madison, and John Jay to the people of New York in defense of the Constitution and for the government it described. That this treatise may share any part of such a monumental work strikes me as somewhat arrogant. In my defense, the logic of the name is inseparably intertwined with the purpose of the work's task; for if Hamilton, Madison, and Jay set out to defend their proposed Constitution with a series of federalist papers under separate cover, then shouldn't a work written some 227 years later whose sole focus is to justify the continued relevance of the Constitution and bound by a single cover be named *The Federalist Pages*?

Undeserving as this work's title may be, the task of salvaging the foundations of our nation is far too great to worry about issues of unworthiness and unsuitability. For if the creation of this great nation required the labor of every tattered hand capable of carrying a musket, every frostbitten foot able to propel a warrior onto the path of battle, and every visionary able to transcribe his ideas for a better future onto a blank page, then the effort to restore the magnificence of what they created will require the same selfless sacrifice of every abled soul believing in the cause of liberty and the fight against oppression and tyranny.

And lest we forget what's at stake in this mission. If we do not succeed at salvaging our great Republic, then America and her great experiment will be remembered as the idealistic but doomed dream of a bunch of farmers who became intoxicated with visions of a human existence that could never be sustained.

Many will call out the incompleteness of the historical considerations within the pages of this volume. That shortcoming is, I admit, completely and indefensibly accurate. But this is due only to the sheer magnitude and complexity of addressing the consequences of the actions of our politicians, our judges, and our citizens over the span of eleven score and seven years. I set out only to address those issues that, to me, are the most impactful upon the nation's character, her collective soul, and her future. These issues include the erosion of the limitations of power upon our federal government, the intrusions into the freedom of the people to publicly and collectively worship their Creator, the existence of a legislative environment caustic to the preeminence of the family as a primary societal pillar, the hatred and injustice that thus far has characterized the interactions between the races, and the disregard of the self-imposed constitutional restrictions placed upon our elected officials. These are the issues I chose to tackle, not because they are the only ones that challenge us, but because they are, in my opinion, the most imminently threatening to our continued existence. Consequently, if this work suffers from historical incompleteness, then may the limited considerations it does undertake be equally as measured and just.

Finally, and ironically, there are those who say I spend too much time on historical considerations. They inform me of their anticipation at hearing some recommendation at solving the problems that afflict us, but instead find that I continue to elicit the historical context of the issues. That so called problem, I believe, is not the work's weakness, but its strength, for if we are truly to solve the problems afflicting our great nation, then we must understand how it is that we got into the mess we find ourselves in today; if we are to quote our Founders, then we must acknowledge their biases, shortcomings and downright mistakes; and if we are to propose changes to our most sacred document, then we can only benefit from considering the unintended effects of those who have tread the perilous paths we find ourselves pursuing.

So it is into history that I dive, sometimes exhaustingly and sometimes incompletely, but it is that very history upon which I will rely in rectifying our station. However, if it is my recommendations you seek, then I invite you to jump to Chapter 5 where I make my proposals for a better nation and a grander American society. But know that these recommendations, without the historical insights leading to their formulation, will seem hollow and perhaps even unfounded. I remind you that it is only through the thorough evaluation of the paths we have traversed that the necessary corrections to our future become painfully clear.

Ultimately, despite this work's strengths and weaknesses, I submit it only with the greatest love for, and deference to, our great country.

Julio Gonzalez, M.D., J.D.
Venice, Florida
August 2016

Prologue

Undoubtedly, our United States of America is an exceptional country. No other nation has afforded such a wealth of opportunities to its citizens, and none has provided an environment conducive to such immense achievements in such little time. But these are not the primary reasons for her exceptionality. Rather, America's greatness stems from three foundational qualities: 1) her people's fervent faith in God; 2) a constitutional foundation for laws that protect the rights, properties, and liberties of her citizens; and 3) an economic system that incentivizes personal achievement and rewards innovation.

Over the past century, however, America has relaxed her jealous protections over these precious foundational attributes. Her peoples' reliance on government has increased at the expense of their reliance on God and family. Her citizens' sense of morals and ethics has diminished. Americans valuation of individual achievement has eroded. And these trends have continued unchecked at a time when she is faced with some of the most daunting challenges in her history.

Traditionally, when faced with common enemies, Americans have relied on their strength and on their seemingly unending resolve to persevere. However, today, Americans doubt whether their great country will meet the overwhelming challenges facing her. They wonder if their nation even has the capacity to succeed. But in their doubts, they forget the tools that propelled the nation to greatness.

Two hundred twenty seven years ago, our country was on the brink of collapse. There was no set of rights enshrined around the individual, no workable structure for governance, no centralized system of currency, no authority for creating and maintaining a standing militia, no ability to compel the states or the people to supply funds in support of the national government, no consolidated leader, no ability to regulate commerce between the various states, and no unified approach to relations with other nations. Faced with these overwhelming challenges, the nation's leaders united to create a groundbreaking framework through which to forge a new nation. Despite the immensity of the issues that divided them, despite their wide cultural differences, and despite their questionable authority to even engage in a meeting to create a new government, these men identified the problems poised to destroy their country and arrived at a solution. That solution was the United States Constitution. This astonishing document not only saved the nation from certain ruin, it propelled the United States to unparalleled greatness.

True to their belief in a government grounded upon the will of the people, the Framers would not force their plan upon their fellow citizens. Instead, they demanded it be the citizenry's decision whether to approve their blueprint for a new government.

In the state of New York, three men—Alexander Hamilton, James Madison, and John Jay—combined their efforts to dispel the misrepresentations and skepticisms that emerged among the populace. Towards this end, they wrote a series of 85 articles between 1787 and 1788 designed for publication in the popular press. The articles, named *The Federalist* by Hamilton, were eventually known as *The Federalist Papers*, and through them, these men created, in the words of Thomas Jefferson, "the best commentary on the principles of government which ever was written."* Largely due to their efforts cataloguing these timeless principles, the Constitution was ultimately adopted, the country was saved, and the United States was born.

Today, we face different challenges, some of which are possibly as threatening as those that afflicted our fledging country at the time of its formation. Once again, the citizenry finds itself looking for solutions. Now, as then,

---

* Thomas Jefferson to James Madison, November 18, 1788, Paris, France.

there is a need for leadership to rise and boldly face these problems. But our abilities to respond are in many ways more hampered than they were in the 1780s and 1790s, for back then, the people had faith that they would eventually overcome their challenges. Today's America finds itself questioning whether the tools necessary to solve the problems plaguing modern American society are even available.

I submit that the solutions and tools needed to meet and overcome the nation's challenges are not unobtainable. They have merely been abandoned.

Corresponding with this idea, the purpose of this work is to reexamine and re-acknowledge the greatness of America's foundations and to identify how those foundations are as equally applicable today as they were 227 years ago. Our voyage begins by recounting the events leading to the creation of our Constitution and the forces of human nature the Framers tried to address in devising their new government. We will visit the original workings of our Constitution as the Framers intended them and discuss how its present manifestation differs from the original version. We will then examine some of the factors that weakened our great nation and evaluate how they may be overcome with the aim of restoring a nation.

Ultimately, I hope this effort will be part of a bigger movement aimed at allowing our nation to overcome the challenges afflicting her. Most of all, I hope the insights gained from this work endow its readers with a renewed vigor for the pursuit of a greater happiness and a resolve to aim for levels of national greatness that had not previously been achieved.

Julio Gonzalez

Chapter 1

The Most Wonderful Document Ever Created by Man

It has been called "the most wonderful work ever struck off at a given time by the brain and purpose of man" by no less a figure than William E. Gladstone, the prime minister of the country whose oppression and abuses inevitably led to its ratification. [1] Two hundred twenty seven years later, the Constitution is still the supreme law of the American Republic and the oldest active constitutional document in existence.

But no colossal achievement in human development occurs in a vacuum, and the events leading to the creation of the United States Constitution are no less remarkable than the document itself. The miraculous circumstances leading to the drafting of the Constitution trace back to North America's geography. The presence of the Atlantic Ocean separating North America from Europe, the absence of a western passage to the Indies, and the lack of gold are no less responsible for the creation of the Constitution than the Stamp Act. If the North American seaboard possessed a transcontinental aquatic passage to the Pacific, if it were separated from Europe by a lesser distance, or most importantly, if it glimmered with gold, England would have guarded her American colonies with greater zeal and meticulously imposed her will upon its inhabitants, robbing them of the opportunity to practice self-governance. Without this experience, there would not be a Declaration, a set of Articles, or a Constitution.

Instead, North America was a land devoid of rapidly available riches. The treasures of the continent were ones mined through the sweat of the brow, the toil of the farmer, the perseverance of the hunter, the audacity of the mariner, and the measured peril of the trader. Although valuable in the long term, these were not the kinds of rewards that entertained the fancies of monarchs eager to fund military campaigns and international exploits. And so, those who battled the elements and challenged the misery of their circumstances to tame a wilderness and conquer a continent were largely left alone by the European power structures to lead their lives in a manner most conducive to their survival.

Of course, forging a working community out of a virgin forest requires organization, and such organization demands a legal framework dictating the relationship of its members. Consequently, the various communities were left to create legal corpuses that would define their new societies. Moreover, each of those communities was largely devoid of direct interactions with adjoining ones through distance and geography, allowing them to develop and experiment in relative isolation. Those that were successful naturally grew and through their expansion eventually absorbed the adjacent smaller and less successful societies.

By 1787, the men assembled in Philadelphia were armed with over 150 years of legislative and regional experience, insights that would be invaluable in framing their document.

But if experience with self-governance was the cornerstone of the Framers' qualifications to engage in a project of radical governmental design, there were other attributes that prepared them for the undertaking. These men were a new breed; one bold enough to leave the safety and comforts of a familiar societal order and venture into an unknown land equipped only with resolve and faith in a more prosperous and happier future. The Framers were the product of stubborn survivalists who had trained themselves to persevere no matter the challenges before them. They were a people that clung to their families and valued the products of hard work. They were staunch individualists who, by necessity, found themselves living next to people of different backgrounds, people with whom they would have never interacted had they remained in Europe. More importantly, they were people stripped of a predestined or universally accepted claim of societal superiority. And yes, they carried with them a deep reverence and belief in a Christian God, a level of religious conviction that for many served as the impetus to embark on a permanent, one-way trip across the Atlantic. The importance of pursuing their Christian faith in the way their consciences dictated cannot be overstated as this is foundational to the governing document developed for the new nation.

These people also brought with them some philosophical preconceptions that would be weaved into the fabric of the Constitution. For starters, they believed in natural law, or God's law—a set of incontrovertible rules that dictated the interactions between men, the Creator, and government; a divinely-created set of rules that began with the presumption that every man has a direct and immutable relationship with God. Such a relationship originated with each and every man's individual, divine creation and with a gift of a life equipped with certain rights, described in the Declaration of Independence as "unalienable," which afforded each individual with a sense of dignity.

Natural law also acknowledges that man is a social creature needing the presence and assistance of others to survive. That association between men naturally leads to a social structure, which in its purest form, arises from a "social contract"—an accord that men would live under certain rules dictating and limiting their behavior. Such limitations represented concessions of a portion of each man's liberties, but they were voluntary restrictions imposed for the betterment of each member's condition and undertaken with the consent and cooperation of those whose liberties were being partly curtailed. A corollary to that reasoning was that the concessions made for society's betterment were to be minimal in scope, as the greater the intrusion on man's liberties, the further away he existed from his most natural and happiest state. These philosophies can be traced to the writings of Cicero, Montesquieu, Bacon, Hume, and Locke and represented a radical departure from those philosophical assertions that had given rise to monarchies and kingdoms.

Prior to man's understanding of the concept of natural law and of his divine relationship with the Creator, the divine right of kings worked as the sociopolitical precept that explained and governed the existence of nations. Under this concept, the King was a direct descendant, if traced far enough, to Adam and Eve. As such, these men, and a few women, who headed nations were the product of divine intervention, and therefore, the product of God's direct placement onto the thrown. Their *subjects* existed only to serve them, and any rights afforded to the general population were courtesy of the benevolence of the king.[i] Advocates for the divine rights of kings, like Thomas Hobbes, reminded their followers that there was no inherent right to resist the king or to assert one's rights against him. Rebellion, or even passive resistance, was sacrilegious and simply against the laws of divine ordination. The king, as the prime and sole representative of God and supreme superintendent of the state, reigned supreme. His was the final word on all matters, even on the continuation of any of his subjects' lives.

But neither the Founders nor the Framers accepted those precepts. For them, molded by more than 100 years of self-rule, the power of government came not from the king, but from the people. *All* of the people, and not just the kings, had a direct relationship with God, and it was they whom God imparted with these unalienable rights. Consequently, it was the peoples' rights that were being leased to the government for the purposes of building a peaceful society, not the king's to distribute amongst his subjects.

---

[i] It is telling that in one of his earlier drafts of the Declaration of Independence, Thomas Jefferson referred to the people of the United States as "subjects," only to scratch out the term and replace it with "citizens." [Marc Kaufman, "Jefferson Changed 'Subjects' to 'Citizens' Declaration of Independence." *Washington Post*, July 3, 2012,*http://www.washingtonpost.com/wp-dyn/content/article/2010/07/02/AR2010070205525.html* (January 20, 2015)]

This whole concept of a nation being built under the precepts of natural law was unheard of before 1776. In fact, it was such a radical departure from the philosophies of the day that it made America a remarkable exception to the accepted norms. Indeed, it is this radical departure from all preconceived notions, coupled with the mindset required to be a part of such a special and unique society that served to make America truly exceptional in every sense of the word.

But the Framers did not base their work on any idealized visions of man. Utopian as the concept of a peacefully contrived social contract may appear, the Framers were also intimately aware of man's shortcomings. "Unlimited power is apt to corrupt the minds of those who possess it," said William Pitt the Elder, Prime Minister of England, to the House of Lords in 1770. The Framers were entirely aware of the dangers of unlimited power. If power corrupts those who have it, then the Framers' aim was to fragment it.

They were also keenly aware of the concept of special interests, but unlike the calls of many in today's political discussions, the Framers embraced their existence and influence. For them, the promotion of specific interests by the various segments of society was expected and employed within the framework of government like fuel powering the engine of innovation and debate. Their objective was to enable the representation of sufficient interests through active roles in policy creation and legislation so as to prevent any single interest from achieving an insurmountable advantage. It was this continuous battle among the various interests that would facilitate a better-suited society.

And then there was the healthy and very appropriate disdain for tyranny. The Framers' common experience sensitized them to the horrors of a war fought to ward off a tyrannical government. For that reason, if there was one goal each of the Framers of the Constitution shared, it was to ensure that they had not escaped the grip of one tyrannical state merely to land in the jaws of another.

The Declaration of Independence, adopted on July 2, 1776, resonated with those concerns. Highly influenced by the writings of John Locke, the

Declaration laid out not only the reasons for the separation from England, but described the Founding Fathers' visions of what this new nation should strive to become. Inherent to the Founders' core beliefs were some truths they held to be "self-evident." Their belief in the equality of all men before the law and of man's endowment with certain unalienable rights not limited to Life, Liberty, and the pursuit of Happiness rings loudly throughout the document. The statement stands, not merely as a florid example of inspired and elevated prose, but as a repudiation of the assigned, aristocratic status they knew under George III.[ii]

Closely related to the concept of societal liberties is the emergence of capitalism, or free market economics. Although the Constitution does not expressly subscribe to a particular economic philosophy, it follows that a free-market system devoid of governmental intervention would be the prescribed model for the nation. If the government is to play a minimal role in society, then vendors and buyers alike should be able to freely determine the manner in which they conduct business. The invisible hand of opportunity and the drive for profit would propel the economic system of the new nation, not government fiat or regulatory direction. The resulting economic system is parallel to that described by Adam Smith in *The Wealth of Nations*, published the very year that gave rise to the nation subscribing to its views.

The Founders envisioned a radically new society, one devoid of a familial aristocracy. Never would a person be elevated merely because of lineage. Every person would be viewed as equal, and his eventual standing would be determined through the toils of his life and fruits of his labor.

[ii] Also, notice that in denoting certain unalienable rights within the Declaration, the Founders mention Life and Liberty, and the *pursuit* of Happiness. This is for good reason as it is not the *right* to Happiness that the Creator guaranteed to man, but merely the right to pursue it, a concept emphasized by Benjamin Franklin himself. The distinction is important as it forces policymakers and political leaders to understand they cannot guarantee the Happiness of their citizens in a free and democratic society. The distinction will also serve as a central tenet behind modern-day discussions regarding civil rights and whether the nation's public policies should strive for all to enjoy equal standing before the law, or whether they ought to ensure an equality in outcomes.

America's first attempt at creating a government fitted for free peoples resulted in the Articles of Confederation. Ratified on March 1, 1781, the Articles were created with the aim of uniting the colonies in the battle against the British, but the endeavor of creating a unifying government did not include a long-range vision for the needs of a new nation.

The Articles called for a loose association of states preserving many of the powers they had prior to the establishment of the Confederation. Indeed, the text of the Articles reads more like a treaty between sovereigns than a blueprint from which a new nation could be forged. Consider the aspirational language of Article I:

> *The said states hereby severally enter into a firm league of friendship with each other for their common defense, the security of their Liberties, and their mutual and general welfare, binding themselves to assist each other, against all force offered to, or attacks made upon them, or any of them, on account of religion, sovereignty of trade, or any other pretense whatever. . .*
>
> (Articles of Confederation of 1781, art. III)

Predictably, shortcomings abounded. For example, each state retained the ability to print its own money, and each state had the authority to not recognize another state's currency. Each state could prohibit or impede commerce with another. Although there was a congress, there was no centralized executive power figure. There was no ability to maintain standing armies, and the confederate militia was dependent on voluntary contributions from each state for its funding. With such a weak, decentralized, unorganized, and unenforceable relationship, the Confederation was bound for failure.

The dispute over water and navigation rights also strained the relationships between the states, particularly Maryland and Virginia, and propelled the search for solutions to the weaknesses of the Articles. In March 1785, delegates from Maryland and Virginia met, initially in Alexandria and later, at the invitation of General George Washington, at Mount Vernon. The delegates arrived at a consensus report known as the Mount Vernon Compact detailing the agreement regarding navigation rights. The Compact was eventually ratified by the Virginia and Maryland legislatures, but the dispute and the process of settling it brought attention to the void within the Articles in regulating the relationship between states.

In response, a delegation met in Annapolis for the purpose of remedying the defects of the federal government. Although all states were invited to attend, only a total of twelve delegates from five states (New York, Pennsylvania, New Jersey, Delaware, and Virginia) attended the Annapolis Convention held between September 11 and September 14, 1786. Despite the poor attendance, the meeting heralded the growing dissatisfaction with the decentralized governmental structure and culminated in a recommendation for Congress to call a formal convention to rectify the Articles' deficiencies.

Shays' Rebellion, gripping Massachusetts between the latter months of 1786 and into 1787, emphasized the pressing nature of the recommendations made by the delegates in Annapolis. Indeed, Congress acted swiftly, and on February 21, 1787, it passed a resolution authorizing a convention to be held on the second Monday of May 1787, in Philadelphia, "for the sole and express purpose of revising the Articles of Confederation."[2]

To say that James Madison was the prime motivator of the Constitutional Convention would only slightly overstate his role in the events. It was Madison who pushed for a meeting in Annapolis following the very successful negotiations at Mount Vernon.[3] It was Madison who arrived in Philadelphia about a month early to prepare for the Constitutional Convention. And most importantly, it was Madison who introduced the Virginia Plan, a vision that fundamentally transformed the relationship between the people and government from a state-centered one ("we the states") to one founded on the consent of the people ("We, the People. . . ").[4]

But such an aggrandizing claim regarding Madison unduly diminishes the roles played by other crucial actors of the time. Alexander Hamilton was rather silent during the convention, but his ideas for economic reforms would help define the nation.[5] Moreover, the Convention would have carried only a fraction of its authority had the ever noble George Washington not agreed to preside over the reunion. If Madison was the promoter of the Constitutional Convention, Washington was the great stabilizer of the process.

And what effort at securing the peaceful reform of a young American nation could ever succeed without the wisdom and stature afforded by the presence of the monumentally influential Benjamin Franklin?

The stage being set for the revision of the Articles of Confederation, the delegates assembled in earnest to accomplish the task. In all, 70 delegates from twelve states (only Rhode Island failed to send a delegation) were appointed to the Convention, and 55 attended, ranging in age from 26 in Jonathan Dayton to 81 in Benjamin Franklin.[6] Among these delegates were businessmen, merchants, landowners, shippers, statesmen, and thirty-five lawyers[7] with positions on issues and national governance as varied as their backgrounds.

But all harbored an intense distrust of monarchical systems of governance. Their skepticism was so great that many were willing to risk the further fragmentation of the Confederation rather than yield their authorities to a national government. The suspicion of a centralized run on power and the insurmountable wariness over the consequences of yielding any authority to any umbrella organization is why some of the signers of the Declaration of Independence would not attend the Constitutional Convention. Chief amongst these was Patrick Henry, who is said to have famously explained his absence from the Convention by declaring, "I smelt a rat in Philadelphia."

Even after the decision to hold a convention, the same anxieties that led to its creation would threaten to derail it. Discordance abounded within the Convention, as even the most elemental issues gnawed at its members. The smaller states distrusted the larger states. They favored a state-centric system where each state was afforded equal representation within the government. The larger states, predictably, favored proportional representation. In the meantime, the agrarian states feared the potential of a taxation model that would excessively burden them over the wealthier, more industrial states.

Among the delegates, some believed the power of the federal government should be conceded by the various states. There were those who believed no personified executive official should exist (a president), and those who believed more than one person should be endowed with that authority. There were those who believed state tribunals should have precedence over any national judiciary, if one were to even exist, and those who felt the federal judiciary's decisions should reign supreme. There were those who felt the new national government could exert its authority directly upon the people and those who insisted the national government only have authority upon the states. Many feared the presence of a standing army during times of peace, and others found such an instrument indispensable to the security of the nation. There were even a few who felt the states should be obliterated altogether in favor of one unified, homogenous jurisdiction.

And although a review of the public discussions of the time would reveal a myriad of other concerns relating to governance in the new nation, by far the issue of greatest historical consequence to the future of the nation was slavery. The agrarian and more southern states demanded its continued existence while the mercantilist, northern states recognized its inherent injustice.

But there was an even more elemental question plaguing the delegation as it worked to draft a constitution: whether it even possessed the authority to propose a new government. After all, Congress had specifically chartered the delegates with the task of *revising* the Articles, not *replacing* them. And so, when it became apparent that the leadership of the Convention—men like Hamilton, Madison, Washington, and to some extent, Franklin—were intent on presenting a model for a new form of government to Congress rather than improving on the Confederation, some within the Convention vociferously objected.[iii]

Ultimately, the delegates labored to formulate the best possible plan for the fledgling country rather than subject themselves to restrictions arising from a strict interpretation of their charter. As Madison explained, since the

[iii] In fact, on September 26 and 27, Congress considered censuring the delegates assembled in Philadelphia for having exceeded their authority in recommending the formation of a new government. ["Teaching with Documents: The Ratification of the Constitution," *Teachers*, accessed October 25, 2014, *http://www.archives.gov/education/lessons/constitution-day/ratification.html*]

proposed Constitution was to be ratified by the people, any unauthorized liberties the delegates had taken in creating and submitting the document would be forever forgiven.[8]

Although these tensions tore at the delegates, none would circumvent the supreme priority of keeping some form of union together. Without a union, the Framers feared that the loose federation would descend into chaos. The various states would devolve into small European-styled nations, which would inevitably settle their contests through the power of the musket and the canon, not through that of the pen and the vote. Each delegate was aware that failure at maintaining a strong and united government, one that could quell civil unrest internally, defend itself from external attack, and provide enough rewards for its thirteen regional members so as to win their loyalties would inevitably result in armed conflict. Indeed, the Framers had little concern for the patriotic and nationalistic ideals conjured by later-day historians. No, for the Framers, failure to produce a unified government for the thirteen states would translate to the needless deaths of thousands of its inhabitants and even the eventual occupation by the French and the British.[9]

While posterity will question the wisdom of the delegates in their failure to eradicate slavery at this critical juncture in history, when viewed from the Framers' viewpoint, the greatest affront to human life and the country's continued and peaceful existence was the fragmentation of the Confederation and the erosion of its people's confidence. As long as the country remained together, there would always be another day to extract from it the infestations of slavery.

Truly, the impact the Constitution had on history and on the relationship between man and government is unparalleled. No document prior to the Constitution created a new system of centralized and coordinated government where there once was none. No document prior to the Constitution defined a social order free of an aristocracy or favored class. No document prior to the Constitution allocated specific, enumerated, and limited powers to the government. In short, the Constitution represents the first time a government was created by the will of the people. The fact that such a document representing the initial attempt by mankind to create a governmental structure based on the principle of putting the citizen first is still in existence serves as a testament to its splendor and to the collective genius of the men who created it.

The Constitution of the United States

We the People of the United States, in Order to form a more perfect Union, establish Justice, insure domestic Tranquility, provide for the common defence, promote the general Welfare, and secure the Blessings of Liberty to ourselves and our Posterity, do ordain and establish this Constitution for the United States of America.

Article I

Section 1

All legislative Powers herein granted shall be vested in a Congress of the United States, which shall consist of a Senate and House of Representatives.

Section 2

The House of Representatives shall be composed of Members chosen every second Year by the People of the several States, and the Electors in each State shall have the Qualifications requisite for Electors of the most numerous Branch of the State Legislature.

No Person shall be a Representative who shall not have attained to the Age of twenty five Years, and been seven Years a Citizen of the United States, and who shall not, when elected, be an Inhabitant of that State in which he shall be chosen.

Representatives and direct Taxes shall be apportioned among the several States which may be included within this Union, according to their respective Numbers, which shall be determined by adding to the whole Number of free Persons, including those bound to Service for a Term of Years, and excluding Indians not taxed, three fifths of all other Persons. The actual Enumeration shall be made within three Years after the first Meeting of the Congress of the United States, and within every subsequent Term of ten Years, in such Manner as they shall by Law direct. The Number of Representatives shall not exceed one for every thirty Thousand, but each State shall have at Least one Representative; and until such enumeration shall be made, the State of New Hampshire shall be entitled to chuse three, Massachusetts eight, Rhode-Island and Providence Plantations one, Connecticut five, New-York six, New Jersey four, Pennsylvania eight, Delaware one, Maryland six, Virginia ten, North Carolina five, South Carolina five, and Georgia three.

When vacancies happen in the Representation from any State, the Executive Authority thereof shall issue Writs of Election to fill such Vacancies.

The House of Representatives shall chuse their Speaker and other Officers; and shall have the sole Power of Impeachment.

Section 3

The Senate of the United States shall be composed of two Senators from each State, chosen by the Legislature thereof, for six Years; and each Senator shall have one Vote.

Immediately after they shall be assembled in Consequence of the first Election, they shall be divided as equally as may be into three Classes. The Seats of the Senators of the first Class shall be vacated at the Expiration of the second Year, of the second Class at the Expiration of the fourth Year, and of the third Class at the Expiration of the sixth Year, so that one third may be chosen every second Year; and if Vacancies happen by Resignation, or otherwise, during the Recess of the Legislature of any State, the Executive thereof may make temporary Appointments until the next Meeting of the Legislature, which shall then fill such Vacancies.

No Person shall be a Senator who shall not have attained to the Age of thirty Years, and been nine Years a Citizen of the United States, and who shall not, when elected, be an Inhabitant of that State for which he shall be chosen.

The Vice President of the United States shall be President of the Senate, but shall have no Vote, unless they be equally divided.

The Senate shall chuse their other Officers, and also a President pro tempore, in the Absence of the Vice President, or when he shall exercise the Office of President of the United States.

The Senate shall have the sole Power to try all Impeachments. When sitting for that Purpose, they shall be on Oath or Affirmation. When the President of the United States is tried, the Chief Justice shall preside: And no Person shall be convicted without the Concurrence of two thirds of the Members present.

Judgment in Cases of impeachment shall not extend further than to removal from Office, and disqualification to hold and enjoy any Office of honor, Trust or Profit under the United States: but the Party convicted shall nevertheless be liable and subject to Indictment, Trial, Judgment and Punishment, according to Law.

Section 4

The Times, Places and Manner of holding Elections for Senators and Representatives, shall be prescribed in each State by the Legislature thereof; but the Congress may at any time by Law make or alter such Regulations, except as to the Places of chusing Senators.

The Congress shall assemble at least once in every Year, and such Meeting shall be on the first Monday in December, unless they shall by Law appoint a different Day.

Section 5

Each House shall be the Judge of the Elections, Returns and Qualifications of its own Members, and a Majority of each shall constitute a Quorum to do Business; but a smaller Number may adjourn from day to day, and may be authorized to compel the Attendance of absent Members, in such Manner, and under such Penalties as each House may provide.

Each House may determine the Rules of its Proceedings, punish its Members for disorderly Behaviour, and, with the Concurrence of two thirds, expel a Member.

Each House shall keep a Journal of its Proceedings, and from time to time publish the same, excepting such Parts as may in their Judgment require Secrecy; and the Yeas and Nays of the Members of either House on any question shall, at the Desire of one fifth of those Present, be entered on the Journal.

Neither House, during the Session of Congress, shall, without the Consent of the other, adjourn for more than three days, nor to any other Place than that in which the two Houses shall be sitting.

Section 6

The Senators and Representatives shall receive a Compensation for their Services, to be ascertained by Law, and paid out of the Treasury of the United States. They shall in all Cases, except Treason, Felony and Breach of the Peace, be privileged from Arrest during their Attendance at the Session of their respective Houses, and in going to and returning from the same; and for any Speech or Debate in either House, they shall not be questioned in any other Place.

No Senator or Representative shall, during the Time for which he was elected, be appointed to any civil Office under the Authority of the United States, which shall have been created, or the Emoluments whereof shall have been encreased during such time; and no Person holding any Office under the United States, shall be a Member of either House during his Continuance in Office.

Section 7

All Bills for raising Revenue shall originate in the House of Representatives; but the Senate may propose or concur with Amendments as on other Bills.

Every Bill which shall have passed the House of Representatives and the Senate, shall, before it become a Law, be presented to the President of the United States; If he approve he shall sign it, but if not he shall return it, with his Objections to that House in which it shall have originated, who shall enter the Objections at large on their Journal, and proceed to reconsider it. If after such Reconsideration two thirds of that House shall agree to pass the Bill, it shall be sent, together with the Objections, to the other House, by which it shall likewise be reconsidered, and if approved by two thirds of that House, it shall become a Law. But in all such Cases the Votes of both Houses shall be determined by yeas and Nays, and the Names of the Persons voting for and against the Bill shall be entered on the Journal of each House respectively. If any Bill shall not be returned by the President within ten Days (Sundays excepted) after it shall have been presented to him, the Same shall be a Law, in like Manner as if he had signed it, unless the Congress by their Adjournment prevent its Return, in which Case it shall not be a Law.

Every Order, Resolution, or Vote to which the Concurrence of the Senate and House of Representatives may be necessary (except on a question of Adjournment) shall be presented to the President of the United States; and before the Same shall take Effect, shall be approved by him, or being disapproved by him, shall be repassed by two thirds of the Senate and House of Representatives, according to the Rules and Limitations prescribed in the Case of a Bill.

Section 8

The Congress shall have Power To lay and collect Taxes, Duties, Imposts and Excises, to pay the Debts and provide for the common Defence and general Welfare of the United States; but all Duties, Imposts and Excises shall be uniform throughout the United States;

To borrow Money on the credit of the United States;

To regulate Commerce with foreign Nations, and among the several States, and with the Indian Tribes;

To establish an uniform Rule of Naturalization, and uniform Laws on the subject of Bankruptcies throughout the United States;

To coin Money, regulate the Value thereof, and of foreign Coin, and fix the Standard of Weights and Measures;

To provide for the Punishment of counterfeiting the Securities and current Coin of the United States;

To establish Post Offices and post Roads;

To promote the Progress of Science and useful Arts, by securing for limited Times to Authors and Inventors the exclusive Right to their respective Writings and Discoveries;

To constitute Tribunals inferior to the supreme Court;

To define and punish Piracies and Felonies committed on the high Seas, and Offences against the Law of Nations;

To declare War, grant Letters of Marque and Reprisal, and make Rules concerning Captures on Land and Water;

To raise and support Armies, but no Appropriation of Money to that Use shall be for a longer Term than two Years;

To provide and maintain a Navy;

To make Rules for the Government and Regulation of the land and naval Forces;

To provide for calling forth the Militia to execute the Laws of the Union, suppress Insurrections and repel Invasions;

To provide for organizing, arming, and disciplining, the Militia, and for governing such Part of them as may be employed in the Service of the United States, reserving to the States respectively, the Appointment of the Officers, and the Authority of training the Militia according to the discipline prescribed by Congress;

To exercise exclusive Legislation in all Cases whatsoever, over such District (not exceeding ten Miles square) as may, by Cession of particular

States, and the Acceptance of Congress, become the Seat of the Government of the United States, and to exercise like Authority over all Places purchased by the Consent of the Legislature of the State in which the Same shall be, for the Erection of Forts, Magazines, Arsenals, dock-Yards, and other needful Buildings; And

To make all Laws which shall be necessary and proper for carrying into Execution the foregoing Powers, and all other Powers vested by this Constitution in the Government of the United States, or in any Department or Officer thereof.

Section 9

The Migration or Importation of such Persons as any of the States now existing shall think proper to admit, shall not be prohibited by the Congress prior to the Year one thousand eight hundred and eight, but a Tax or duty may be imposed on such Importation, not exceeding ten dollars for each Person.

The Privilege of the Writ of Habeas corpus shall not be suspended, unless when in Cases of Rebellion or Invasion the public Safety may require it.

No Bill of Attainder or ex post facto Law shall be passed.

No Capitation, or other direct, Tax shall be laid, unless in Proportion to the Census or Enumeration herein before directed to be taken.

No Tax or Duty shall be laid on Articles exported from any State.

No Preference shall be given by any Regulation of Commerce or Revenue to the Ports of one State over those of another: nor shall Vessels bound to, or from, one State, be obliged to enter, clear, or pay Duties in another.

No Money shall be drawn from the Treasury, but in Consequence of Appropriations made by Law; and a regular Statement and Account of the Receipts and Expenditures of all public Money shall be published from time to time.

No Title of Nobility shall be granted by the United States: And no Person holding any Office of Profit or Trust under them, shall, without the Consent of the Congress, accept of any present, Emolument, Office, or Title, of any kind whatever, from any King, Prince, or foreign State.

Section 10

No State shall enter into any Treaty, Alliance, or Confederation; grant Letters of Marque and Reprisal; coin Money; emit Bills of Credit; make any Thing but gold and silver Coin a Tender in Payment of Debts; pass any Bill of Attainder, ex post facto Law, or Law impairing the Obligation of Contracts, or grant any Title of Nobility.

No State shall, without the Consent of the Congress, lay any Imposts or Duties on Imports or Exports, except what may be absolutely necessary for executing it's inspection Laws: and the net Produce of all Duties and Imposts, laid by any State on Imports or Exports, shall be for the Use of the Treasury of the United States; and all such Laws shall be subject to the Revision and Controul of the Congress.

No State shall, without the Consent of Congress, lay any Duty of Tonnage, keep Troops, or Ships of War in time of Peace, enter into any Agreement or Compact with another State, or with a foreign Power, or engage in War, unless actually invaded, or in such imminent Danger as will not admit of delay.

Article II

Section 1

The executive Power shall be vested in a President of the United States of America. He shall hold his Office during the Term of four Years, and, together with the Vice President, chosen for the same Term, be elected, as follows

Each State shall appoint, in such Manner as the Legislature thereof may direct, a Number of Electors, equal to the whole Number of Senators and Representatives to which the State may be entitled in the Congress: but no Senator or Representative, or Person holding an Office of Trust or Profit under the United States, shall be appointed an Elector.

The Electors shall meet in their respective States, and vote by Ballot for two Persons, of whom one at least shall not be an Inhabitant of the same State with themselves. And they shall make a List of all the Persons voted for, and of the Number of Votes for each; which List they shall sign and certify, and transmit sealed to the Seat of the Government of the United States, directed to the President of the Senate. The President of the Senate shall, in the Presence of the Senate and House of Representatives, open all the Certificates, and the Votes shall then be counted. The Person having the greatest Number of Votes shall be the President, if such Number be a Majority of the whole Number of Electors appointed; and if there be more than one who have such Majority, and have an equal Number of Votes, then the House of Representatives shall immediately chuse by Ballot one of them for President; and if no Person have a Majority, then from the five highest on the List the said House shall in like Manner chuse the President. But in chusing the President, the Votes shall be taken by States, the Representation from each State having one Vote; A quorum for this Purpose shall consist of a Member or Members from two thirds of the States, and a Majority of all the States shall be necessary to a Choice. In every Case, after the Choice of the President, the Person having the greatest Number of Votes of the Electors shall be the Vice President. But if there should remain two or more who have equal Votes, the Senate shall chuse from them by Ballot the Vice President.

The Congress may determine the Time of chusing the Electors, and the Day on which they shall give their Votes; which Day shall be the same throughout the United States.

No Person except a natural born Citizen, or a Citizen of the United States, at the time of the Adoption of this Constitution, shall be eligible to the Office of President; neither shall any Person be eligible to that Office who shall not have attained to the Age of thirty five Years, and been fourteen Years a Resident within the United States.

In Case of the Removal of the President from Office, or of his Death, Resignation, or Inability to discharge the Powers and Duties of the said Office, the Same shall devolve on the VicePresident, and the Congress may by Law provide for the Case of Removal, Death, Resignation or Inability, both of the President and Vice President, declaring what Officer shall then act as President, and such Officer shall act accordingly, until the Disability be removed, or a President shall be elected.

The President shall, at stated Times, receive for his Services, a Compensation, which shall neither be encreased nor diminished during the Period for which he shall have been elected, and he shall not receive within that Period any other Emolument from the United States, or any of them.

Before he enter on the Execution of his Office, he shall take the following Oath or Affirmation—"I do solemnly swear (or affirm) that I will faithfully execute the Office of President of the United States, and will to the best of my Ability, preserve, protect and defend the Constitution of the United States."

Section 2

The President shall be Commander in Chief of the Army and Navy of the United States, and of the Militia of the several States, when called into the actual Service of the United States; he may require the Opinion, in writing, of the principal Officer in each of the executive Departments, upon any Subject relating to the Duties of their respective Offices, and he shall have Power to grant Reprieves and Pardons for Offences against the United States, except in Cases of Impeachment.

He shall have Power, by and with the Advice and Consent of the Senate, to make Treaties, provided two thirds of the Senators present concur; and he shall nominate, and by and with the Advice and Consent of the Senate, shall appoint Ambassadors, other public Ministers and Consuls, Judges of the supreme Court, and all other Officers of the United States, whose Appointments are not herein otherwise provided for, and which shall be established by Law: but the Congress may by Law vest the Appointment of such inferior Officers, as they think proper, in the President alone, in the Courts of Law, or in the Heads of Departments.

The President shall have Power to fill up all Vacancies that may happen during the Recess of the Senate, by granting Commissions which shall expire at the End of their next Session.

Section 3

He shall from time to time give to the Congress Information of the State of the Union, and recommend to their Consideration such Measures as he shall judge necessary and expedient; he may, on extraordinary Occasions, convene both Houses, or either of them, and in Case of Disagreement between them, with Respect to the Time of Adjournment, he may adjourn them to such Time as he shall think proper; he shall receive Ambassadors and other public Ministers; he shall take Care that the Laws be faithfully executed, and shall Commission all the Officers of the United States.

Section 4

The President, Vice President and all civil Officers of the United States, shall be removed from Office on Impeachment for, and Conviction of, Treason, Bribery, or other high Crimes and Misdemeanors.

Article III

Section 1

The judicial Power of the United States, shall be vested in one supreme Court, and in such inferior Courts as the Congress may from time to time ordain and establish. The Judges, both of the supreme and inferior Courts, shall hold their Offices during good Behaviour, and shall, at stated Times, receive for their Services, a Compensation, which shall not be diminished during their Continuance in Office.

Section 2

The judicial Power shall extend to all Cases, in Law and Equity, arising under this Constitution, the Laws of the United States, and Treaties made, or which shall be made, under their Authority;–to all Cases affecting Ambassadors, other public Ministers and Consuls;–to all Cases of admiralty and maritime Jurisdiction;–to Controversies to which the United States shall be a Party;–to Controversies between two or more States;–between a State and Citizens of another State; –between Citizens of different States, –between Citizens of the same State claiming Lands under Grants of different States, and between a State, or the Citizens thereof, and foreign States, Citizens or Subjects.

In all Cases affecting Ambassadors, other public Ministers and Consuls, and those in which a State shall be Party, the supreme Court shall have original Jurisdiction. In all the other Cases before mentioned, the supreme Court shall have appellate Jurisdiction, both as to Law and Fact, with such Exceptions, and under such Regulations as the Congress shall make.

The Trial of all Crimes, except in Cases of Impeachment, shall be by Jury; and such Trial shall be held in the State where the said Crimes shall have been committed; but when not committed within any State, the Trial shall be at such Place or Places as the Congress may by Law have directed.

Section 3

Treason against the United States, shall consist only in levying War against them, or in adhering to their Enemies, giving them Aid and Comfort. No Person shall be convicted of Treason unless on the Testimony of two Witnesses to the same overt Act, or on Confession in open Court.

The Congress shall have Power to declare the Punishment of Treason, but no Attainder of Treason shall work Corruption of Blood, or Forfeiture except during the Life of the Person attainted.

Article IV

Section 1

Full Faith and Credit shall be given in each State to the public Acts, Records, and judicial Proceedings of every other State. And the Congress may by general Laws prescribe the Manner in which such Acts, Records and Proceedings shall be proved, and the Effect thereof.

Section 2

The Citizens of each State shall be entitled to all Privileges and Immunities of Citizens in the several States.

A Person charged in any State with Treason, Felony, or other Crime, who shall flee from Justice, and be found in another State, shall on Demand of the executive Authority of the State from which he fled, be delivered up, to be removed to the State having Jurisdiction of the Crime.

No Person held to Service or Labour in one State, under the Laws thereof, escaping into another, shall, in Consequence of any Law or Regulation therein, be discharged from such Service or Labour, but shall be delivered up on Claim of the Party to whom such Service or Labour may be due.

Section 3

New States may be admitted by the Congress into this Union; but no new State shall be formed or erected within the Jurisdiction of any other State; nor any State be formed by the Junction of two or more States, or Parts of States, without the Consent of the Legislatures of the States concerned as well as of the Congress.

The Congress shall have Power to dispose of and make all needful Rules and Regulations respecting the Territory or other Property belonging to the United States; and nothing in this Constitution shall be so construed as to Prejudice any Claims of the United States, or of any particular State.

Section 4

The United States shall guarantee to every State in this Union a Republican Form of Government, and shall protect each of them against Invasion; and on Application of the Legislature, or of the Executive (when the Legislature cannot be convened) against domestic Violence.

Article V

The Congress, whenever two thirds of both Houses shall deem it necessary, shall propose Amendments to this Constitution, or, on the Application of the Legislatures of two thirds of the several States, shall call a Convention for proposing Amendments, which, in either Case, shall be valid to all Intents and Purposes, as Part of this Constitution, when ratified by the Legislatures of three fourths of the several States, or by Conventions in three fourths thereof, as the one or the other Mode of Ratification may be proposed by the Congress; Provided that no Amendment which may be made prior to the Year One thousand eight hundred and eight shall in any Manner affect the first and fourth Clauses in the Ninth Section of the first Article; and that no State, without its Consent, shall be deprived of its equal Suffrage in the Senate.

Article VI

All Debts contracted and Engagements entered into, before the Adoption of this Constitution, shall be as valid against the United States under this Constitution, as under the Confederation.

This Constitution, and the Laws of the United States which shall be made in Pursuance thereof; and all Treaties made, or which shall be made, under the Authority of the United States, shall be the supreme Law of the Land; and the Judges in every State shall be bound thereby, any Thing in the Constitution or Laws of any State to the Contrary notwithstanding.

The Senators and Representatives before mentioned, and the Members of the several State Legislatures, and all executive and judicial Officers, both of the United States and of the several States, shall be bound by Oath or Affirmation, to support this Constitution; but no religious Test shall ever be required as a Qualification to any Office or public Trust under the United States.

Article VII

The Ratification of the Conventions of nine States, shall be sufficient for the Establishment of this Constitution between the States so ratifying the Same.

The Word "the," being interlined between the seventh and eight Lines of the first Page, The Word "Thirty" being partly written on an Erazure in the fifteenth Line of the first Page. The Words "is tried" being interlined between the thirty second and thirty third Lines of the first Page and the Word "the" being interlined between the forty third and forty fourth Lines of the second Page.

done in Convention by the Unanimous Consent of the States present the Seventeenth Day of September in the Year of our Lord one thousand seven hundred and Eighty seven and of the Independence of the United States of America the Twelfth In witness whereof We have hereunto subscribed our Names,

Attest William Jackson Secretary

Go: Washington -Presidt. and deputy from Virginia

Delaware:
Geo: Read, Gunning Bedford jun, John Dickinson
Richard Bassett, Jaco: Broom
Maryland:
James McHenry, Dan of St, Thos. Jenifer, Danl Carroll.

Virginia:

John Blair, James Madison Jr.

North Carolina:

Wm Blount, Richd. Dobbs Spaight, Hu Williamson

South Carolina:

J. Rutledge, Charles Cotesworth Pinckney, Charles Pinckney
Pierce Butler.

Georgia:

William Few, Abr Baldwin

New Hampshire:

John Langdon, Nicholas Gilman

Massachusetts:

Nathaniel Gorham, Rufus King

Connecticut:

Wm. Saml. Johnson, Roger Sherman

New York:

Alexander Hamilton

New Jersey:

Wil. Livingston, David Brearley, Wm. Paterson, Jona: Dayton

Pennsylvania

B Franklin, Thomas Mifflin, Robt Morris, Geo. Clymer
Thos. FitzSimons, Jared Ingersoll, James Wilson.
Gouv Morris

PREAMBLE

Congress of the United States begun and held at the City of New-York, on Wednesday the fourth of March, one thousand seven hundred and eighty nine.

THE Conventions of a number of the States, having at the time of their adopting the Constitution, expressed a desire, in order to prevent misconstruction or abuse of its powers, that further declaratory and restrictive clauses should be added: And as extending the ground of public confidence in the Government, will best ensure the beneficent ends of its institution.

RESOLVED by the Senate and House of Representatives of the United States of America, in Congress assembled, two thirds of both Houses concurring, that the following Articles be proposed to the Legislatures of the several States, as amendments to the Constitution of the United States, all, or any of which Articles, when ratified by three fourths of the said Legislatures, to be valid to all intents and purposes, as part of the said Constitution; viz.

ARTICLES in addition to, and Amendment of the Constitution of the United States of America, proposed by Congress, and ratified by the Legislatures of the several States, pursuant to the fifth Article of the original Constitution.

(Articles I through X are known as the Bill of Rights)

AMENDMENT I

Congress shall make no law respecting an establishment of religion, or prohibiting the free exercise thereof; or abridging the freedom of speech, or of the press, or the right of the people peaceably to assemble, and to petition the Government for a redress of grievances.

AMENDMENT II

A well regulated Militia, being necessary to the security of a free State, the right of the people to keep and bear Arms, shall not be infringed.

AMENDMENT III

No Soldier shall, in time of peace be quartered in any house, without the consent of the Owner; nor in time of war, but in a manner to be prescribed by law.

AMENDMENT IV

The right of the people to be secure in their persons, houses, papers, and effects, against unreasonable searches and seizures, shall not be violated, and no Warrants shall issue, but upon probable cause, supported by Oath or affirmation, and particularly describing the place to be searched, and the persons or things to be seized.

AMENDMENT V

No person shall be held to answer for a capital, or otherwise infamous crime, unless on a presentment or indictment of a Grand Jury, except in cases arising in the land or naval forces, or in the Militia, when in actual service in time of War or public danger; nor shall any person be subject for the same offence to be twice put in jeopardy of life or limb; nor shall be compelled in any criminal case to be a witness against himself; nor be deprived of life, liberty, or property, without due process of law; nor shall private property be taken for public use without just compensation.

AMENDMENT VI In all criminal prosecutions, the accused shall enjoy the right to a speedy and public trial, by an impartial jury of the State and district wherein the crime shall have been committed; which district shall have been previously ascertained by law, and to be informed of the nature and cause of the accusation; to be confronted with the witnesses against him; to have compulsory process for obtaining witnesses in his favor; and to have the assistance of counsel for his defence.

AMENDMENT VII

In Suits at common law, where the value in controversy shall exceed twenty dollars, the right of trial by jury shall be preserved, and no fact tried by a jury shall be otherwise reexamined in any Court of the United States, than according to the rules of common law.

AMENDMENT VIII

Excessive bail shall not be required, nor excessive fines imposed, nor cruel and unusual punishments inflicted.

AMENDMENT IX

The enumeration in the Constitution of certain rights shall not be construed to deny or disparage others retained by the people.

AMENDMENT X

The powers not delegated to the United States by the Constitution, nor prohibited by it to the States, are reserved to the States respectively, or to the people.

AMENDMENT XI

Passed by Congress March 4, 1794. Ratified February 7, 1795.

The Judicial power of the United States shall not be construed to extend to any suit in law or equity, commenced or prosecuted against one of the United States by Citizens of another State, or by Citizens or Subjects of any Foreign State.

AMENDMENT XII

Passed by Congress December 9, 1803. Ratified June 15, 1804.

The Electors shall meet in their respective states and vote by ballot for President and Vice-President, one of whom, at least, shall not be an inhabitant of the same state with themselves; they shall name in their ballots the person voted for as President, and in distinct ballots the person voted for as Vice-President, and they shall make distinct lists of all persons voted for as President, and of all persons voted for as Vice-President, and of the number of votes for each, which lists they shall sign and certify, and transmit sealed to the seat of the government of the United States, directed to the President of the Senate; -- the President of the Senate shall, in the presence of the Senate and House of Representatives, open all the certificates and the votes shall then be counted; -- The person having the greatest number of votes for President, shall be the President, if such number be a majority of the whole number of Electors appointed; and if no person have such majority, then from the persons having the highest numbers not exceeding three on the list of those voted for as President, the House of Representatives shall choose immediately, by ballot, the President. But in choosing the President, the votes shall be taken by states, the representation from each state having one vote; a quorum for this purpose shall consist of a member or members from two-thirds of the states, and a majority of all the states shall be necessary to a choice. And if the House of Representatives shall not choose a President whenever the right of choice shall devolve upon them, before the fourth day of March next following, then the Vice-President shall act as President, as in case of the death or other constitutional disability of the President. The person having the greatest number of votes as Vice-President, shall be the Vice-President, if such number be a majority of the whole number of Electors appointed, and if no person have a majority, then from the two highest numbers on the list, the Senate shall choose the Vice-President; a quorum for the purpose shall consist of two-thirds of the whole number of Senators, and a majority of the whole number shall be necessary to a choice. But no person constitutionally ineligible to the office of President shall be eligible to that of Vice-President of the United States.

AMENDMENT XIII

Passed by Congress January 31, 1865. Ratified December 6, 1865.

Section 1. Neither slavery nor involuntary servitude, except as a punishment for crime whereof the party shall have been duly convicted, shall exist within the United States, or any place subject to their jurisdiction.

Section 2. Congress shall have power to enforce this article by appropriate legislation.

AMENDMENT XIV

Passed by Congress June 13, 1866. Ratified July 9, 1868.

Section 1. All persons born or naturalized in the United States, and subject to the jurisdiction thereof, are citizens of the United States and of the State wherein they reside. No State shall make or enforce any law which shall abridge the privileges or immunities of citizens of the United States; nor shall any State deprive any person of life, liberty, or property, without due process of law; nor deny to any person within its jurisdiction the equal protection of the laws.

Section 2. Representatives shall be apportioned among the several States according to their respective numbers, counting the whole number of persons in each State, excluding Indians not taxed. But when the right to vote at any election for the choice of electors for President and

Vice-President of the United States, Representatives in Congress, the Executive and Judicial officers of a State, or the members of the Legislature thereof, is denied to any of the male inhabitants of such State, being twenty-one years of age, and citizens of the United States, or in any way abridged, except for participation in rebellion, or other crime, the basis of representation therein shall be reduced in the proportion which the number of such male citizens shall bear to the whole number of male citizens twenty-one years of age in such State.

Section 3. No person shall be a Senator or Representative in Congress, or elector of President and Vice-President, or hold any office, civil or military, under the United States, or under any State, who, having previously taken an oath, as a member of Congress, or as an officer of the United States, or as a member of any State legislature, or as an executive or judicial officer of any State, to support the Constitution of the United States, shall have engaged in insurrection or rebellion against the same, or given aid or comfort to the enemies thereof. But Congress may by a vote of two-thirds of each House, remove such disability.

Section 4. The validity of the public debt of the United States, authorized by law, including debts incurred for payment of pensions and bounties for services in suppressing insurrection or rebellion, shall not be questioned. But neither the United States nor any State shall assume or pay any debt or obligation incurred in aid of insurrection or rebellion against the United States, or any claim for the loss or emancipation of any slave; but all such debts, obligations and claims shall be held illegal and void.

Section 5. The Congress shall have the power to enforce, by appropriate legislation, the provisions of this article.

AMENDMENT XV

Passed by Congress February 26, 1869. Ratified February 3, 1870.

Section 1. The right of citizens of the United States to vote shall not be denied or abridged by the United States or by any State on account of race, color, or previous condition of servitude--

Section 2. The Congress shall have the power to enforce this article by appropriate legislation.

AMENDMENT XVI

Passed by Congress July 2, 1909. Ratified February 3, 1913.

The Congress shall have power to lay and collect taxes on incomes, from whatever source derived, without apportionment among the several States, and without regard to any census or enumeration.

AMENDMENT XVII

Passed by Congress May 13, 1912. Ratified April 8, 1913.

The Senate of the United States shall be composed of two Senators from each State, elected by the people thereof, for six years; and each Senator shall have one vote. The electors in each State shall have the qualifications requisite for electors of the most numerous branch of the State legislatures.

When vacancies happen in the representation of any State in the Senate, the executive authority of such State shall issue writs of election to fill such vacancies: Provided, That the legislature of any State may empower the executive thereof to make temporary appointments until the people fill the vacancies by election as the legislature may direct.

This amendment shall not be so construed as to affect the election or term of any Senator chosen before it becomes valid as part of the Constitution.

AMENDMENT XVIII

Passed by Congress December 18, 1917. Ratified January 16, 1919. Repealed by amendment 21.

Section 1. After one year from the ratification of this article the manufacture, sale, or transportation of intoxicating liquors within, the importation thereof into, or the exportation thereof from the United States and all territory subject to the jurisdiction thereof for beverage purposes is hereby prohibited.

Section 2. The Congress and the several States shall have concurrent power to enforce this article by appropriate legislation.

Section 3. This article shall be inoperative unless it shall have been ratified as an amendment to the Constitution by the legislatures of the several States, as provided in the Constitution, within seven years from the date of the submission hereof to the States by the Congress.

AMENDMENT XIX

Passed by Congress June 4, 1919. Ratified August 18, 1920.

The right of citizens of the United States to vote shall not be denied or abridged by the United States or by any State on account of sex.

Congress shall have power to enforce this article by appropriate legislation.

AMENDMENT XX

Passed by Congress March 2, 1932. Ratified January 23, 1933.

Section 1. The terms of the President and the Vice President shall end at noon on the 20th day of January, and the terms of Senators and Representatives at noon on the 3rd day of January, of the years in which such terms would have ended if this article had not been ratified; and the terms of their successors shall then begin.

Section 2. The Congress shall assemble at least once in every year, and such meeting shall begin at noon on the 3d day of January, unless they shall by law appoint a different day.

Section 3. If, at the time fixed for the beginning of the term of the President, the President elect shall have died, the Vice President elect shall become President. If a President shall not have been chosen before the time fixed for the beginning of his term, or if the President elect shall have failed to qualify, then the Vice President elect shall act as President until a President shall have qualified; and the Congress may by law provide for the case wherein neither a President elect nor a Vice President shall have qualified, declaring who shall then act as President, or the manner in which one who is to act shall be selected, and such person shall act accordingly until a President or Vice President shall have qualified.

Section 4. The Congress may by law provide for the case of the death of any of the persons from whom the House of Representatives may choose a President whenever the right of choice shall have devolved upon them, and for the case of the death of any of the persons from whom the Senate may choose a Vice President whenever the right of choice shall have devolved upon them.

Section 5. Sections 1 and 2 shall take effect on the 15th day of October following the ratification of this article.

Section 6. This article shall be inoperative unless it shall have been ratified as an amendment to the Constitution by the legislatures of three-fourths of the several States within seven years from the date of its submission.

AMENDMENT XXI

Passed by Congress February 20, 1933. Ratified December 5, 1933.

Section 1. The eighteenth article of amendment to the Constitution of the United States is hereby repealed.

Section 2. The transportation or importation into any State, Territory, or Possession of the United States for delivery or use therein of intoxicating liquors, in violation of the laws thereof, is hereby prohibited.

Section 3. This article shall be inoperative unless it shall have been ratified as an amendment to the Constitution by conventions in the several States, as provided in the Constitution, within seven years from the date of the submission hereof to the States by the Congress.

AMENDMENT XXII

Passed by Congress March 21, 1947. Ratified February 27, 1951.

Section 1. No person shall be elected to the office of the President more than twice, and no person who has held the office of President, or acted as President, for more than two years of a term to which some other person was elected President shall be elected to the office of President more than once. But this Article shall not apply to any person holding the office of President when this Article was proposed by Congress, and shall not prevent any person who may be holding the office of President, or acting as President, during the term within which this Article becomes operative from holding the office of President or acting as President during the remainder of such term.

Section 2. This article shall be inoperative unless it shall have been ratified as an amendment to the Constitution by the legislatures of three-fourths of the several States within seven years from the date of its submission to the States by the Congress.

AMENDMENT XXIII

Passed by Congress June 16, 1960. Ratified March 29, 1961.

Section 1. The District constituting the seat of Government of the United States shall appoint in such manner as Congress may direct:

A number of electors of President and Vice President equal to the whole number of Senators and Representatives in Congress to which the District would be entitled if it were a State, but in no event more than the least populous State; they shall be in addition to those appointed by the States, but they shall be considered, for the purposes of the election of President and Vice President, to be electors appointed by a State; and they shall meet in the District and perform such duties as provided by the twelfth article of amendment.

Section 2. The Congress shall have power to enforce this article by appropriate legislation.

AMENDMENT XXIV

Passed by Congress August 27, 1962. Ratified January 23, 1964.

Section 1. The right of citizens of the United States to vote in any primary or other election for President or Vice President, for electors for President or Vice President, or for Senator or Representative in Congress, shall not be denied or abridged by the United States or any State by reason of failure to pay any poll tax or other tax.

Section 2. The Congress shall have power to enforce this article by appropriate legislation.

AMENDMENT XXV

Passed by Congress July 6, 1965. Ratified February 10, 1967.

Section 1. In case of the removal of the President from office or of his death or resignation, the Vice President shall become President.

Section 2. Whenever there is a vacancy in the office of the Vice President, the President shall nominate a Vice President who shall take office upon confirmation by a majority vote of both Houses of Congress.

Section 3. Whenever the President transmits to the President pro tempore of the Senate and the Speaker of the House of Representatives his written declaration that he is unable to discharge the powers and duties of his office, and until he transmits to them a written declaration to the contrary, such powers and duties shall be discharged by the Vice President as Acting President.

Section 4. Whenever the Vice President and a majority of either the principal officers of the executive departments or of such other body as Congress may by law provide, transmit to the President pro tempore of the Senate and the Speaker of the House of Representatives their written declaration that the President is unable to discharge the powers and duties of his office, the Vice President shall immediately assume the powers and duties of the office as Acting President.

Thereafter, when the President transmits to the President pro tempore of the Senate and the Speaker of the House of Representatives his written declaration that no inability exists, he shall resume the powers and duties of his office unless the Vice President and a majority of either the principal officers of the executive department or of such other body as Congress may by law provide, transmit within four days to the President pro tempore of the Senate and the Speaker of the House of Representatives their written declaration that the President is unable to discharge the powers and duties of his office. Thereupon Congress shall decide the issue, assembling within forty-eight hours for that purpose if not in session. If the Congress, within twenty-one days after receipt of the latter written declaration, or, if Congress is not in session, within twenty-one days after Congress is required to assemble, determines by two-thirds vote of both Houses that the President is unable to discharge the powers and duties of his office, the Vice President shall continue to discharge the same as Acting President; otherwise, the President shall resume the powers and duties of his office.

AMENDMENT XXVI

Passed by Congress March 23, 1971. Ratified July 1, 1971.

Section 1. The right of citizens of the United States, who are eighteen years of age or older, to vote shall not be denied or abridged by the United States or by any State on account of age.

Section 2. The Congress shall have power to enforce this article by appropriate legislation.

AMENDMENT XXVII

Originally proposed Sept. 25, 1789. Ratified May 7, 1992.

No law, varying the compensation for the services of the Senators and Representatives, shall take effect, until an election of representatives shall have intervened.

Chapter 2

The Workings of the United States Constitution

Any attempt at applying the concepts that created a nation to today's challenges must begin with a thorough understanding of the fabric the Framers weaved into their governmental design. Although there are multiple angles through which their efforts may be examined, two will be developed here: the structural design of the government created by the Constitution and the treatment of religion in the eyes of the Framers. We begin with the Framers' governmental design.

1. The Structure of the Government Designed by the Framers

At the conclusion of the Convention, it is said that a woman approached Benjamin Franklin and inquired about the type of government the Framers had created. Franklin famously answered, "A republic, if you can keep it."

Indeed, the Framers placed a great importance in creating a republic. They valued a government based on the consent of the people and dependent upon them as the source of its power. That ideal screamed for a democracy, but a pure democracy would be doomed to failure. Not only would such a government collapse under the weight of its inefficiency—with every single law being put to a mass vote of the people—but the unadultered administration of the people's voices would inevitably result in anarchy as the masses voted to disarm the oligarchy and eventually bring the nation's organizational structure to a grinding halt.

Indeed, the tensions and anxieties confronted by the Framers led to the design of a government rich in roadblocks and limitations, the so called checks and balances. These hurdles to the access of power were placed horizontally, with the separation of powers and the various branches of government, and vertically, with the interdependence of the states and the national governments in the execution of their duties.

The vertical component of their governmental design, in particular, was integral to the creation of the new republic because it allowed for a framework through which the sovereignties of the states would be preserved. The blueprint also allowed for those same states to yield some limited, specifically enumerated authorities to the national government with the aim of developing a stronger and more cohesive nation. The result was a complicated lattice of competing, yet interdependent departments that endowed the people with a governmental body that was minimally intrusive and respectful of its citizens' freedoms and rights.

In designing the national government, the Framers began by borrowing a concept dating back to the teachings of Aristotle and formalized by Montesquieu; the concept of splitting government into legislative, executive, and judicial branches. By dividing the responsibilities and authorities of the federal government among separately functioning departments, the Framers hoped no single branch would become excessively powerful.

The first branch would be the legislative branch, composed of Congress and responsible for creating the laws for the new republic. Essentially, Congress would be the driving force of the national government. Because it was the only branch capable of passing laws, it defined federal authority. But the powers of Congress to pass laws and shape policy could not be unlimited, as doing so would allow the federal government an unfettered opportunity to grow at the expense of the sovereignty of the states. To combat this, the Framers employed the concept of enumerated powers.

When the Framers discarded the Articles of Confederation, they erased the umbrella organization that united the thirteen states. Being that the national government was a creature of the states, the Framers envisioned the national government as initially having no powers. It was therefore up to the states to cede to this new national government the powers they collectively felt necessary to its proper and limited functions. The powers vested upon the federal government were specifically enumerated in Article I, Section 8 of the Constitution. It followed that if an activity was not listed, the federal government could not engage in it. The matter was, therefore, left for the states to govern.

The only exception was the conduct of international affairs, a power the Framers felt appropriate for the federal government since the nation needed a solitary, unifying voice to represent it when dealing with other nations. This largely unchecked power would be placed at the hands of the chief executive.

The Framers placed even greater restraints upon the Congress by splitting it into two chambers. The first, the House of Representatives, or the lower chamber, would be elected directly by the people. The number of representatives would be based on each state's population, but each representative would be responsible for a similar number of constituents. Consequently, the weight of representation of each person within the House of Representatives would be similar. This enabled each state to possess a delegation of representatives in the House whose size was proportional to that state's populations. Each representative would serve two years, creating a chamber quickly responsive to the passions of the people. The House of Representatives, then, was designed to be a rapidly changing body, closely attuned to the concerns of the electorate.

The Senate would be the higher chamber and would be composed of two representatives from each state. The term would be for six years, and the members of the Senate would not be elected directly by the people of the state, but by the state's legislature. Only one third of the Senate would change every two years so that there would always be members who had served in prior legislative sessions within the Senate. Such a staggered election arrangement would impart stability and continuity of representation to the higher chamber. The Senate would be an august body providing for a more temperate and wiser influence upon legislation than would the House. This higher degree of austerity would also be the reason for senators to be at least thirty years of age and nine years a citizen of the United States at the time they take office compared to twenty-five years of age and seven years of citizenship for representatives.

In their writings, Madison and Hamilton saw the legislature as the strongest of the three branches because it was the only one that could define the nation's laws. A proposed law would be presented in the form of a bill, and it could only be eligible to become law when both chambers agreed on identical language.[i] That approved bill would then be presented to the President, and only upon approval of the President, or upon his failure to sign the bill within ten days, would it become law. The only orders, resolutions, or votes, which the Framers exempted from presentation to the President were votes on adjournment, votes regarding the rules of the inner workings of each chamber, votes relating to impeachments, and votes on the elections of the chambers' officers. There was also one exception to the chambers' discretion at selecting its officers, and that was the President of the Senate who would always be the Vice President of the United States.

The administrative branch would be the executive, and its powers would be vested in one person, the President of the United States, who would serve four-year terms. On that person would rest all the executive powers of the national government. The President was to "take Care that the Laws be faithfully executed."[10] As previously noted, those laws would consist of bills passed by Congress and would be either signed by the President, or not signed

[i] Many, modern political observers criticize the executive and the judiciary for their abilities to create law. The merits and inherent weaknesses of these charges will be further explored.

within ten days. The President would also be given the opportunity to reject a bill by returning it to the chamber from which it had originated, but he or she would have to do this within ten days of the bill's presentation. This power of rejecting a bill from the legislature presently known as the presidential veto was referred to as "a negative" by the Framers.[11] However, the Framers did not award an absolute negative to the Chief Executive like was seen in the crown in its relations with Parliament. Rather, the President would have a "qualified negative" subject to override by a two-thirds vote of each chamber.[12] Interestingly, the Framers did not provide Congress a deadline within which it could override a presidential veto, leaving it instead to the "Rules and limitations prescribed in the Case of a Bill."[13]

Although the President would have very limited lawmaking powers in domestic matters, his authorities would be virtually unlimited in the international arena. The President, essentially, would serve as the nation's chief ambassador, representing the United States before the community of nations. The President would singlehandedly negotiate treaties with foreign powers, although such treaties had to be approved by a two-thirds vote of the Senate. The President would also be the Commander in Chief, able to lead the nation's military into war, but he could not declare war. Only the Congress would be given that authority. Additionally, only Congress would have the power to provide the necessary funding to execute a war, not the president.

The President would be given wide powers of appointments: ambassadors, consuls, justices of the Supreme Court, and other public ministers. But once again, the Framers restricted the President by requiring such appointments be subject to approval of the Senate.

Because of the high esteem with which the President would be held and the great responsibility the person serving as President would carry, the Framers devised an elaborate scheme through which the President would be chosen. With the goal of ensuring that the President remain beholden to the States, the Framers placed the responsibility of selecting the President directly upon them. However, they did not desire the state legislatures be responsible to the President. Consequently, the Framers required that every four years the legislatures of each state select a number of electors from that State that was equal to the number of Representatives and Senators allotted to that State. Those electors, none of whom could be senators or representatives serving in Congress, would then meet and select two candidates for President, at least one of which was not from that state. Once the Electors had created the list of candidates, the body of Electors would be dissolved in order to avoid any ongoing allegiance to the elected President.

The list of all the persons for whom they voted and the number of votes each member had garnered would then be sealed and sent to the President of the Senate who would open and count the certificates in the presence of the House and the Senate. The person obtaining the majority of votes would be President. If more than one person obtained a majority, then the House of Representatives would "immediately"[14] select a President from those receiving the majority. If there were no majority, then the House would choose from amongst the five candidates with the highest number of votes. In all cases, the States would each have one vote regardless of the number of members each state had appointed to the House.

The process would be similar for the Vice President, who would be the second highest receiver of votes, except in this case, a tie would be decided by the Senate.

The Framers did not impose term limits on either the President or the Vice President, except that each would be subject to impeachment proceedings by the House in cases of "Treason, Bribery, or other High Crimes and Misdemeanors."[15] The trial would be conducted by the Senate.[ii]

In order to guarantee the maturity of the President and to ensure his allegiance to the nation, he or she was to be at least 35 years old, a resident

[ii] Although the Framers did define treason as "levying War against [the United States] or in adhering to their Enemies, [and in] giving them Aid and Comfort," (U.S. Const. art. III, § 3) they did not define any of the other terms for which the President and high officials could be subject to impeachment.

of the United States for at least fourteen years prior to serving,[16] and be "a natural born citizen."[17]

Lastly, and perhaps most importantly, the President would be required to make the following Oath or Affirmation before taking office, "I do solemnly swear (or affirm) that I will faithfully execute the Office of President of the United States, and will to the best of my Ability, preserve, protect and defend the Constitution of the United States."[18, iii]

The third branch of government was the judiciary, charged with the responsibility of interpreting the laws of the United States. According to Hamilton, the judiciary was the weakest branch. [19] Without the power to legislate, a purse of its own, or the power to execute, the judiciary was devoid of all influences except the power of the legal opinion. However, through these opinions, the judiciary could disqualify the laws of the Congress and the actions of the President. The Framers designated only one Supreme Court upon which the judicial power of the United States was vested,[20] but endowed Congress with the authority to fund and create such inferior courts as it saw necessary,[21] and equipped the President with the responsibility, under the advice and consent of the Senate, of appointing judges.[22]

Interestingly, federal courts would not be allowed to hear all cases. Rather, they were to be given specific jurisdictions. Crimes violating state laws would be the jurisdiction of the state whose laws were broken and would be prosecuted by that state's court. Similarly, criminal cases arising out of violations of federal law would be the responsibility of the federal courts to try.[23]

In civil (non-criminal) matters, the Constitution gave federal courts the authority to try all cases dealing with the Constitution, the laws of the United States or its treaties, admiralty cases, and all cases to which the United States should be a party.[24] And although the Supreme Court was the one court specifically created by the Constitution, it would primarily serve as an

---

[iii] The words, "so help me God," were added through precedent by President George Washington who uttered the plea at the end of his oath of office, just before leaning over to kiss the Bible.

appellate court responsible for reviewing the correctness of the decisions made in the lower courts. Only when cases affected ambassadors, public ministers and consuls, and those in which a State would be a party, would the Supreme Court actually "try a case."[25]

The Constitution also gave federal courts the power to hear certain cases that did not arise out of controversies regarding federal laws. These included cases involving two or more States; a state and a citizen of another state, citizens of different states, citizens of the same state claiming lands under grants of different states, and between a State, or the Citizens thereof, and foreign States, Citizens or Subjects.[26]

But the Constitution did not prohibit state courts from hearing civil cases involving federal law, thus affording the country with a large body of cases where the state and federal courts shared jurisdiction.[iv]

All cases arising within a state that did not involve a question of federal law, were to be tried by the states and could not be heard by any federal court. The greater mass of exclusive jurisdiction, meaning cases that may only be heard by the federal *or* the state courts, was therefore afforded to the states. As Hamilton explained, "The States will retain the jurisdictions they now have, unless it appears to be taken away in one of the enumerated modes."[27]

There were also many issues outside of the direct organization of the various branches of government that needed to be addressed. For example, a republican form of government was guaranteed to every state in the Union,[28] and the method under which new states would be created was defined.[29]

The original Constitution also protected a number of civil rights. For example, the Framers fought against the possibility of a politician judging the guilt of a citizen by prohibiting The Bill of Attainder, or a legislatively passed declaration of a person's guilt.[30] Similarly, ex post facto laws, or ones making previously committed acts into a crime, were made illegal.[31] Additionally, the

---

[iv] Congress has further limited the diversity cases the federal courts may try to ones where the matters in controversy are valued at greater than $75,000.00. Rest assured that lawyers are well aware of how well their cases would be received in their state court versus their federal courts and choose accordingly.

right to a trial by jury in all crimes was guaranteed, except in cases of impeachment where the Senate would try the accused.[32] Even more importantly, the right to a writ of habeas corpus was guaranteed,[33] meaning that any person who believed he or she was wrongly held by the authorities, could file a petition before the court to determine the appropriateness of his or her arrest.[34, v]

To a significant degree, the Constitution also limited the powers of the states, as they were not allowed to impose taxes or duties upon articles exported from any other state,[35] and no state was allowed to enter into any treaty, alliance, or confederation.[36] The states were also prohibited from coining money[37] and from laying any imposts or duties on articles leaving or entering it, except those necessary to pay the costs of inspection.[38] A state was also not allowed to keep troops or warships in times of peace, or engage in a war with a foreign nation unless it was actually invaded, or in imminent danger of being invaded.[39] And in order to guarantee the subservience of the states to the new Constitution, the Framers included a supremacy clause, establishing the Constitution's authority over them.[40] For this reason, all officials, even those in state or local governments would be bound by oath or affirmation to support the Constitution of the United States.[41] Finally, the full faith and credit of one state was to be honored by every other state,[42] as would the privileges and immunities of its citizens.[43]

The issue of slavery was a difficult one for the Framers. The overwhelming majority of the Delegates to the Constitutional Convention, even some slave owners like Washington and Franklin, wished to bring that vile institution to a brisk end. But as we will see, they were unable to achieve consensus, so slavery would continue in America.

This then, was the working framework of the American Republic. Although truly revolutionary in its scope, the Constitution was nowhere near perfect. For one, it did not crisply define the extent of state autonomy.

---

[v] Congress *could* temporarily repeal this right for public safety reasons during times of Rebellion or Invasion.

Unacceptably, it allowed a state to be dragged into federal court by a party or another state, directly offending the concept of state sovereignty before federal judges. But worst of all, it left uncorrected the tragic circumstance that would inevitably result in the abuse and torment of countless black men and women and in the deaths of hundreds of thousands of Americans of all races.

2. Religion in the Nation's Founding and Constitutional Standing

Arguably, the passages of the Constitution dealing with religion have the most profound effects on American society and governance. Their misapplication has led to the extrication of worship from American schools, the removal of religious symbols from public lands and public squares, and the relegation of God and religion to a corollary position within American society—virtually the opposite of the "free exercise" the Framers envisioned. The consequences of these actions have been stark, with the profound deterioration of American ethics and morality through the latter half of the twentieth century and into the twenty-first.

The argument for God's removal from the public square has been laced with incorrect affirmations about a secular United States and with incredulous assertions of an insignificant role played by religion in the nation's founding. Indeed, these opinions have figured prominently in twentieth and twenty-first century jurisprudence.

However, if an informed analysis of the original intent of the Constitution and of the nation's founding is undertaken, the assault on the religious rights of the individual is easily repelled, and America can continue to rely on the same ethical and cultural presumptions that gave rise to this most exceptional nation.

We will begin where we always should, with a visit to America's past.

The Role of Religion and Worship in Colonial Establishment

From their earliest experiences, the American people have had a deeply rooted relationship with Christ. Indeed, the motivations behind the foundations of the various colonies offer incontrovertible evidence of the inextricable role religious freedom played in America's foundation.

For the religiously oppressed residing in seventeenth century Europe, emigration to North America offered an escape from the tyrannical nature of European governance. And so, the Puritans fled to Massachusetts. The Huguenots settled in New York and Virginia. The Catholics migrated (as a minority to their Protestant recruits) to Baltimore. Jews fled to colonial New York, New England, and Pennsylvania. And the Quakers sought refuge in Pennsylvania.

Perhaps no document captures the religiously based motivations of the settlers traveling to the New World better than the Mayflower Compact:

> *Having undertaken, for the glory of God, and the advancement of the Christian faith, and honor of our King and Country, a voyage to plant the first colony in the northern parts of Virginia, do these presents solemnly and mutually, in the presence of God, and one of another, covenant and combine our selves together in a civil body politic, for our better ordering and preservation and furtherance of the ends aforesaid. . .*
>
> (Mayflower Compact. Nov. 11, 1620)

Interestingly, the same religiously oppressive tendencies that forced the North American colonialists to flee Europe began to take root within the colonies, giving rise to yet another set of colonial migrations. In Massachusetts, Roger Williams found himself at odds over his religious beliefs, not only with the crown in the Old World, but with the fledgling leadership in the New. This conflict led to his banishment from the Massachusetts Bay Colony. Williams made his way to Rhode Island where he established a colony named Providence whose mission was to observe the religious freedoms of its inhabitants. Providence quickly earned a reputation as a safe haven for religious outcasts and Jews.

Despite these events, there are those who argue the foundation of the North American colonies was economically driven, not religiously so. They cite the elusive search for the Northwest Passage that drove England's first expeditions westward with the foundation of Roanoke and Jamestown. They argue that Jamestown was not founded because of religious persecution, but because of the economic allure of a burgeoning tobacco industry. They also argue that, for New Amsterdam in Manhattan Island, it was the establishment of a trading post that gave the colony its life.

While there is truth to an economic drive among these colonies, the pivotal role of religion and religious worship in creating and fortifying the colonies is unmistakable. In 1612, Sir Thomas Dale, the Deputy Governor of the Jamestown Colony in Virginia, enacted a series of laws that would govern the inhabitants of the colony. Its very title denotes God's central role in the colony's mission and in the lives of its inhabitants, "Articles, Lawes, and Orders, Divine, Politique, and Martiall for the Colony in Virginia." And the mission statement for the colony is riddled with references to God, God's blessings, the colony's duty to God, and God's supremacy.

Even in New Amsterdam, which would eventually become New York, religious liberty played an integral role in its development even though it was a colony primarily established for the purposes of furthering trade in the New World. By the seventeenth century, the Dutch had made significant advances toward respecting individuals' freedoms of conscience. Consequently, within the Netherlands, the strong urge for citizens to migrate to the New World did not exist as it did in nearby England where religious oppression motivated a substantial segment of society to seek alternative living arrangements. It comes as no surprise, then, that when the Dutch embarked on establishing trade- and business-centered colonies in the New World, they would be more tolerant of religious nonconformists than the rigid and essentially oppressive policies of the Massachusetts Bay Colonies. Additionally, because of the relative acceptance of diverse views within the Netherlands, the Dutch were amenable to having their colony inhabited by non-Dutch, and certainly, non-Calvinist people.

By 1645, the Dutch had appointed Willem Kieft as New Amsterdam's Director General. Kieft did not have the progression of Calvinist Christianity as a major pillar of his agenda but was keenly interested in promoting New Amsterdam's habitation. At the same time, a group of British colonists, including William Thorne and Lady Deborah Moody, were either banished from the Massachusetts Bay Colonies for religious non-compliance or found it uncomfortable to remain there. They turned their eyes to New Amsterdam as a place where they could live peacefully while practicing their faith.

On October 10, 1645, Kieft signed a Charter patenting a tract of land in Flushing to a group of transplanted British colonists. Integral to the patent was a provision granting the right ". . . to have and Enjoy the liberty of Consciousness, according to Custome and manner of Holland, without molestation or disturbance, from any Magistrate or Magistrates, or any other Ecclesiastical Minister, that may extend Jurisdiccon over them. . . . "[44]

On December 19, 1645, another patent issued by Kieft granted similar rights to another group of transposed British colonists headed by Lady Deborah Moody in Grevesend.[vi]

But the calm of religious tolerance would not remain. Kieft would be replaced by Petrus Stuyvesant in 1647, largely in response to a number of ill-advised, violent confrontations Kieft had with local tribes. A strict disciplinarian, Stuyvesant took a much firmer approach to enforcing the laws of the colony. With regard to religion, he insisted upon the supremacy of the Dutch Reformed Church and employed a stance of absolute intolerance against a Quaker presence in New Amsterdam. His views were so intolerant that when the *Woodhouse*, a trading vessel carrying Quakers, arrived in New Amsterdam Stuyvesant refused the ship entry and hunted down some of the passengers that had managed to escape and remain behind.[45]

In his zeal for persecuting Quakers, Stuyvesant arrested anyone who housed a Quaker, confiscated ships carrying Quakers, and even tortured Quakers captured in New Amsterdam. As word spread of the harsh treatment of religious non-comformists in New Amsterdam, a group of inhabitants of Flushing, including the sheriff, some of its founders, and the town clerk, gathered on December 27, 1657, to fashion a response. They drafted and signed a remarkable document written by Edward Hart, one of

---

vi The Gravesend patent was also unique in that it was the only patent naming a woman, Lady Deborah Moody, as the lead patentee. [Joseph Ditta, *Gravesend, Brooklyn, Then and Now* (Charleston, S.C : Arcadia Publishing,2009), ix]

Flushing's inhabitants, that would serve as the first written assertion of religious liberty in North America.[46] It is reproduced below in its entirety:

December 27, 1657 Right Honorable,

You have been pleased to send up unto us a certain prohibition or command that we should not receive or entertain any of those people called Quakers because they are supposed to be by some, seducers of the people. For our part we cannot condemn them in this case, neither can we stretch out our hands against them, to punish, banish or persucute them, for out of Christ god is a consuming fire, and it is a fearful thing to fall into the hands of the living God.

We desire therefore in this case not to judge least we be judged, neither to condemn least we be condemned, but rather let every man stand and fall to his own Master. Wee are bounde by the Law to doe good unto all men, especially to those of the household of faith. And though for the present we seem to be unsensible of the law and the Law giver, yet when death and the Law assault us, if wee have our advocate to seeke, who shall plead for us in this case of conscience betwixt god and our own souls; the power of this world can neither attack us, neither excuse us, for if God justifye who can condemn and if God condemn there is none can justifye.

And for those jealousies and suspicions which some have of them, that they are destructive unto Magistracy and Ministerye, that can not bee, for the magistrate hath the sword in his hand and the minister hath the sword in his hand, as witnesse those two great examples which all magistrates and ministers are to follow, Moses and Christ, whom god raised up maintained and defended against all the enemies both of flesh and spirit; and therefore that which is of God will stand, and that which is of man will come to nothing. And as the Lord hath taught Moses or the civil power to give an outward liberty in the state by the law written in his heart designed for the good of all, and can truly judge who is good, who is civil, who is true and who is false, and can pass definitive sentence of life or death against that man which rises up against the fundamental law of the States General; soe he hath made his ministers a savor of life unto life, and a savor of death unto death.

The law of love, peace and liberty in the states extending to Jews, Turks, and Egyptians, as they are considered the sonnes of Adam, which is the glory of the outward state of Holland, soe love, peace and liberty, extending to all in Christ Jesus, condemns hatred, war and bondage. And because our Saviour saith it is impossible but that offenses will come, but woe unto him by whom they cometh, our desire is not to offend one of his little ones, in whatsoever form, name or title hee appears in, whether Presbyterian, Independent, Baptist or Quaker, but shall be glad to see anything of God in any of them, desiring to doe unto all men as wee desire all men should doe unto us, which is the true law both of Church and State; for our Saviour saith this is the law and the prophets.

Therefore if any of these said persons come in love unto us, we cannot in conscience lay violent hands upon them, but give them free egresse and regresse unto our Town, and houses, as God shall persuade our consciences. And in this we are true subjects both of Church and State, for we are bounde by the law of God and man to doe good unto all men and evil to noe man. And this is according to the patent and charter of our Towne, given unto us in the name of the States General, which we are not willing to infringe, and violate, but shall houlde to our patent and shall remaine, your humble servants, the inhabitants of Vlishing.

Written this 27th day of December, in the year 1657, by mee EDWARD HART, *Clericus Tobias Feake Nathaniel Tue*

The Mark of *William Noble Nicholas Blackford*

The Mark of *Micah Tue William Thorne, seignor*

The Mark of *William Thorne, junior* The Mark of *Philipp Ud Edward Tarne Robert Field, senior John Store Robert Field, junior Nathaniel Hefferd Nick Colas Parsell Benjamin Hubbard Michael Milner*

The Mark of *Henry Townsend William Pigion George Wright*

The Mark of *John Foard George Clere Henry Semtel Elias Doughtie*

Edward Hart Antonie Feild John Mastine Richard Stockton John Townesend Edward Griffine Edward Farrington

Stuyvesant was so unimpressed with the magnificence of this document that he promptly arrested those responsible for its execution including the sheriff of Flushing and Edward Hart, its author.

Despite the overt oppression, the colonists, particularly those of Flushing, continued to be sympathetic to the Quakers, hiding them when necessary and allowing them to hold meetings in the homes of non-Quakers. In one noteworthy case, John Bowne, the husband of a Quaker, was arrested in 1662 for allowing Quakers to congregate in his home. He was tried and fined, but Bowne refused to remit.

In an attempt to have Bowne banished, Stuyvesant placed him on a ship to Ireland along with a letter of explanation bound for Holland. Arriving in Ireland, Bowne proceeded to Holland and presented the letter and his case to the Dutch West India Company, which responded with an order for Stuyvesant to moderate his crackdown on religious liberty stating, "The consciences of men ought ever to remain free and unshackled."[47] In short, the Dutch West India Company told the Stuyvesant to "allow everyone to have his own belief."[48]

The effects of the Dutch West India Company's order upon New Amsterdam would be short-lived as the colony would be handed to the British a year later, but its effects upon religious liberty and the free exercise of religion would be more permanent. The renamed New York was a place tolerant of men's consciences, and the willingness of its people to stand up for their right to worship would be indelibly etched upon the colony's character. New York, like New Amsterdam before it, would be viewed as a sanctuary for many of North America's religiously oppressed, including Quakers and Jews. The actions and written words of the settlers in Flushing would serve as foundational steps that would eventually lead to the monumental pursuit of religious freedom within the Declaration of Independence, the Revolutionary War, and the First Amendment to the Constitution.

But Flushing and New York were not alone in their zealous pursuit of freedom of conscience. Among the most overt expressions of freedom of worship was seen in Maryland. Maryland was decreed to George Calvert, a Catholic, by Charles I, a protestant king. Despite their religious differences, George Calvert had a strong relationship with the king. Calvert had previously attempted to establish a colony in Newfoundland but had been unsuccessful. Although he died before he could receive the charter, his son, Cecilius Calvert, was granted the land to the north of the Potomac River in 1632, which was named Maryland after Charles's wife, Queen Mary.

George Calvert initially intended the colony to serve as a respite for oppressed Catholics in England, but too few were interested in moving to North America. As a result, the invitation was extended to Protestants in the form of the Toleration Act of 1649. The Toleration Act inscribed into law the respect government would have for any person with regard to worship. Specifically, it held:

> *. . .noe person or persons whatsoever within this Province, or the Islands, Ports, Harbors, Creekes, or havens thereunto belonging professing to beleive in Jesus Christ, shall from henceforth bee any waies troubled, Molested or discountenanced for or in respect of his or her religion nor in the free exercise thereof within this Province or the Islands thereunto belonging nor any way compelled to the beleife or exercise of any other Religion against his or her consent, soe as they be not unfaithfull to the Lord Proprietary, or molest or conspire against the civill Governement established or to bee established in this Province under him or his heires.*
>
> (Maryland Toleration Act Sept. 21, 1649)

Despite its name, the Toleration Act offered harsh punishments for those blaspheming the Holy Trinity or the supremacy of the Lord Jesus Christ. Punishments included fines, confiscation of property, and even death. But the Toleration Act did inscribe one view of institutional tolerance within the New World, a view that would drive the Founders in the formation of the new Republic. Although the State was free to engage in the regulation religious speech and establishment regarding Christianity, it was restricted from selecting any one sect over the others, and it was prohibited from punishing a person for belonging to any such sect so long as the subject did not blaspheme God, Jesus Christ, or the Holy Trinity, or failed to observe the Sabbath on Sunday.

The central role of religious worship in society did not end with North American colonization. The foothold Puritanism and Calvinism initially had on the colonies receded over the eighteenth century, replaced by a new form of Christianity that was uniquely American. This new Christianity was "undogmatic, moralistic rather than credal, tolerant but strong, and all-pervasive of society. . . ,"[49] and gave rise to a renewed sense of religious discussion and debate within the emerging country; a movement that would be known as the Great Awakening.

Regardless of the dynamics of the Great Awakening, the movement, informal as it was, fortified Christianity in the colonial psyche. In fact, Protestant Christianity was so important to the colonists during the run-up to the American Revolution that it led to increasing tensions with the Crown and played a role in the road to revolution.

The French and Indian War had taxed the Crown greatly. The war ended with the Treaty of Paris of 1763 where France ceded Canada to the British. Suddenly, England found itself in the awkward predicament of having to rule over a population of North American colonists that were decidedly French. To help appease them, the British Parliament passed the Quebec Act of 1774, redefining the boundaries of the now renamed colony of Quebec[vii] and creating new rules restricting westward expansion among the British colonists. Additionally, Parliament, hoping to avert discontent among their new French subjects, allowed Catholicism to legally flourish within Quebec and permitted the French to employ French law in governing the territory. This capitulation inflamed the Anglo (and very Protestant) colonists who concluded that the new regulations would allow French Catholics to impede their westward expansion. Instead of instilling peace and harmony within the colonies, the Quebec Act served only to drive the British colonists to even greater levels of disdain against George III and Parliament.

As the colonies careened towards war with the British, North American political leaders relied heavily on religion and divine guidance, publicly invoking the assistance of God, not only for themselves, but also for their emerging nation. When the First Continental Congress convened in 1774 to consider a response to increasingly hostile British acts, one of the questions

---

[vii] Under the new borders, what was known as Canada under French rule would now include the areas encompassing present-day Ontario, Illinois, Indiana, Michigan, Ohio, Wisconsin, and Minnesota.

considered was whether it ought to engage in an opening prayer. After a debate regarding the appropriateness of prayer ended in the affirmative, the delegates invited Reverend Jacob Duché, a local minister, to read prayers to the assembled body.[50] According to John Adams, after reading some formal prayers, Duché engaged in an "unplanned and extemporary prayer, . . . which filled the Bosom of every Man present. . . . [and] has had an excellent Effect upon every Body here."[51]

By the next year, the colonies found themselves engaged in overt acts of aggression against the British. They assembled a Second Continental Congress, which continued the trend of reliance on divine inspiration and intervention by declaring national days of "Humiliation, Fasting, and Prayer" and recommending that "Christians of all denominations, . . . assemble for public worship [in order that God] animate our officers and soldiers with invincible fortitude."[52]

This intimate relationship with God would work its way into the nation's initial foundational document, the Declaration of Independence. From its opening sentence, the Declaration relies on "Laws of Nature" and "Nature's God" to support the Founders' assertions ". . . that all men are created equal, that they are endowed by their Creator with certain unalienable Rights, that among these are Life, Liberty and the Pursuit of Happiness."[53]

In this regard, William Blackstone, one of the eighteenth century's preeminent legal scholars, had a great influence upon the Founders. His writings provide further proof of the direct, inseparable role God and Divinity played upon the nation's foundation. Blackstone viewed human law as creations of God waiting to be discovered by man.[54] He succinctly summarized his unabashed view regarding the role Christianity plays in British jurisprudence when he said, ". . . Christianity is part of the laws of England."[55] In other words, according to Blackstone, it is from Christianity that Anglo-American law gains its awareness of wrong and right.[56] In Blackstone's view, the Ten Commandments and Christ's teachings had a direct and controlling influence on the laws of man, such that God was not to be separated from the worldly legal structure. For this reason, Blackstone would argue that Biblical teachings and the Christian religion had a direct and breathing relationship with British jurisprudence. Through their adoption of British law, the Founders extended that relationship to American jurisprudence.[57]

Thomas Jefferson, like all the preeminent American lawyers of his day, was especially familiar with Blackstone's work. His familiarity with the notions of "laws of nature" and "natural law" in Blackstone's writings facilitated Jefferson's use of the concepts in the Declaration of Independence.[viii]

There are other associations between Blackstone and the Founders. Thomas Paine's concept of certain laws being of a higher authority than the laws of man alludes to God's role in the moral justification for separating the colonies from the rule of England. From this follows yet another concept promoted by Blackstone (although in his case, he was using it in support of the authority of the British Crown), the notion that there are certain laws running counter to the laws of nature. It was such contrarian laws that, according to the Declaration of Independence, imparted upon man the duty to throw off the governments that upheld them. Each of these concepts weaved into the Declaration of Independence was based on the Founders' assertions of a direct relationship between each man, as an individual, and God—a relationship that could not be interrupted by civil institutions.

So, from the very beginning, the Second Continental Congress cloaked itself with the supremacy of God and the direct, unbreakable relationship between all men and the Creator as the justification for their separation from the Crown, thus entrenching the country's very foundation in the premise of religious freedom and the acknowledgment of every person's unique and uninterrupted relationship with God.

[viii] Interestingly, Jefferson's was a love hate relationship with Blackstone, for although he relied upon him in invoking the concepts of natural law within the Declaration of Independence, he absolutely abhorred Blackstone's use of these concepts in defending the same monarchy Jefferson was risking his life to defeat. He also sternly disagreed with the concept of adoption of British common law in American jurisprudence, a concept also borrowed from Blackstone's Commentaries.

Religion and the Law Under the Articles of Confederation

The time under the Articles of Confederation bore great insights as to the direction the Founders intended the nation to go regarding religion and public worship. One of the crowning achievements of the Confederation was the passage in 1787 of the Northwest Ordinance, which created the Northwest Territory and encompassed the areas known today as Ohio, Indiana, Illinois, Michigan, and Wisconsin. The Northwest Ordinance embraced the central importance of religion to the nation's future and to man's development. Specifically, in authorizing the creation of schools, it held, "Religion, morality, and knowledge, being necessary to good government and the happiness of mankind, schools and the means of education shall forever be encouraged."[58] This language is particularly significant since it expressly allows for religious education in schools created and funded by the state. This same Continental Congress imported 20,000 Bibles in 1787 and commissioned the printing of an American version of the Scriptures in 1783.[59] Through its actions, one can conclude that the Continental Congress's wall of separation between church and state was very porous indeed—if one was even intended to exist.

But it was in Virginia where arguably the most influential events regarding the role of religion and religious governance transpired, a place where no less than four of America's giant political thinkers of the era interacted, debated, and fought: George Mason, Thomas Jefferson, James Madison, and Patrick Henry. The initial volley dates back to the days immediately preceding the Declaration of Independence.

During the run-up to the Revolutionary War, Virginia took steps to maintain communications and coordinate actions with its surrounding colonies against England. In 1774, Virginia engaged in the first of many Conventions manned by delegates from its various counties. With the reality of an impending secession from the Crown, Virginia assembled its Fifth Convention on May 6, 1776. This was the assembly that would declare Virginia's independence from England and replace the British flag with the colonial colors. Faced with the reality of independent rule, the Convention embarked on the creation of two key documents. The first was a constitution, which it ratified on June 29, 1776, and the second, the Virginia Bill of Rights, was adopted on June 12, 1776. It is this latter document, reproduced below, that holds some of the key building blocks to America's eventual position on religious liberties.[ix, x]

> A DECLARATION OF RIGHTS *made by the representatives of the good people of Virginia, assembled in full and free convention which rights do pertain to them and their posterity, as the basis and foundation of government.*
>
> **Section 1.** *That all men are by nature equally free and independent and have certain inherent rights, of which, when they enter into a state of society, they cannot, by any compact, deprive or divest their posterity; namely, the enjoyment of life and liberty, with the means of acquiring and possessing property, and pursuing and obtaining happiness and safety.*[x]
>
> **Section 2.** *That all power is vested in, and consequently derived from, the people; that magistrates are their trustees and servants and at all times amenable to them.*[31]
>
> **Section 3.** *hat government is, or ought to be, instituted for the common benefit, protection, and security of the people, nation, or community; of all the various modes and forms of government, that is best which is capable of producing the greatest degree of happiness and safety and is most effectually secured against the danger of maladministration. And that, when any government shall be found inadequate or contrary to these purposes, a majority of the community has an indubitable, inalienable, and indefeasible right to reform, alter, or abolish it, in such manner as shall be judged most conducive to the public weal.* [31]
>
> **Section 4.** *hat no man, or set of men, is entitled to exclusive or separate emoluments or privileges from the community, but in consideration of public services; which, nor being descendible,neither ought the offices of magistrate, legislator, or judge to be hereditary.* [31]

[ix] The document is in George Mason's handwriting up to the part referring to the press, which appears to have been written by Thomas Ludwell Lee.

[x] Originally drafted by Mason.

Section 5. *That the legislative and executive powers of the state should be separate and distinct from the judiciary; and that the members of the two first may be restrained from oppression, by feeling and participating the burdens of the people, they should, at fixed periods, be reduced to a private station, return into that body from which they were originally taken, and the vacancies be supplied by frequent, certain, and regular elections, in which all, or any part, of the former members, to be again eligible, or ineligible, as the laws shall direct.* [31]

Section 6. *That elections of members to serve as representatives of the people, in assembly ought to be free; and that all men, having sufficient evidence of permanent common interest with, and attachment to, the community, have the right of suffrage and cannot be taxed or deprived of their property for public uses without their own consent or that of their representatives so elected, nor bound by any law to which they have not, in like manner, assembled for the public good.* [31]

Section 7. *That all power of suspending laws, or the execution of laws, by any authority, without consent of the representatives of the people, is injurious to their rights and ought not to be exercised.*

Section 8. *That in all capital or criminal prosecutions a man has a right to demand the cause and nature of his accusation, to be confronted with the accusers and witnesses, to call for evidence in his favor, and to a speedy trial by an impartial jury of twelve men of his vicinage, without whose unanimous consent he cannot be found guilty; nor can he be compelled to give evidence against himself; that no man be deprived of his liberty except by the law of the land or the judgment of his peers.*

Section 9. *That excessive bail ought not to be required, nor excessive fines imposed, nor cruel and unusual punishments inflicted.*

Section 10. *That general warrants, whereby an officer or messenger may be commanded to search suspected places without evidence of a fact committed, or to seize any person or persons not named, or whose offense is not particularly described and supported by evidence, are grievous and oppressive and ought not to be granted.*

Section 11. *That in controversies respecting property, and in suits between man and man, the ancient trial by jury is preferable to any other and ought to be held sacred.* [31]

Section 12. *That the freedom of the press is one of the great bulwarks of liberty, and can never be restrained but by despotic governments.*

Section 13. *That a well-regulated militia, composed of the body of the people, trained to arms, is the proper, natural, and safe defense of a free state; that standing armies, in time of peace, should be avoided as dangerous to liberty; and that in all cases the military should be under strict subordination to, and governed by, the civil power.*

Section 14. *That the people have a right to uniform government; and, therefore, that no government separate from or independent of the government of Virginia ought to be erected or established within the limits thereof.*

Section 15. *That no free government, or the blessings of liberty, can be preserved to any people but by a firm adherence to justice, moderation, temperance, frugality, and virtue and by frequent recurrence to fundamental principles.*

Section 16. *That religion, or the duty which we owe to our Creator, and the manner of discharging it, can be directed only by reason and conviction, not by force or violence; and therefore all men are equally entitled to the free exercise of religion, according to the dictates of conscience; and that it is the mutual duty of all to practise Christian forbearance, love, and charity toward each other.*

Unanimously adopted, June 11, 1776, at the Virginia Convention.

Section 16, relating to the role of religion in Virginia society and governance, carries with it several premises and suppositions. First, it acknowledges that man owes a duty to his Creator, and that such a duty is both individual, in each person, and collective, in society.

The second concept confirms the manner in which members of society are to discharge that duty, namely through individual reason and conviction. That religious duty is an innately personal one, which is not imposed by force or violence, but by the omnipotent Creator. From this assertion springs the third concept: the state cannot punish or restrain a person based on religious beliefs except when such beliefs disturb peace, happiness, or safety.

Finally, there is the absolute requirement that all citizens of Virginia practice Christian forbearance, love, and charity. This concept of Christianity guiding the actions of the people is of seminal importance, and not merely because Christianity was the prevailing religion of the day. The reason Christianity, specifically, *must* be the principal religious force within a free society is because of the unique, central message that Christianity brought to the Jewish faith: the concept of loving service to one's neighbor stated, amongst other places, in the Gospel according to Mark.

> *"You must love the Lord your God with all your heart, with all your soul, with all your mind and with all your strength. . . . You must love your neighbor as yourself. There is no commandment greater than these. . . To love Him with all you heart, with all your understanding and strength, and to love your neighbor as yourself, this is far more important than any burnt offering or sacrifice."*
>
> (Mk. 12:30-33)

This concept of love and its inextricable ties to religious service is unique to Christianity. With this assertion that man's purpose includes loving those around him comes the responsibility of service to others. In a free society, unencumbered by external restraints, the selfish pursuit of a man's interest will push him inexorably toward amassing more possessions and more power. Naturally, those with the greatest abilities will eventually tower over those with lesser ones and squander them with their overwhelming might.

A pure republic respecting the unencumbered motivations and accomplishments of its citizens rightfully would allow these proclivities to proceed unchecked, unless its people were restricted by the Christian edict of loving others as they would love themselves. The people would then possess an inherent code of conduct not needing to be laid down by the Republic.

It is through this prism of Christian forbearance that the actions and interventions of the Founders and the Framers need to be viewed. These men were working on the assumption that their society and social customs were decidedly Christian in nature. Whether they advocated for religious freedom, rights of conscience, or separation of church and state, their testimonies and arguments were based on the precept that American society and the American people were inherently Christian and acted under the moral presumptions afforded by Christianity. This fundamental assumption regarding the color of American society at the time of its founding is the reason George Mason declared it the "mutual duty of all to practice Christian forbearance, love, and charity to each other," in Section 16 of the Virginia Bill of Rights.

This is also the reason why when Madison entered the debate as a twenty-six year-old legislator at the Virginia Convention and preached a strict adherence to religious freedom in Virginia's laws regardless of whether the religion be Christian or not, the delegates at the Virginia Convention did not accept his radical contention.

Just look at Madison's response to Mason's religious freedom draft within the proposed Virginia Bill of Rights and compare it to Section 16:

> *That religion, or the duty we owe our creator, and the manner of discharging it, being under the direction of reason and conviction only, not of violence, or compulsion, all men are entitled to the full and free exercise of it according to the dictates of conscience; and therefore no man or class of men ought on account of religion be invested with particular emoluments or privileges, nor subjected to any penalties or disabilities, unless under color of religion the preservation of equal liberty, and the existence of the State be manifestly endangered.*[xi]

There are significant differences between Madison's version and Mason's, not the least of these is the removal of Christian forbearance, love, and charity as the central pillar for society.

It is evident that regardless of Madison's personal faith, he did not place a great deal of importance upon Christianity as the guiding force in a republic. His greater quest was for equal standing for all regardless of the observed religion. Madison based his reasoning on the presumption that if there is a direct and intimate relationship between an individual and his

---

xi James Madison in Rodney K. Smith, "Getting Off On the Wrong Foot and Back On Again: A Reexamination of the History of the Framing of the Religion Clauses of the First Amendment And a Critique of the Reynolds And Everson Decisions." Wake Forest Law Review vol. 20, (1984): 580.

Creator, a relationship not to be decayed by the power of the state, then there would be no room for the state to influence the person on his or her selection of his or her beliefs. This prohibition, Madison argued, would not be limited to the selection or preference of a particular Christian sect, but in the selection of any religious belief, Christian or not.[60]

But the Fifth Convention would have none of it. Instead, it would adopt a hybrid version of Mason's and Madison's statements, retaining the acknowledgement of a duty borne upon all to practice Christian forbearance, love, and charity:

> **Section 16.** *That religion, or the duty which we owe to our Creator, and the manner of discharging it, can be directed only by reason and conviction, not by force or violence; and therefore all men are equally entitled to the free exercise of religion, according to the dictates of conscience; and that it is the mutual duty of all to practise Christian forbearance, love, and charity toward each other.*
>
> (Va. Bill of Rights, Jun. 11, 1776)

From the final actions of the Fifth Convention, we can conclude that Madison was not in the majority in the matter of removing Christianity from the Virginia Bill of Rights. We can also glean that the retention of Christianity as a named religion was a matter of significant importance to the revolutionary leaders in Virginia. That twentieth-century justices selectively ignored this fact in rulings regarding religious liberty is evidence of either a lack of understanding on the matter, or the presence of an artificially contrived agenda to extricate Christianity from serving as America's overarching moral compass.

Interestingly, Thomas Jefferson did not participate in the Fifth Convention's discussions as he was serving in Congress. Consequently, although he was aware of the results of the Convention, he was not nearly as familiar with its actual discussions and deliberations. This is of particular importance when considering the weight courts place on Jefferson's personal letter regarding religious freedom.

But the Virginia Bill of Rights is by no means the only source providing insight into the intent of the Framers regarding religion and public worship.

Much can be learned as well from the events that transpired thirteen years later involving Thomas Jefferson, James Madison, and Patrick Henry in the Virginia Assembly.

Jefferson was always a grandiose thinker and concerned over the condition of man. In keeping with his preoccupations on this issue and the possible interference of government with man's pursuit of truth, he introduced his Bill for Religious Freedom at the Virginia Assembly in 1779.[xii] Based on the positions espoused in this statute, Jefferson's view on religious freedom was seemingly even stricter than Madison's. For Jefferson, any interference with religious worship and liberty must be avoided.[61] Jefferson was not only an ardent follower of natural law, but also of the promotion of the uncorrupted pursuit of truth. For as Jefferson articulated as one of his assumptions in the recitals of his Bill for Establishing Religious Freedom:

> *And finally, that truth is great and will prevail if left to herself; that she is the proper and sufficient antagonist to error, and has nothing to fear from the conflict unless by human interposition disarmed of her natural weapons, free argument and debate; errors ceasing to be dangerous when it is permitted freely to contradict them. . .*
>
> (An Act for Establishing Religious Freedom,
> Va, Assembly, Jan. 16, 1786)

And if truth is to be sought free from obstructions, then government interference or the magistrate should not corrupt the pursuit of the ultimate truth, the truth governing the meaning and the purpose of man. For this reason, Jefferson would write within the substance of the same bill,

> *That to suffer the civil magistrate to intrude his powers into the field of opinion and to restrain the profession or propagation of principles on supposition of their ill tendency is a dangerous falacy, which at once destroys all religious liberty. . .* (An Act for Establishing Religious Freedom,
> Va, Assembly, Jan. 16, 1786)

---

xii Jefferson listed the Statute as one of three accomplishments for which he most wished to be remembered. The others were the drafting of the Declaration of Independence and the founding of the University of Virginia. (Thomas Jefferson, undated memorandum quoted in epitaph.)

But even for Jefferson, there was some room for interference in the beliefs of an individual, such as "when principles break out into overt acts against peace and good order."[62] So even though Jefferson advocated for strict avoidance of interference by government with the religious beliefs of men, neither one's religious beliefs nor conscience was to be employed for the purposes of disrupting the safety of the citizenry or to disrupt the social order. In 1779, at least, Jefferson's focus was not on a complete separation of church and state, but rather on a prohibition of interference by government in the person's pursuit of truth, religious or otherwise.

Nor was Jefferson's purpose in submitting his bill the prohibition of public worship. Truer to his vision was the prevention of government interference with the consciences of men. From his Bill Establishing Religious Freedom:

> *We the General Assembly of Virginia do enact that no man shall be compelled to frequent or support any religious worship, place, or ministry whatsoever, nor shall be enforced, restrained, molested, or burthened in his body or goods, nor shall otherwise suffer, on account of his religious opinions or belief; but that all men shall be free to profess, and by argument to maintain, their opinions in matters of religion, and that the same shall in no wise diminish, enlarge, or affect their civil capacities.*
>
> (An Act for Establishing Religious Freedom,
> Va, Assembly, Jan. 16, 1786)

By 1784, Jefferson's bill had not successfully passed through the Virginia Assembly, but at this time, another bill dealing with religious worship, introduced by Patrick Henry, arrived at the Assembly's floor.

At the time, Virginians were allowed to worship in established churches that were supported by taxes. As one could imagine, the disestablishment of a church by the legislature served as an existential threat to its existence.

Even though the House of Burgess did not officially recognize it until 1619, the Anglican Church had been the established church of Virginia since its inception, but Virginians did not hold the Anglican Church in high esteem during the time of the Revolutionary War. Consequently, a number of provisions were passed to weaken its position within the new state, including the passage of a law that would discontinue the collection of tithes designed to support the salaries of the Anglican clergy. By 1784, the Anglican Church was in danger of disestablishment, and some members within Virginia's House of Delegates wished to strengthen its position in Virginia to prevent its complete decimation.[63] Ultimately, Virginia disestablished the Anglican Church within its boundaries and created the Episcopal Church out of its vestiges.[xiii]

Powered by the momentum of the establishment of the Episcopal Church, Patrick Henry, on the day following the establishment bill's passage, introduced a "Bill Establishing a Provision for Teachers of Christian Religion" of 1784. If passed, Henry's bill, cloaked in a concern over the deteriorating state of morality in Virginia, would require Virginians to pay a tax that would go toward the support of the Episcopal Church in Virginia.

The initial incarnation of Henry's Bill saw limited support and was modified to allow the taxpayer to designate the church to which the funds would be allocated. If the taxpayer preferred, the funds would not be allocated to any church, but rather to the treasury ". . . for the encouragement of seminaries of learning within the Counties whence such sums shall arise. . ."[64]

Although Jefferson chaired the Committee on Religion, it was Madison who most aggressively acted in opposition to Henry's bill. As we have seen, Madison strongly disagreed with Henry's view on government support for religion. For Madison, which faith one espoused was a question solely for the individual to answer, and government had no place in influencing it, directly or indirectly.[65]

Henry, however, was an impassioned and powerful orator, arguably the best in America at the time, and his speech was winning great affection for his bill. Madison recognized the swell of support that Henry was garnering and feared his bill's passage. On its surface, it would appear that Madison's objection to Henry's Bill centered around the preferential treatment the State would provide the Episcopal church, a proposition that ran counter to Madison's views of equality among religions before government. Yet, his

---

[xiii] Interestingly, James Madison's cousin of the same name was ordained the first Archbishop of the Episcopal Church in Virginia.

opposition continued despite the discretionary provisions amended onto the bill obviating the validity of that argument.

However, under Henry's leadership, the Bill came so close to passing that Madison found no other viable alternative than to have it tabled.

Having earned a respite from the debate, Madison quickly went to work to garner public support in opposing Henry's Bill. His approach of directly appealing to the people resulted in the "Memorial and Remonstrance Against Religious Assessments," which Madison authored and anonymously published on June 20, 1785. In his "Memorial," Madison laid out the arguments against Henry's Bill, creating what would later be considered his treatise on his views regarding the relationship between government, the governed, and religion. Interestingly, unbeknownst to Madison, the language in his Remonstrance would serve as one of the most heavily cited texts in civil law regarding religion and religious freedom.

> *To the Honorable the General Assembly of the Commonwealth of Virginia A Memorial and Remonstrance*
>
> *We the subscribers, citizens of the said Commonwealth, having taken into serious consideration, a Bill printed by order of the last Session of General Assembly, entitled "A Bill Establishing a Provision for Teachers of Christian Religion," and conceiving that the same if finally armed with the sanctions of a law, will be a dangerous abuse of power, are bound as faithful members of a free State to remonstrate against it, and to declare the reasons by which we are determined. We remonstrate against the said Bill,*
>
> *1. Because we hold it for a fundamental and undeniable truth, "that Religion or the duty which we owe to our Creator and the manner of discharging it, can be directed only by reason and conviction, not by force or violence." [Virginia Declaration of Rights, art. 16] The Religion then of every man must be left to the conviction and conscience of every man; and it is the right of every man to exercise it as these may dictate. This right is in its nature an unalienable right. It is unalienable, because the opinions of men, depending only on the evidence contemplated by their own minds cannot follow the dictates of other men: It is unalienable also, because what is here a right towards men,*

is a duty towards the Creator. It is the duty of every man to render to the Creator such homage and such only as he believes to be acceptable to him. This duty is precedent, both in order of time and in degree of obligation, to the claims of Civil Society. Before any man can be considered as a member of Civil Society, he must be considered as a subject of the Governour of the Universe: And if a member of Civil Society, who enters into any subordinate Association, must always do it with a reservation of his duty to the General Authority; much more must every man who becomes a member of any particular Civil Society, do it with a saving of his allegiance to the Universal Sovereign. We maintain therefore that in matters of Religion, no mans right is abridged by the institution of Civil Society and that Religion is wholly exempt from its cognizance. True it is, that no other rule exists, by which any question which may divide a Society, can be ultimately determined, but the will of the majority; but it is also true that the majority may trespass on the rights of the minority.

2. Because if Religion be exempt from the authority of the Society at large, still less can it be subject to that of the Legislative Body. The latter are but the creatures and vicegerents of the former. Their jurisdiction is both derivative and limited: it is limited with regard to the co-ordinate departments, more necessarily is it limited with regard to the constituents. The preservation of a free Government requires not merely, that the metes and bounds which separate each department of power be invariably maintained; but more especially that neither of them be suffered to overleap the great Barrier which defends the rights of the people. The Rulers who are guilty of such an encroachment, exceed the commission from which they derive their authority, and are Tyrants. The People who submit to it are governed by laws made neither by themselves nor by an authority derived from them, and are slaves.

3. Because it is proper to take alarm at the first experiment on our liberties. We hold this prudent jealousy to be the first duty of Citizens, and one of the noblest characteristics of the late Revolution. The free men of America did not wait till usurped power had strengthened itself by exercise, and entangled the question in precedents. They saw all the consequences in the principle, and they avoided the consequences by denying the principle. We revere this lesson too much soon to forget it. Who does not see that the same authority which can establish Christianity, in exclusion of all other Religions, may establish with the same ease any particular sect of Christians, in exclusion of all other Sects? that the same authority which can force a citizen to contribute three pence only of his property for the support of any one establishment, may force him to conform to any other establishment in all cases whatsoever?

4. Because the Bill violates that equality which ought to be the basis of every law, and which is more indispensible, in proportion as the validity or expediency of any law is more liable to be impeached. If "all men are by nature equally free and independent," [Virginia Declaration of Rights, art. 1] all men are to be considered as entering into Society on equal conditions; as relinquishing no more, and therefore retaining no less, one than another, of their natural rights. Above all are they to be considered as retaining an "equal title to the free exercise of Religion according to the dictates of Conscience." [Virginia Declaration of Rights, art. 16] Whilst we assert for ourselves a freedom to embrace, to profess and to observe the Religion which we believe to be of divine origin, we cannot deny an equal freedom to those whose minds have not yet yielded to the evidence which has convinced us. If this freedom be abused, it is an offence against God, not against man: To God, therefore, not to man, must an account of it be rendered. As the Bill violates equality by subjecting some to peculiar burdens, so it violates the same principle, by granting to others peculiar exemptions. Are the Quakers and Menonists the only sects who think a compulsive support of their Religions unnecessary and unwarrantable? Can their piety alone be en trusted with the care of public worship? Ought their Religions to be e dowed above all others with extraordinary privileges by which prosel may be enticed from all others? We think too favorably of the j and good sense of these denominations to believe that they eithe pre-eminences over their fellow citizens or that they will be sed them from the common opposition to the measure.

5. Because the Bill implies either that the Civil Magistra petent Judge of Religious Truth; or that he may employ Re engine of Civil policy. The first is an arrogant pretension f contradictory opinions of Rulers in all ages, and throug the second an unhallowed perversion of the means of sa

6. Because the establishment proposed by the Bill is not requisite for the support of the Christian Religion. To say that it is, is a contradiction to the Christian Religion itself, for every page of it disavows a dependence on the powers of this world: it is a contradiction to fact; for it is known that this Religion both existed and flourished, not only without the support of human laws, but in spite of every opposition from them, and not only during the period of miraculous aid, but long after it had been left to its own evidence and the ordinary care of Providence. Nay, it is a contradiction in terms; for a Religion not invented by human policy, must have pre-existed and been supported, before it was established by human policy. It is moreover to weaken in those who profess this Religion a pious confidence in its innate excellence and the patronage of its Author; and to foster in those who still reject it, a suspicion that its friends are too conscious of its fallacies to trust it to its own merits.

7. Because experience witnesseth that ecclesiastical establishments,
nstead of maintaining the purity and efficacy of Religion, have had a
ntrary operation. During almost fifteen centuries has the legal estab-
ment of Christianity been on trial. What have been its fruits? More
s in all places, pride and indolence in the Clergy, ignorance and
y in the laity, in both, superstition, bigotry and persecution. En-
the Teachers of Christianity for the ages in which it appeared in
t lustre; those of every sect, point to the ages prior to its incor-
ith Civil policy. Propose a restoration of this primitive State
Teachers depended on the voluntary rewards of their flocks,
predict its downfall. On which Side ought their testimo-
test weight, when for or when against their interest?

e establishment in question is not necessary for the
ernment. If it be urged as necessary for the support
only as it is a means of supporting Religion, and
he latter purpose, it cannot be necessary for the
t within the cognizance of Civil Government
ent be necessary to Civil Government? What
stical establishments had on Civil Society?
een seen to erect a spiritual tyranny on
in many instances they have been seen
tyranny: in no instance have they

influence on the health and prosperity of the State. If with the salutary effects of this system under our own eyes, we begin to contract the bounds of Religious freedom, we know no name that will too severely reproach our folly. At least let warning be taken at the first fruits of the threatened innovation. The very appearance of the Bill has transformed "that Christian forbearance, love and charity," [Virginia Declaration of Rights, art. 16] which of late mutually prevailed, into animosities and jealousies, which may not soon be appeased. What mischiefs may not be dreaded, should this enemy to the public quiet be armed with the force of a law?

12. Because the policy of the Bill is adverse to the diffusion of the light of Christianity. The first wish of those who enjoy this precious gift ought to be that it may be imparted to the whole race of mankind. Compare the number of those who have as yet received it with the number still remaining under the dominion of false Religions; and how small is the former! Does the policy of the Bill tend to lessen the disproportion? No; it at once discourages those who are strangers to the light of revelation from coming into the Region of it; and countenances by example the nations who continue in darkness, in shutting out those who might convey it to them. Instead of Levelling as far as possible, every obstacle to the victorious progress of Truth, the Bill with an ignoble and unchristian timidity would circumscribe it with a wall of defence against the encroachments of error.

13. Because attempts to enforce by legal sanctions, acts obnoxious to so great a proportion of Citizens, tend to enervate the laws in general, and to slacken the bands of Society. If it be difficult to execute any law which is not generally deemed necessary or salutary, what must be the case, where it is deemed invalid and dangerous? And what may be the effect of so striking an example of impotency in the Government, on its general authority?

14. Because a measure of such singular magnitude and delicacy ought not to be imposed, without the clearest evidence that it is called for by a majority of citizens, and no satisfactory method is yet proposed by which the voice of the majority in this case may be determined, or its influence secured. "The people of the respective counties are indeed requested to signify their opinion respecting the adoption of the Bill to the next Session of Assembly." But the representation must be made equal, been seen the guardians of the liberties of the people. Rulers who wished to subvert the public liberty, may have found an established Clergy convenient auxiliaries. A just Government instituted to secure & perpetuate it needs them not. Such a Government will be best supported by protecting every Citizen in the enjoyment of his Religion with the same equal hand which protects his person and his property; by neither invading the equal rights of any Sect, nor suffering any Sect to invade those of another.

9. Because the proposed establishment is a departure from that generous policy, which, offering an Asylum to the persecuted and oppressed of every Nation and Religion, promised a lustre to our country, and an accession to the number of its citizens. What a melancholy mark is the Bill of sudden degeneracy? Instead of holding forth an Asylum to the persecuted, it is itself a signal of persecution. It degrades from the equal rank of Citizens all those whose opinions in Religion do not bend to those of the Legislative authority. Distant as it may be in its present form from the Inquisition, it differs from it only in degree. The one is the first step, the other the last in the career of intolerance. The magnanimous sufferer under this cruel scourge in foreign Regions, must view the Bill as a Beacon on our Coast, warning him to seek some other haven, where liberty and philanthrophy in their due extent, may offer a more certain repose from his Troubles.

10. Because it will have a like tendency to banish our Citizens. The allurements presented by other situations are every day thinning their number. To superadd a fresh motive to emigration by revoking the liberty which they now enjoy, would be the same species of folly which has dishonoured and depopulated flourishing kingdoms.

11. Because it will destroy that moderation and harmony which the forbearance of our laws to intermeddle with Religion has produced among its several sects. Torrents of blood have been spilt in the old world, by vain attempts of the secular arm, to extinguish Religious discord, by proscribing all difference in Religious opinion. Time has at length revealed the true remedy. Every relaxation of narrow and rigorous policy, wherever it has been tried, has been found to assuage the disease. The American Theatre has exhibited proofs that equal and compleat liberty, if it does not wholly eradicate it, sufficiently destroys its malignant

6. Because the establishment proposed by the Bill is not requisite for the support of the Christian Religion. To say that it is, is a contradiction to the Christian Religion itself, for every page of it disavows a dependence on the powers of this world: it is a contradiction to fact; for it is known that this Religion both existed and flourished, not only without the support of human laws, but in spite of every opposition from them, and not only during the period of miraculous aid, but long after it had been left to its own evidence and the ordinary care of Providence. Nay, it is a contradiction in terms; for a Religion not invented by human policy, must have pre-existed and been supported, before it was established by human policy. It is moreover to weaken in those who profess this Religion a pious confidence in its innate excellence and the patronage of its Author; and to foster in those who still reject it, a suspicion that its friends are too conscious of its fallacies to trust it to its own merits.

7. Because experience witnesseth that ecclesiastical establishments, instead of maintaining the purity and efficacy of Religion, have had a contrary operation. During almost fifteen centuries has the legal establishment of Christianity been on trial. What have been its fruits? More or less in all places, pride and indolence in the Clergy, ignorance and servility in the laity, in both, superstition, bigotry and persecution. Enquire of the Teachers of Christianity for the ages in which it appeared in its greatest lustre; those of every sect, point to the ages prior to its incorporation with Civil policy. Propose a restoration of this primitive State in which its Teachers depended on the voluntary rewards of their flocks, many of them predict its downfall. On which Side ought their testimony to have greatest weight, when for or when against their interest?

8. Because the establishment in question is not necessary for the support of Civil Government. If it be urged as necessary for the support of Civil Government only as it is a means of supporting Religion, and it be not necessary for the latter purpose, it cannot be necessary for the former. If Religion be not within the cognizance of Civil Government how can its legal establishment be necessary to Civil Government? What influence in fact have ecclesiastical establishments had on Civil Society? In some instances they have been seen to erect a spiritual tyranny on the ruins of the Civil authority; in many instances they have been seen upholding the thrones of political tyranny: in no instance have they does not see that the same authority which can establish Christianity, in exclusion of all other Religions, may establish with the same ease any particular sect of Christians, in exclusion of all other Sects? that the same authority which can force a citizen to contribute three pence only of his property for the support of any one establishment, may force him to conform to any other establishment in all cases whatsoever?

4. Because the Bill violates that equality which ought to be the basis of every law, and which is more indispensible, in proportion as the validity or expediency of any law is more liable to be impeached. If "all men are by nature equally free and independent," [Virginia Declaration of Rights, art. 1] all men are to be considered as entering into Society on equal conditions; as relinquishing no more, and therefore retaining no less, one than another, of their natural rights. Above all are they to be considered as retaining an "equal title to the free exercise of Religion according to the dictates of Conscience." [Virginia Declaration of Rights, art. 16] Whilst we assert for ourselves a freedom to embrace, to profess and to observe the Religion which we believe to be of divine origin, we cannot deny an equal freedom to those whose minds have not yet yielded to the evidence which has convinced us. If this freedom be abused, it is an offence against God, not against man: To God, therefore, not to man, must an account of it be rendered. As the Bill violates equality by subjecting some to peculiar burdens, so it violates the same principle, by granting to others peculiar exemptions. Are the Quakers and Menonists the only sects who think a compulsive support of their Religions unnecessary and unwarrantable? Can their piety alone be entrusted with the care of public worship? Ought their Religions to be endowed above all others with extraordinary privileges by which proselytes may be enticed from all others? We think too favorably of the justice and good sense of these denominations to believe that they either covet pre-eminences over their fellow citizens or that they will be seduced by them from the common opposition to the measure.

5. Because the Bill implies either that the Civil Magistrate is a competent Judge of Religious Truth; or that he may employ Religion as an engine of Civil policy. The first is an arrogant pretension falsified by the contradictory opinions of Rulers in all ages, and throughout the world: the second an unhallowed perversion of the means of salvation.

before the voice either of the Representatives or of the Counties will be that of the people. Our hope is that neither of the former will, after due consideration, espouse the dangerous principle of the Bill. Should the event disappoint us, it will still leave us in full confidence, that a fair appeal to the latter will reverse the sentence against our liberties.

15. Because finally, "the equal right of every citizen to the free exercise of his Religion according to the dictates of conscience" is held by the same tenure with all our other rights. If we recur to its origin, it is equally the gift of nature; if we weigh its importance, it cannot be less dear to us; if we consult the "Declaration of those rights which pertain to the good people of Virginia, as the basis and foundation of Government," it is enumerated with equal solemnity, or rather studied emphasis. Either then, we must say, that the Will of the Legislature is the only measure of their authority; and that in the plenitude of this authority, they may sweep away all our fundamental rights; or, that they are bound to leave this particular right untouched and sacred: Either we must say, that they may controul the freedom of the press, may abolish the Trial by Jury, may swallow up the Executive and Judiciary Powers of the State; nay that they may despoil us of our very right of suffrage, and erect themselves into an independent and hereditary Assembly or, we must say, that they have no authority to enact into law the Bill under consideration. We the Subscribers say, that the General Assembly of this Commonwealth have no such authority: And that no effort may be omitted on our part against so dangerous an usurpation, we oppose to it, this remonstrance; earnestly praying, as we are in duty bound, that the Supreme Lawgiver of the Universe, by illuminating those to whom it is addressed, may on the one hand, turn their Councils from every act which would affront his holy prerogative, or violate the trust committed to them: and on the other, guide them into every measure which may be worthy of his blessing, may redound to their own praise, and may establish more firmly the liberties, the prosperity and the happiness of the Commonwealth.

[James Madison, "Memorial and Remonstrance Against Religious Assessments," (Jun. 20, 1785)].

Interestingly, although Madison, in his Memorial, takes great pains to defend the concept of equality for the various religions, he does not explicitly state that government must be devoid of religion, nor does he call for a separation of church and state.[66] In fact, he opens by referring to the duty owed to the Creator, calling it an undeniable truth. He then asserts, "It is the duty of every man to render to the Creator such homage and such only as he believes to be acceptable to him."[67] He also voices concern over the ability of the majority to trespass on the rights of the minority, [68] and remarkably, even advocates for the rights of the atheist, affirming that they could not be denied an equal freedom to that observed for the faithful.[69] Finally, he defends his minority belief that even Christianity as a whole ought not have a special place in Virginian society since the establishment of Christianity to the exclusion of all other religions would essentially mean giving government the authority to select one sect over all others.[70, xiv]

Madison's "Memorial" made a monumental impact on twentieth century American society as it has been embraced not only by those who honestly advocate for religious freedom, but also by those who use the concept to banish worship from the public square.

However, there are a number of substantive and even fatal arguments to Madison's contentions not only as they apply to the Assembly debates relating to Patrick Henry's Bill, but also to the application of the argument regarding the national government and his selective use of the Virginia Bill of Rights. First, despite Madison's claim, Henry's Bill did not establish a predominant religious sect, nor for that matter, did it establish Christianity as an official religion of Virginia.[71] In fact, the Bill allowed the taxpayer to select a preferred church for which to contribute, or no church at all.[72]

Additionally, the preamble of the Bill describes the *secular* purpose of supporting religion.[73] Patrick Henry asserts that the diffusion of Christian knowledge is necessary, not for the self-serving purpose of promoting religion, but because such knowledge ". . . hath a natural tendency to correct

---

[xiv] Of course, here Madison makes the mistake of considering one of the world's great religions a mere "sect."

the morals of men, restrain their vices, and preserve the peace of society. . . ,"[74] goals that Henry believed could not be accomplished without learned teachers of religion.

As fate would have it, the Governor's office in Virginia would become vacant at the same time Madison's Memorial was being circulated. Because of this development, Madison saw an opportunity to remove his opponent from the Virginia Assembly and astutely arranged to have Henry elected Governor of Virginia, successfully carrying out the ploy in November, 1784.

Predictably, devoid of Henry's influence, the measure providing for state support for teachers of religion died upon its return to the Assembly during the 1785 session. In 1786, the Assembly then passed Jefferson's Act for Establishing Religious Freedom.

The passage of Jefferson's Bill, seemingly at the expense of Henry's, served to incorrectly promulgate the impression that the Framers believed in a strict separation between church and state; a sense that would be misused almost two centuries later in calling for the government's sterilization of every form of religious influence.

Interestingly, however, Henry's Bill would not have clashed with Jefferson's Bill since Henry's provisions did not compel taxpayers to frequent or support any form of religious worship or belief and allowed all to profess and maintain their religious opinions. Indeed, one of the great historical ironies in this regard is that the debate in the Virginia Assembly led by Madison against Henry was, in reality, not required at all.[75]

The Fight for Religious Freedom at the Constitutional Convention

Madison continued his fight for religious liberty within the Constitutional Convention in Philadelphia. But, despite his monumental presence there, he would not have many opportunities to define his views on religious freedom and its relationship to the government. The Delegates in Philadelphia would be crafting a government of limited powers and none was prepared to cede to the new national government any authority at directing, or repressing, the religious proclivities of any state. Their task was delineating legal relationships among men, stripped of any philosophical comments.

Moreover, Madison wanted nothing to do with a delineation of rights, as the mere act of creating such a list was antithetical to the Convention's purpose of creating a government of enumerated powers. Why, Madison asked, if the new federal government was limited in its scope of powers to only those in Article I of the Constitution, include a list of guaranteed rights?

But here again, men like Madison's longtime opponent, Governor Patrick Henry, forced Madison's hand. These men so distrusted the new federal government, so distrusted man's innate thirst for power and the tyrannical predispositions of government that they refused to even participate in the Constitution's construction. These men represented a real obstacle to the ratification of the new Constitution, particularly when the esteemed defender of states' rights, George Mason, joined their cause. They demanded, at the very least, an express guarantee that the new government would honor the rights belonging to the people and the states. It was this faction and its concerns that finally forced Madison to concede the point and promise that upon ratification of the new national constitution, he would begin work at defining a list of freedoms protected from encroachment by the new national government.

Consequently, because the federal government was not going to play a role in legislation regarding religious freedoms, there was no significant opportunity to engage in a discussion about it during the convention. Some have contended that the relative absence of God and religious worship within the Constitutional Convention is evidence of the secular nature of the nation the Framers were constructing. They claim, in fact, that in the ten years between the time of the Declaration of Independence and the Constitutional Convention, the country and its leaders steered away from religion and God toward a more secular existence. This explains, they argue, the reason why God is essentially stripped from the Constitution.

The argument of these secularists collapses under the weight of historical realities. The state constitutions ratified during that time, for example, resoundingly remove any doubt as to the importance of Christianity in eighteenth century American society. Of the original thirteen states, eleven had constitutions drafted around the time of the Declaration of Independence.[xv] In each of those eleven, the existence of God was acknowledged in some manner greater than merely declaring a year of our Lord, and each, except for the Constitution of New York, overtly declared Christianity as the observed religion of the state. This is hardly evidence of a move towards secularism.

Here are some of the many examples of the intermingling between church and state in the various state constitutions of the time. Delaware required each of its officers and legislators to take an oath declaring that he had ". . . faith in God the Father, and in Jesus Christ, His Only Son, and in the Holy Ghost, one God, blessed for evermore, . . ."[76] and to ". . . acknowledge the holy scriptures of the Old and New Testament to be given by divine inspiration."[77] In Georgia, all representatives were required to be members of the Protestant religion.[78] In Pennsylvania, an oath was required of every member of the legislature to swear his belief in one God and in the divinity of the Old and New Testaments.[79] South Carolina required a belief in God in order to be an elector,[80] and Protestant Christianity was its official religion.[81] The Constitution of Vermont of 1786 declared Christianity as the religion of the land while affording no Christian sect supremacy over another.[82] The Kentucky Constitution of 1792 also acknowledged government's subservience to God by declaring an oath or affirmation to be ". . . the most solemn appeal to God,"[83] and declared all men's ". . . natural and indefeasible right to worship Almighty God. . . "[84] And in Tennessee, although ministers were prohibited from holding office,[85] a person denying the existence of God or an afterlife full of rewards was not allowed to hold any civil office.[86]

It was not until the Louisiana State Constitution of 1812 that the need to worship God is not proclaimed in some fashion, except that even here, the oath of office for governmental officers included the plea, ". . . so help me

---

[xv] Connecticut created its constitution through its Fundamental Orders of 1638-1639 and will not be considered here. Rhode Island, the last state to adopt the Constitution of the United States did not adopt its own Constitution until 1842.

God."[87, xvi, xvii] Indeed, Christianity was so integral to the soul of the country even after the ratification of the Constitution that John Marshall wrote in 1833,

> *The American population is entirely Christian, & with us, Christianity & Religion are identified. It would not be strange, indeed, if with such a people, our institutions did not presuppose Christianity, & did not often refer to it, & exhibit with it. Legislation on the subject is admitted to require great delicacy, because fredom [sic] of conscience & respect for our religion both claim our most serious regard.*
>
> (John Marshall to Jasper Adams, May 9, 1833)

Is the Constitution Really a Secular Document?

As we have seen, many argue the secularity of the Constitution, citing the absence of any specific reference to a Creator and the express prohibition of a religious test. In reality, the more likely reason the federal constitution does not delve into the relationship between man, God, and government is simply because the Constitution is a document descriptive of the new nation's regulatory machinery and not a philosophical work.

The organizational nature of the document notwithstanding, Christianity and God still enter the Constitution of the United States in at least four instances, 1) the reference to the year of our Lord; 2) the skipping of Sunday in the days by which the President is allowed to return a bill passed by Congress; 3) the prohibition against a religious test as a qualification for any office or public trust; and 4) the inclusion of an oath of affirmation. Of these, the last bears further commentary, as it is an overt action of subservience to the Creator, but has been inappropriately used to support an argument in favor of a strict separation between church and state.

In Article VI, the Framers wrote, "The Senators and Representatives before mentioned, and the members of the several states, shall be bound by oath or affirmation, to support this Constitution." The importance of this

---

[xvi] For an example of such language, see Del. Const. art. 22 (adopted Sept. 10, 1776).

[xvii] Later Constitutions such as the Constitution of Indiana continued to declare man's right to worship Almighty God. (Ind. Const. art. I, § 3 (adopted 1816)

requirement is striking when one considers that an "oath" is often defined as "a solemn promise"[88] with the words "calling on God" as witness included in many definitions.[89] It is viewed as an appeal to God to witness the veracity or solemnity of the words or actions about to be taken.[90] No greater act of contrition, or of subservience to God, can be required of one about to undertake an action than to require the person to make the statement under the direct appeal to God. The oath requirement within the Constitution of the United States is a preeminent acknowledgment of the existence of God and of the subservience of every American elected official to Him.

However, many have argued that in including the option for undertaking an affirmation as an alternative to an oath, the Framers were allowing a vehicle for nonbelievers and atheists to swear their allegiance to the Constitution, thus reinforcing the secular nature of the document. This assertion is not true. The Framers were attempting to appease the faith requirements of the Quakers and those like them, whose fears of God was so great that they were prohibited from undertaking an oath.[91] Consequently, the affirmation inscribed within the Constitution was far from Godless, as some would like to argue today. It was merely an option to be exercised by those whose fear of and respect for God was so great that they could not bring themselves to invoke His name in an oath, but would nevertheless place themselves under the threat of perjury when making their declaration.

Oddly, another argument made in support of a purely secular Constitution centers on a faith intervention that took place during the Constitutional Convention on June 28, 1787. At the time, the Convention had been bogged down with conflict. The issues of slavery, the relative representation of the various states, the number and flavor of each of the chambers, and the rights afforded to each of the sovereigns had taken a toll on the members. In frustration, some were thinking that their great effort of redefining the new nation's government would end in failure.

At about that time, Benjamin Franklin recalled a great difference between the dealings of the Constitutional Convention and those of the Second Continental Congress: prayer. Franklin, recalling the opening prayer delivered by Jacob Duché,[xviii] made an impassioned plea to the delegates on the floor of the Convention. Addressing the delegates, he said,

> *Mr. President,*
> *...In the beginning of the Contest with G. Britain, when we were sensible of danger we had daily prayer in this room for the divine protection. Our prayers, Sir, were heard, & they were graciously answered. All of us who were engaged in the struggle must have observed frequent instances of a superintending providence in our favor. To that kind providence we owe this happy opportunity of consulting in peace on the means of establishing our future national felicity. And have we now forgotten that powerful friend? Or do we imagine that we no longer need his assistance? I have lived, Sir, a long time, and the longer I live, the more convincing proofs I see of this truth- that God Governs in the affairs of men...*
> *I therefore beg leave to move-that henceforth prayers imploring the assistance of Heaven, and its blessings on our deliberations, be held in this Assembly every morning before we proceed to business, and that one or more of the Clergy of this City be requested to officiate in that Service.*
>
> (Benjamin Franklin, Jun. 28, 1787, in James Madison, "Notes of Debates in the Federal Convention of 1787.")

Franklin's were some of the most congealing words of the Constitutional Convention and some of the savviest. But, despite his selfless and insightful plea, the Convention rejected his recommendation. Predictably, the significance of that rejection and the implications of this non-action upon the nature of the Constitution have become a source of partisan squalor. Those professing the secularity of the Constitution promote the rejection by the delegates of Franklin's call to prayer as evidence of the Framers' abandonment of religion. They argue that the Framers had strayed away from a theocentric approach to one that was secular, and perhaps even atheistic, in its foundation.

But then there is the matter of the directed comments made in opposition to Franklin's motion. Bearing in mind that the day's convention was to hire a pastor to pray before those assembled rather than simply having

---

[xviii] See pages 80-81.

an assigned member lead the rest of the group in prayer, Franklin's motion required that ". . . one or more of the Clergy of this City be requested to officiate. . ." the delegates in prayer.[92] The concerns of Alexander Hamilton are the first to be recorded in Madison's notes. Hamilton fretted over the perception outside the Convention when the people saw that the delegates, all of a sudden, were asking for the assistance of a pastor. For him, it was the criticisms and fears their actions would elicit among the general public that caused him to object to Franklin's proposal. Hugh Williamson, on the other hand, had a much more practical reason for objecting to Franklin's motion; namely the Convention had no funds with which to pay the pastor for his assistance.[93]

And with those two pragmatic considerations, we witness the complete demise of the secularists' misinformed contentions.

The Bill of Rights, Freedom of Worship, and the Post-Constitutional Role of Religion

It is arguably in the earliest days of the Constitutional Republic and in the conduct of the national leaders of the day that we gain the most direct insights to the proper role of religion in society and governance as envisioned by the Framers. One of the first steps taken by the First United States Congress was the allocation of $500 from the treasury for the annual salary in support of an elected chaplain.[94] The chaplain, among his other responsibilities, was to deliver a prayer for the Congress assembled; a tradition that continues to this day and a true representation of the importance the members of that First Congress placed on God in the public square.[95, xix]

---

xix House Chaplains have represented a diverse group of religious denominations with the following ditributions: Baptist (7), Christian (1), Congregationalist (2), Disciples of Christ (1), Episcopalian (4), Lutheran (1), Methodist (16), Presbyterian (15), Roman Catholic (1), Unitarian (2), and Universalist (1) ; "History of the Chaplaincy," (Office of the Chaplain, United States House of Representatives), *http://chaplain.house.gov/chaplaincy/history.html* on August 16, 2015; and for the Senate: Episcopalians (19), Methodists (17), Presbyterians (14), Baptists (6), Unitarians (2), Congregationalists (1), Lutherans (1), Roman Catholic (1), and Seventh-day Adventist (1) . "Senate Chaplain," *Senate History* (United States Senate), accessed Aug. 16, 2015, *http://www.senate.gov/artandhistory/history/common/briefing/Senate_Chaplain.htm.*

By June 7, that First Congress was set to further define its limitations in regards to religion when presented with Madison's twelve proposed amendments to the Constitution. Unlike the writing of the Constitution, where the language and the concepts leading to the final draft were widely debated and publicly explained, precious little is known about the evolution of the language that became the First Amendment.

Regarding the religious clause of the First Amendment, we do know the First Congress arrived at the words, "Congress shall make no law respecting an establishment of religion, or prohibiting the free exercise thereof. . . ,"[96] as the final iteration of their conception of the guarantees offered by the Creator regarding religious worship. But how did they arrive at this language? Was this Madison's original proposal? Were there other thoughts that were rejected?

The answers to these questions have led us to at least two conclusions that stand as virtually indisputable: 1) the Framers never intended their proposed Constitution to interfere with the manner in which the states regulated religion within their borders; and 2) the wall between church and state, if there ever was such a thing, was to be very porous. In support of the former, we have many of the events that have previously been reviewed. With regards to the latter, we have the actions of our forefathers and their government.

In his original proposition for the First Amendment, Madison wrote: "the Civil Rights of none shall be abridged on account of religious belief or worship, nor shall any national religion be established, nor shall the full and equal rights of conscience be in any manner, nor on any pretext, infringed."[97]

Although introduced in June, Madison's proposed amendments were not acted upon until August 13, 1789, after a floor debate that only took a number of days to complete. August 15, a Saturday, saw the members turn their attention to the matter of freedom of religion. Some, such as Congressmen Sylvester and Huntington feared Madison's language could be misconstrued to give Congress the authority to restrict religion. More to the point, Sylvester feared the language would allow Congress to abolish religion altogether[98] while Huntington was concerned for the rights of those professing no religion at all.[99]

Madison took the opportunity to explain the intent of his proposed language. In his view, "Congress should not establish a religion, and enforce the legal observation of it by law, nor compel men to worship God in any manner contrary to their conscience."[100]

Congressman Livermore was also concerned about the unintended effects of Madison's language and proposed that the clause read, "Congress shall make no laws touching religion, or infringing the rights of conscience."[101] But on August 20, Congressman Ames proposed that the religious freedom language be once again altered to read, "Congress shall make no law establishing religion, or to prevent the free exercise thereof, or to infringe the rights of conscience."[102] The motion was adopted without any record of a debate or an explanation. It is interesting that this language was passed out of the House over Livermore's. Although both versions disallow congressional infringement upon the rights of conscience, Livermore's use of the words "touching religion" as the object of the prohibition imposes a broader restriction than merely prohibiting Congress from establishing a religion. Ames's language allowed for a greater meddling by Congress in religious affairs than Livermore's while agreeing with the prohibition of religious establishment.

The difference is greatly significant as Ames's language would conceivably allow for the funding of religious schools or governmental support of religious institutions, concepts that were at odds with Madison's position during his time in the Virginia Assembly.

The Senate would consider Ames's language, but unfortunately, it did not keep detailed records of its deliberations, leaving posterity only with the recordings of the motions on the bill. On September 9, 1789, after considering a few proposals including one that would have altogether removed a religious clause from the Bill of Rights, the Senate settled upon the language it would send back to the House: "Congress shall make no law establishing articles of faith or a mode of worship, or prohibiting the free exercise of religion."[103]

The House refused to accept the Senate's language, and so the religious liberty provision, along with the rest of the Bill of Rights, made its way to the Conference Committee. It was the Committee's proposed language that was ultimately adopted as part of the First Amendment of the Constitution, "Congress shall make no law respecting an establishment of Religion, or prohibiting the free exercise thereof."[104]

From these debates and their surrounding events, certain conclusions can be drawn. First, the members of the First Congress were very concerned about any perceived power for Congress to select any religion for any advantage or disadvantage before government. Even though it appears there was a significant faction that would have preferred that Christianity in general be given special consideration relative to the other world religions, this view of religious standing did not prevail.

Second, the members were equally concerned with the possibility of the federal government infringing on the religious beliefs and practices of the people and the states' authorities in regulating religion.

Third, there was no mention, at any time, of the existence of a strict separation between church and state. In other words, even though numerous recitations were made regarding undue preferences or undue intrusions, no one, not even Jefferson, suggested that government should be stripped of any religious or spiritual influence, nor was there any discussion in Congress or at the Constitutional Convention about prohibiting governmental support of religious institutions.

And finally, and most importantly, none of the restrictions in the Constitution were to apply to the states.

Thomas Jefferson's Accidental Role in the Analysis of Religious Freedom

During the years following the ratification of the Constitution, the new government embraced religion. George Washington, at his first inauguration, placed his hand on the Bible and spontaneously added the words, "So help me God," to the oath of office. Congress hired chaplains to attend to the religious needs of the members and led them in daily prayers. The plenary authority of the various states to regulate religion and religious worship remained unquestioned. The first two presidents declared national days of fasting and prayer for various purposes, not the least of which was to show the nation's appreciation to its Creator for the favorable outcome of the Revolutionary War and the freedoms that sprang from it. Even the Thanksgiving observance was undertaken, not as a standing tradition as is done presently, but at the behest of a presidential order calling for the national observance.

In 1801, Jefferson became the nation's third president, bringing with him views regarding religion that were quite distinct from those of his predecessors as well as his distinct background. Jefferson never engaged in a military battle like Washington, nor did he take up arms against the British like Adams. Also, Jefferson kept his faith to himself.

By the time he assumed office, Jefferson had participated in only one open forum debate regarding the role of religion in governance. During the Virginia Convention of 1776, when the Virginia Bill of Rights was drafted, Jefferson was serving in Congress. During the Constitutional Convention, Jefferson was in France. And during the First Amendment debates, Jefferson was serving as Secretary of State. Of all the major pubic discussions taking place during the country's founding regarding religion, Jefferson was only present for the Madison-Henry debates in the Virginia Assembly—meaning that he did not benefit from first hand knowledge of the long debates preceding the final wording of the Constitution or the First Amendment.

That is not to say that Jefferson's views did not have ample opportunity to develop and evolve. Clearly, Jefferson's impact on Virginia's legal corpus regarding religion was significant. After all, he did draft and pass his Statute for Religious Freedom through the Virginia Assembly. However, there is no telling what impact Jefferson's presence at the nation's other formative events would have had on the future president.

We can surmise the following regarding Jefferson's views on the nexus between religion and government. He viewed the separation between church and government more strictly than his contemporaries, more so than even Madison.[105] According to Jefferson, government was not to intermingle with religion. His views of separation were so strict that he even objected to the directing of any religious exercise by the national government through the presidential calls for days of fasting or prayer.[106] But Jefferson's objections to any intermingling between government and religion were apparently focused much more on restricting the federal government than the states, as he sponsored state legislation declaring days for fasting and thanksgiving.[107]

Oddly, history would hand Jefferson one opportunity to formally present a position on church and state by way of a letter. The Congregationalist Church was Connecticut's official church since the colony's founding by a Congregationalist minister named Thomas Hooker. Other churches residing in Connecticut, such as the Baptists, were therefore subject to substantial disadvantages, including unequal taxation and fees, merely because of their religious positions. Frustrated with their persistently unequal treatment despite the ratification of the new federal Constitution, the leaders of the Danbury Baptist Association wrote a letter to the President of the United States, then Thomas Jefferson, sharing with him the difficulties they were facing. Their letter, dated October 7, 1801, read as follows:

> *Sir,*
>
> *Among the many millions in America and Europe who rejoice in your Election to office; we embrace the first opportunity which we have enjoy'd in our collective capacity, since your Inauguration, to express our great satisfaction, in your appointment to the chief Magistracy in the United States: And though our mode of expression may be less courtly and pompious than what many others clothe their addresses with, we beg you, Sir to believe, that none are more sincere.*
>
> *Our Sentiments are uniformly on the side of Religious Liberty—That Religion is at all times and places a Matter between God and Individuals—That no man aught to suffer in Name, person or effects on account of his religious Opinions—That the legetimate Power of civil Goverment extends no further than to punish the man who works ill to his neighbour: But Sir, our constitution of goverment is not specific. Our antient charter, together with the Laws made coincident therewith, were adopted as the Basis of our goverment. At the time of our revolution; and such had been our Laws & usages, & such still are; that religion is*

consider'd as the first object of Legislation; & therefore what religious privileges we enjoy (as a minor part of the State) we enjoy as favors granted, and not as inalienable rights: and these favors we receive at the expence of such degrading acknowledgements as are inconsistant with the rights of freemen. It is not to be wondred at therefore; if those, who seek after power & gain under the pretence of goverment & Religion should reproach their fellow men—should reproach their chief Magistrate, as an enemy of religion Law & good order because he will not, dares not assume the prerogative of Jehovah and make Laws to govern the Kingdom of Christ.

Sir, we are sensible that the President of the united States, is not the national Legislator, & also sensible that the national goverment cannot destroy the Laws of each State; but our hopes are strong that the sentiments of our beloved President, which have had such genial Effect already, like the radiant beams of the Sun, will shine & prevail through all these States and all the world till Hierarchy and tyranny be destroyed from the Earth. Sir when we reflect on your past services, and see a glow of philanthropy and good will shining forth in a course of more than thirty years we have reason to believe that America's God has raised you up to fill the chair of State out of that good will which he bears to the Millions which you preside over. May God strengthen you for the arduous task which providence & the voice of the people have cal'd you to sustain and support you in your Administration against all the predetermin'd opposition of those who wish to rise to wealth & importance on the poverty and subjection of the people.

And may the Lord preserve you safe from every evil and bring you at last to his Heavenly Kingdom throug Jesus Christ our Glorious Mediator.

Signed in behalf of the Association
NEHH. DODGE
EPHM. ROBBINS The Committee
STEPHEN S NELSON

Interestingly, although the letter had been written in October, 1801, there is no evidence Jefferson received it until December 30, 1801.

At the time he received the letter, Jefferson was facing some political turmoil. Jefferson and his Republicans had just survived a very tumultuous election against Adams and his Federalists. Not the least of Jefferson's difficulties was the problems he had developed from his strict views on the separation of church and state dating back to his days in the Virginia State Assembly.

Among other charges, Jefferson was accused of being an atheist, no small charge in that day. Evidence to that claim was his refusal to proclaim times of thanksgiving and national fasts in contrast to the habits of Washington and Adams. Having faced such ardent and continuous attacks regarding the role of government in religious worship and of his personal convictions, Jefferson saw the Danbury letter as an opportunity to discuss his views on religious worship and freedom.[108] So anxious was Jefferson to respond that he immediately crafted a draft and submitted it to Postmaster General Gildeon Granger and Attorney General Levi Lincoln. By December 31, Granger had responded to Jefferson. The next day, Jefferson sent the letter with a cover note to Lincoln who also immediately responded. Jefferson, despite a busy New Years Day, finalized his answer and sent it on January 1, 1802. His final letter read as follows:

> *Gentlemen*
>
> *The affectionate sentiments of esteem and approbation which you are so good as to express towards me, on behalf of the Danbury Baptist association, give me the highest satisfaction. My duties dictate a faithful and zealous pursuit of the interests of my constituents, & in proportion as they are persuaded of my fidelity to those duties, the discharge of them becomes more and more pleasing.*
>
> *Believing with you that religion is a matter which lies solely between Man & his God, that he owes account to none other for his faith or his worship, that the legitimate powers of government reach actions only, & not opinions, I contemplate with sovereign reverence that act of the whole American people which declared that their legislature should "make no law respecting an establishment of religion, or prohibiting the free exercise thereof," thus building a wall of separation between Church & State. Adhering to this expression of the supreme will of the nation in behalf of the rights of conscience, I shall see with sincere satisfaction the progress of those sentiments which tend to restore to man all his natural rights, convinced he has no natural right in opposition to his social duties.*

I reciprocate your kind prayers for the protection & blessing of the common father and creator of man, and tender you for yourselves & your religious association, assurances of my high respect & esteem.

Thomas Jefferson Jan. 1. 1802. [xx]

The next few days would interest the observers of Jefferson's actions regarding government and religious worship. On the same day that Jefferson finalized his letter to the Danbury Baptist Association, he publicly met with John Leland, a Baptist minister whom he had invited to deliver a sermon at the House of Representatives. In a public demonstration of friendship, Leland presented Jefferson with a 1,250-pound cheese produced by his parishioners.[109] That Sunday, January 3, 1802, Jefferson personally attended the sermon at the House of Representatives that his friend delivered. How many of these actions were specifically due to political expediency will never be answered. However, it is said that subsequent to this letter Jefferson 'constantly' attended House services.[110]

These events notwithstanding, after some limited initial and regional play that was largely led by the Danbury Baptist Association, Jefferson's letter disappeared from the national conscience for more than seventy years, until it reappeared in the writings of a Supreme Court Justice.

The Barbary Pirates' Influence on Separation of Church and State

Remarkably, a group of harassers from what is known today as Libya provided scholars and laypersons alike with one of the most hotly debated controversies regarding the role of Christianity in the nation's founding.

---

xx The various incarnations of the language of his drafts have been reconstructed as follows: "confining myself therefore to the duties of my station, which are merely temporal, be assured that your religious rights shall never be infringed by any act of mine and that. . ." (There now appear some crossed out lines followed by:) "concurring with"; (which he also crossed out, then continued) "Adhering to this great act of national legislation in behalf of the rights of conscience" (he crossed out these words and then wrote) "Adhering to this expression of the supreme will of the nation in behalf of the rights of conscience I shall see with friendly dispositions the progress of those sentiments which tend to restore to man all his natural rights, convinced that he has no natural rights in opposition to his social duties." ["Jefferson's Letter to the Danbury Baptists; The Draft and Recently Discovered Text" (Library of Congress: June 1998)]

During the colonial period, American merchants transporting goods throughout the Mediterranean relied on the British navy to protect them from opportunists in the high seas. With the onset of the Revolutionary War, France assisted these American vessels, but with the Treaty of Paris, American mariners doing business in the Mediterranean were left to themselves in protecting their vessels.

In 1785, abductions began of American merchant vessels by corsairs from Algiers, Tunis, Tripoli, and Morocco. Not only did these Barbary pirates steal the goods and the vessels, but the passengers and crewmembers were taken as slaves and forced to work under harsh conditions, frequently leading to their deaths. This became a problem for the Washington administration, which received petitions from prisoners and free merchants alike demanding the new American government do something to obtain their freedoms and protect the sea-lanes for American vessels. The problem became more pressing under an impending peace accord being fashioned in Lisbon involving the North African states. Americans feared this peace treaty would allow the Barbary pirates to spill out into the open ocean, free to terrorize American vessels in the Atlantic. The matter was exacerbated by the influence of the English who were only too happy to have American merchants disadvantaged in trade.

Washington authorized negotiations in France to secure the safety of American vessels. A series of peace talks and treaties ensued spanning Washington's administration and those of his early nineteenth century successors. One of the treaties that resulted from these talks was the "Treaty of Peace and Friendship between the United States of America and the Bey and Subjects of Tripoli of Barbary" signed on November 4, 1796. The treaty was written in Arabic and translated to English by Joel Barlow, the Consul General at Algiers. In his English translation, Barlow included a paragraph that was not included in the Arabic text of the treaty; language contained in Article 11 that has caused significant fodder for secularists in the battle for strict separation of church and state:

> *As the government of the United States of America is not in any sense founded on the Christian Religion, as it has in itself no character of*

enmity against the laws, religion or tranquility of Musselmen, and as the said States never have entered into any war or act of hostility against any Mehomitan nation, it is declared by the parties that no pretext arising from religious opinions shall ever produce an interruption of the harmony existing between the two countries.

(Treaty of Peace and Friendship between the United States of America and the Bey and Subjects of Tripoli of Barbary, Nov. 4, 1796)

Virtually no information exits regarding the dynamics behind the inclusion of this language into the English translation. Regardless, it was presented before the Senate for ratification, which it unanimously did on June 10, 1797, and Adams subsequently signed. The treaty was then published in New York and Philadelphia.

For our purposes, the controversy lies not in the authenticity of the language and the dynamics of how such a phrase would enter the text of a treaty, but in the apparent open admission by the United States government that the United States was not founded on Christianity. Secularists have used this outlying event to support the argument that the Founders and Framers did not base the foundation of the United States on any religion.

The notion that this single, corollary phrase in a treaty holds greater weight than the mountains of evidence pointing to the contrary strains credulity. As this analysis has already demonstrated America was born as a direct result of the pursuit of religious liberty. Its foundation was fueled by it as was its revolution, and its new system of government was restrained by it. Moreover, the religious liberty sought was inherently Christian, and the moral conscience that was upheld was Judeo-Christian. It is for this reason that both the Founders and the Framers were so comfortable with an active and robust presence of religious worship in their public lives. Nevertheless, as will be explored later, the Courts would change that crucial, existential relationship.

Chapter 3

From Minor Repairs to Civil War

At the close of the Constitutional Convention, the Framers had drafted a government whose power was grounded in the people; a federal government where the sovereignty of the thirteen states was respected and where any effort at expanding its powers was sufficiently hindered. But there remained ambiguities within the document, some of which were recognized during the ratification process and others afterward. These imperfections and ambiguities would be handled, either through the process of judicial interpretation or amendment, as they represented roadblocks to the nation's proper development, and sometimes, to the proper function of government. Indeed, not a year would pass before the first conflict arose, and they continued throughout America's history, even to the present day. How these uncertainties were handled are integral to understanding our nation's evolution. We begin with the Framers' first experience in the area of constitutional interpretation dealing with the issue of money, financing, and the meaning of "necessary and proper."

1. The National Bank: Hamilton, Jefferson, and Madison Go to War Over "Necessary and Proper"

The nation's first two decades were mired with economic strife. The various states, particularly the northern ones, had borrowed copiously from foreign nations and investors in order to finance the war. At the time of the Constitution's ratification, the nation's debt stood at over $55 million[111] with no feasible plan to pay it back. Specie was sparse, and there was little capital with which to pursue investments or moneymaking ventures.

Moreover, there was a difference of opinion as to the future direction of the young country. For men like Jefferson, the nation's future lay in agriculture. So long as families farmed, he maintained, the traditional lifestyles and beliefs that had given rise to the Declaration of Independence and the Constitution would remain secure. Alexander Hamilton saw the country's future differently. His was a more industrial view, imagining a myriad of opportunities for investors and manufacturers.

Upon being elected President, George Washington appointed Hamilton Secretary of the Treasury because of his knowledge of banking and financing. Jefferson, with his prior ambassadorial experience in Paris, was appointed Secretary of State. Hamilton's friendship with President Washington was longstanding and well developed. Jefferson did not share such an intimate relationship with the nation's first president, but his reputation was Herculean among the nation's leadership. Jefferson also had a strong ally in another national giant, James Madison.

With Congress struggling to deal with the nation's financial hardships, it turned to the Secretary of the Treasury to provide it with ideas on how to address its economic woes. A prolific writer, Hamilton quickly obliged, writing his First and Second Reports on the Public Credit. In them, he laid out a multifaceted approach at solving the nation's fiscal difficulties. His plans called for raising money through tariffs on certain products like alcohol and tea, imposing land taxes, and honoring the national and states' debts accrued in prosecuting the Revolutionary War.[i]

[i] In his First Report on Public Credit, Hamilton called the debts accrued as a result of the Revolutionary War, the price of liberty.

Almost immediately, impassioned arguments ensued. Although most agreed with honoring foreign debt, the issue of paying off the domestic debt was much more caustic. During the Revolutionary War, many American patriots were given promissory notes deferring their payments for their military service. With the government in virtual financial ruin and the prospect of payment bleak, many of those soldiers sold their promissory notes to investors at pennies on the dollar. Hamilton's plan to repay these debts called for payment of the notes to the bondholders (the investors who had purchased the promissory notes at the risk of not getting paid at all). A sense of injustice ensued as people considered the prospect of those soldiers who had undertaken immense sacrifices for the country's inception not getting paid what they deserved. Even Madison uncharacteristically called for the federal government to intervene by paying the original owners of the notes rather than the present holders.

Hamilton, however, held strong, insisting that the debt be paid to the current holders and arguing in favor of the merits of the speculators and the risk they had undertaken in purchasing the notes. Additionally, Hamilton thought the difficulties and costs of identifying the original creditors made the prospects of Madison's approach untenable.

Hamilton prevailed, and Congress agreed to honor the current holders of the nation's domestic debt. The move would help permanently define American financing law and policy.

Hamilton also successfully argued that the national government should honor the states' debts, a concept known as "assumption." During the Revolutionary War, the states had borrowed extensively, particularly from the French and Dutch. The total debt amassed by the states stood at about $25 million.[112] In light of the nation's financial hardships, dismissing these loans and not paying them back was a very tempting proposition. Hamilton correctly argued the importance of honoring those debts, even though they had been amassed by the states and not by the national government. Again, Hamilton prevailed, and the states' debts to foreign nations were secured.

However controversial Hamilton's positions on debt repayment may have been, they paled in comparison to his final proposal: the creation of a national bank. Hamilton reasoned that the nation needed a repository for its funds as well as an institution capable of lending money to investors and American businesses. Further, Hamilton referred to the multiple advantages a similar model had offered to England, allowing it to undertake such pressing and expensive tasks as financing European wars and building up defenses. Of course, Hamilton would have to cite the constitutional authority for such a bank. For this, he employed the General Welfare Clause allowing Congress to collect taxes "to provide for the . . . general welfare,"[113] and the Necessary and Proper Clause authorizing Congress "to make all Laws which shall be necessary and proper for carrying into Execution" the powers vested in the Constitution.[114]

Predictably, the proposal resulted in a firestorm of opposition. Within the House of Representatives, Madison led the charge against the idea of a federally created national bank. Rising within the well of the House of Representatives on February 2, 1791, Madison gave a powerful speech about the inappropriateness of the act.

First, he argued that the creation of a national bank was not in the best interests of the United States.[115] He told of how the whole matter represented an unconstitutional misuse of congressional authority and cited the Constitutional Convention where the issue of allowing Congress to grant charters of incorporation had been considered and rejected.[116] Second, Madison reminded the House of the federal government's enumerated powers. He explained that the government was allowed only to act in the manner in which it had been given authority, and no enumeration granted Congress the authority to create a bank. He spoke of the General Welfare Clause, explaining that the powers it gave to Congress applied only to taxation, not to the creation of a bank. If the General Welfare Clause were to be successfully employed as the foundation for creating a national bank, Madison said, it would "give Congress an unlimited power; would render nugatory the enumeration of particular powers; [and] would supersede all the powers reserved to the State Governments."[117]

As to the Necessary and Proper Clause, for the same reasons applicable to the General Welfare Clause, Madison cautioned against its interpretation as anything other than a provision limiting congressional authority. Those powers authorized by the Necessary and Proper Clause were those "necessary to an end, and incident to the nature of the specified powers."[118] Any other interpretation would destroy all limitations within the enumerated powers.[119]

Despite Madison's ardent plea, the controversial proposal passed and went to the new president for review. Washington immediately asked one of the bill's major opponents, Secretary of State Thomas Jefferson, to discuss the constitutionality of the creation of a bank. Jefferson's response amounted to a beautiful rendition of constitutional restraint and strict constitutional construction.[120] He reminded the President that the federal government was not empowered to engage in any activities not specifically enumerated in the Constitution, and that there was no constitutional provision allowing the federal government to establish a corporation, much less a national bank. To Jefferson, the Necessary and Proper Clause was designed to give Congress the power to make only those laws required to carry out the authorities granted in Article I, Section 8. In other words, if the power that Congress was seeking to deploy was not an enumerated one, then the Necessary and Proper Clause could not be used to justify it. Consequently, just like Madison, Jefferson thought the Necessary and Proper Clause was not an expansive one.

Jefferson's interpretation of the word "necessary" was even more restrictive. In his view, the word "necessary" was to be differentiated from "convenient," which was a word specifically not chosen by the Framers. For Jefferson, this meant that Congress could only pass laws that were *necessary* to the implementation of its enumerated authorities and not merely convenient. And because all the roles to be played by the proposed national bank were achievable without a national bank, the creation of one was not a necessity, and therefore, an unconstitutional act.[121]

Instead of rushing to a veto under the weight of Jefferson's arguments, Washington presented Jefferson's Opinion to Hamilton, who hurriedly crafted his response. Hamilton's views on federalism were decidedly different from Jefferson's. Instead of fearing a centralized power that would overwhelm the sovereignties of the various states, Hamilton advocated for a strong centralized government and felt the federal government was endowed with certain implied powers that went beyond those expressed in Article I, Section 8.[122] Hamilton viewed the establishment and operation of a bank as a necessity for running the nation.[123] For Hamilton, the establishment of a national bank for the purpose of maintaining the nation's revenues and facilitating the lending of money was not only proper, but necessary to the running of a country. Therefore, he saw the creation of a national bank by the federal government as authorized by the Constitution even though it was not specifically delineated.

Hamilton's was the first progressive, expansive argument regarding congressional authority in the nation's history and ultimately convinced Washington to sign the bill creating the United States Bank into law. His victory allowed for the first redefinition of Article I in the young nation's history and developed unimaginable precedents for the nation's future.

As it turns out, the First Bank of the United States was a great success and a key component in allowing the frail country to work its way out of its voluminous debt. The country was in need of an agency to safeguard the country's coffers and manage its borrowing. The First Bank of the United States supplied that service.

But the solution came at a price. The United States would chart a course through history of borrowing more than it could pay back rather than curtailing its borrowing. The United States became, and still is, a chronic borrower, amassing debts to finance the Civil War, World War I, World War II, and other wars, along with its modern and massively expensive social programs, elevating its borrowing powers well beyond what anyone ever imagined, even Hamilton.

Congress would also take on the role of maintaining the nation's economic wellbeing through its spending and printing policies. Its efforts in this regard eventually led to the creation of the Federal Reserve in 1913. But the Federal Reserve would do so much more than what Jefferson feared the United States Bank would ever do. Under the Federal Reserve Act, the Federal Reserve would create as many as twelve regional districts, each with its own Federal Reserve Bank.

The Federal Reserve System, with its Federal Reserve Board, would be responsible for managing the nation's fiscal policies in order to keep the national currency "elastic."[ii] Doing so would help counteract the nation's financial rigors such as those it would encounter during the many panics of the nineteenth century and early twentieth centuries. To accomplish this, the Federal Reserve would be authorized to create a new currency, the Federal Reserve Note, which it would expand and contract as required.

The Federal Reserve also fostered international financing, allowing the dollar, which was already the currency of the largest economy in the world, to flow through the international markets at the expense of European banks. The Federal Reserve would eventually serve as the principal manipulative force in the American economy, setting fiscal policies as a stabilizing and corrective monetary force. Of course, whether the Federal Reserve has succeeded in accomplishing this aim, or whether it has actually furthered the nation's economic woes is a matter of very lively, spirited, and complicated debate.

However, key to all of these governmental fiscal activities is the breadth to which government was given the authority to spend. Did the Constitution allow the federal government to spend money merely for the purpose of correcting and stabilizing the nation's markets? Did Congress have the authority to act through a third party as a manipulative force upon the economy?

Predictably, the Supreme Court has been asked to comment on this matter, most directly in 1936 when Congress authorized spending for the sole purpose of manipulating the market prices of certain commodities. In *United States v. Butler*,[124] the Supreme Court did not agree that Congress's spending authority should be able to artificially control market prices, but it did recognize a wide scope of congressional spending authority.[125] As a matter of fact, the Court held that Congress's powers to spend were not limited by the enumerated powers, but by the furtherance of the general welfare,

[ii] The elasticity of a currency refers its ability to expand and contract the amount of money within the economy in response to financial pressures.

signaling a dramatic increase in congressional spending powers. Later, in *Steward Machine Co. v. Davis*,[126] the Court further expanded congressional spending authority by holding that Congress had the authority to define what it viewed as general welfare. This latter ruling essentially nullified the enumerated powers' restrictions on spending and functionally ended the Hamilton-Jefferson debate in favor of Hamilton, but to an extent beyond Hamilton's most permissive dreams.

The results of *Butler* and *Steward Machine Co.* were catastrophic to federalism and state autonomy as they caused the concept of state sovereignty to become little more than illusory.[127] As Madison pointed out, being that virtually all legislative actions involve funding, the concept of a government able to spend without limitations essentially is a government whose power knows no bounds.[128] We see today how this court-expanded power for the federal government essentially ended all of the critical restrictions the Framers put into place and allowed for the seemingly unstoppable expansion of federal government spending, power, and intrusion.

2. The Bill of Rights Comes Into Existence

Despite the great care in designing a system with sufficient checks and balances to keep the federal government constrained, the concern over its expansion of powers remained. Some of the country's most famous leaders, men like Patrick Henry and George Mason, either refused to attend the Constitutional Convention or did not sign the document because of that concern. As seen in the confrontations between Hamilton and Jefferson, the fear was not only that the federal government would overrun the states with its powers, but also that it would directly intrude upon the rights of the people. Many believed that without an enumeration of the rights of the individual, rights that could not be infringed by the federal government, the vulnerability of the citizenship to such an oppressive relationship was simply too great.

Initially, the prime proponents of a constitution and a stronger centralized government did not see the need for an enumeration of individual rights since they viewed the Constitution itself as a bill of rights.[129]

Hamilton contended that the necessary protections of the people's rights were already included within the Constitution in 1) the guarantee of a trial by jury in criminal cases;[130] 2) the guarantee that criminal trials would be performed in the state where the crime was committed;[131] 3) the guarantee of a privilege for a writ of habeas corpus;[132] 4) the prohibition of ex-post-facto laws;[133] 5) the guarantee against titles of nobility; [134] 6) the definition of a charge of treason against the United States with a requirement that at least two witnesses provide testimony of the same act and that there be a confession by the accused;[135] and 7) the guarantee of a republican form of government.[136]

According to the federalists, the inclusion of a bill of rights in the American Constitution was illogical because the national government's scope of authority had already been defined. The addition of a bill of rights was totally unnecessary. In Hamilton's words, "Why declare things that shall not be done which there is no power to do?"[137]

Additionally, Hamilton and Madison saw an inconsistency in a bill of rights restricting a republic. In a monarchy, they explained, the source of power lies with the king. Consequently, a bill of rights such as that seen in the Magna Charta, represents a stipulation between the king and his subjects. However, when the government is a constitutional republic, a bill of rights would be inapplicable since the power of the government proceeded directly from the people through their representatives. The consent of the people is the source of whatever authority they agree to acquiesce to the state, obviating the need for an enumeration of rights still within their hands.[138] According to Hamilton, the words, "'WE, THE PEOPLE of the United States, to secure the blessings of liberty to ourselves and our posterity, do *ordain* and *establish* this Constitution of the United States of America,' is a better recognition of popular rights than volumes of those aphorisms in several of our State bills of rights, and which would sound much better in a treatise of ethics than in a constitution of government." [139] (emphasis added by Hamilton)

Both men also warned that a delineation of enumerated rights created the possibility for the government to argue the absence of an express guarantee as equating to the absence of such a right.[140] Madison took the argument a step further stating, "The powers granted by the proposed constitution are the gift of the people, and may be resumed by them whenever perverted to their oppression, and every power not granted thereby, remains with the people and at their will."[141]

These reassurances and philosophical explanations did not assuage the fears of the anti-federalists who saw a great potential for abuse of the power acquiesced to the national government. They wanted an enumeration of popular rights included in the Constitution. Madison, for one, was willing to compromise, conceding that there could be times, even in a republic, that the instrument of oppression may be the government itself.

As a result, Madison agreed to write the amendments to the Constitution once it was ratified. Although the step was necessary to ensure the implementation of a new national government, the individually undertaken venture of drafting a Bill of Rights robbed posterity of a more robust record of the debates that accompanied its creation.[iii] Consequently, we are largely left to surmise Madison's and Congress's intents in passing each of the amendments contained within the Bill of Rights. And although the language incorporated into the first ten amendments to the Constitution is largely derived from existing state constitutions, particularly Madison's Virginia, differences in interpretation existed regarding the scope and meaning of the various liberties between the thirteen states. We therefore have little opportunity to make definitive assertions about our popular rights when using only the historical record of the time.

Because the Bill of Rights touches on such a varied array of topics, the better approach for a volume such as this is to discuss the historical particularities of the individual amendments. Suffice it for now to acknowledge the language Madison submitted to Congress on June 7, 1789, as the original proposal for a series of amendments to the Constitution:

[iii] For a more detailed analysis on the passage of the religious clause of the First Amendment, see Chapter 2.

Transcription of the 1789 Joint Resolution of Congress Proposing 12 Amendments to the U.S. Constitution

Congress of the United States begun and held at the City of New-York, on Wednesday the fourth of March, one thousand seven hundred and eighty nine.

***THE** Conventions of a number of the States, having at the time of their adopting the Constitution, expressed a desire, in order to prevent misconstruction or abuse of its powers, that further declaratory and restrictive clauses should be added: And as extending the ground of public confidence in the Government, will best ensure the beneficent ends of its institution.*

***RESOLVED** by the Senate and House of Representatives of the United States of America, in Congress assembled, two thirds of both Houses concurring, that the following Articles be proposed to the Legislatures of the several States, as amendments to the Constitution of the United States, all, or any of which Articles, when ratified by three fourths of the said Legislatures, to be valid to all intents and purposes, as part of the said Constitution; viz.*

***ARTICLES** in addition to, and Amendment of the Constitution of the United States of America, proposed by Congress, and ratified by the Legislatures of the several States, pursuant to the fifth Article of the original Constitution.*

***Article the first**... After the first enumeration required by the first article of the Constitution, there shall be one Representative for every thirty thousand, until the number shall amount to one hundred, after which the proportion shall be so regulated by Congress, that there shall be not less than one hundred Representatives, nor less than one Representative for every forty thousand persons, until the number of Representatives shall amount to two hundred; after which the proportion shall be so regulated by Congress, that there shall not be less than two hundred Representatives, nor more than one Representative for every fifty thousand persons.*

***Article the second**... No law, varying the compensation for the services of the Senators and Representatives, shall take effect, until an election of Representatives shall have intervened.*

Article the third... *Congress shall make no law respecting an establishment of religion, or prohibiting the free exercise thereof; or abridging the freedom of speech, or of the press; or the right of the people peaceably to assemble, and to petition the Government for a redress of grievances.*

Article the fourth... *A well regulated Militia, being necessary to the security of a free State, the right of the people to keep and bear Arms, shall not be infringed.*

Article the fifth... *No Soldier shall, in time of peace be quartered in any house, without the consent of the Owner, nor in time of war, but in a manner to be prescribed by law.*

Article the sixth... *The right of the people to be secure in their persons, houses, papers, and effects, against unreasonable searches and seizures, shall not be violated, and no Warrants shall issue, but upon probable cause, supported by Oath or affirmation, and particularly describing the place to be searched, and the persons or things to be seized.*

Article the seventh... *No person shall be held to answer for a capital, or otherwise infamous crime, unless on a presentment or indictment of a Grand Jury, except in cases arising in the land or naval forces, or in the Militia, when in actual service in time of War or public danger; nor shall any person be subject for the same offence to be twice put in jeopardy of life or limb; nor shall be compelled in any criminal case to be a witness against himself, nor be deprived of life, liberty, or property, without due process of law; nor shall private property be taken for public use, without just compensation.*

Article the eighth... *In all criminal prosecutions, the accused shall enjoy the right to a speedy and public trial, by an impartial jury of the State and district wherein the crime shall have been committed, which district shall have been previously ascertained by law, and to be informed of the nature and cause of the accusation; to be confronted with the witnesses against him; to have compulsory process for obtaining witnesses in his favor, and to have the Assistance of Counsel for his defence.*

Article the ninth... *In suits at common law, where the value in controversy shall exceed twenty dollars, the right of trial by jury shall be preserved, and no fact tried by a jury, shall be otherwise re-examined in any Court of the United States, than according to the rules of the common law.*

***Article the tenth**... Excessive bail shall not be required, nor excessive fines imposed, nor cruel and unusual punishments inflicted.*

Article the eleventh... The enumeration in the Constitution, of certain rights, shall not be construed to deny or disparage others retained by the people.

***Article the twelfth**... The powers not delegated to the United States by the Constitution, nor prohibited by it to the States, are reserved to the States respectively, or to the people.*

FREDERICK AUGUSTUS MUHLENBERG,
Speaker of the House of Representatives
JOHN ADAMS,
Vice-President of the United States, and President of the Senate
Attest,
John Beckley, *Clerk of the House of Representatives.*
Samuel A. Otis, *Secretary of the Senate.*

On December 15, 1791, the ten of Madison's twelve amendments were ratified, giving rise to the nation's Bill of Rights. They read as follows:

Amendment I: *Congress shall make no law respecting an establishment of religion, or prohibiting the free exercise thereof; or abridging the freedom of speech, or of the press; or the right of the people peaceably to assemble, and to petition the government for a redress of grievances.*

Amendment II: *A well regulated militia, being necessary to the security of a free state, the right of the people to keep and bear arms, shall not be infringed.*

Amendment III: *No soldier shall, in time of peace be quartered in any house, without the consent of the owner, nor in time of war, but in a manner to be prescribed by law.*

Amendment IV: *The right of the people to be secure in their persons, houses, papers, and effects, against unreasonable searches and seizures, shall not be violated, and no warrants shall issue, but upon probable cause, supported by oath or affirmation, and particularly describing the place to be searched, and the persons or things to be seized.*

Amendment V: *No person shall be held to answer for a capital, or otherwise infamous crime, unless on a presentment or indictment of a grand jury, except in cases arising in the land or naval forces, or in the* *militia, when in actual service in time of war or public danger; nor shall any person be subject for the same offense to be twice put in jeopardy of life or limb; nor shall be compelled in any criminal case to be a witness against himself, nor be deprived of life, liberty, or property, without due process of law; nor shall private property be taken for public use, without just compensation.*

Amendment VI: *In all criminal prosecutions, the accused shall enjoy the right to a speedy and public trial, by an impartial jury of the state and district wherein the crime shall have been committed, which district shall have been previously ascertained by law, and to be informed of the nature and cause of the accusation; to be confronted with the witnesses against him; to have compulsory process for obtaining witnesses in his favor, and to have the assistance of counsel for his defense.*

Amendment VII: *In suits at common law, where the value in controversy shall exceed twenty dollars, the right of trial by jury shall be preserved, and no fact tried by a jury, shall be otherwise reexamined in any court of the United States, than according to the rules of the common law.*

Amendment VIII: *Excessive bail shall not be required, nor excessive fines imposed, nor cruel and unusual punishments inflicted.*

Amendment IX: *The enumeration in the Constitution, of certain rights, shall not be construed to deny or disparage others retained by the people.*

Amendment X: *The powers not delegated to the United States by the Constitution, nor prohibited by it to the states, are reserved to the states respectively, or to the people.*

We must also acknowledge that what Congress produced in its ten amendments to the Constitution essentially amounted to a declaration of the peoples' most elemental foundational freedoms. It listed a set of liberties that by right, and through divine impartation, were inherent to man and never to be encroached on by the actions of government. In the Bill of Rights, Congress also declared certain guarantees that would constrain government in its dealings with the people; restraints that would keep the government from overwhelming the liberties of the American people in their persons and in their properties.

What is fascinating is that the warnings from the anti-federalists about government abuses of powers rang as true as the warnings from Madison and Hamilton regarding attempts by zealous activists to erase those rights that were not specifically enumerated. But neither side discussed the role the courts would have in divining new rights and in curtailing certain others. As we shall see, whether the Framers intended it or not, the courts would play a vital role in defining the actual rights possessed by American citizens.

3. The Eleventh Amendment: Can You Prosecute the King?

A seemingly innocuous phrase in Article III gave rise to America's first constitutional crisis. Section 2 of Article III, gave the federal courts the authority to hear "those [cases] in which a State shall be party." Read in isolation, the phrase meant that a state could be dragged to a federal court against its wishes and made the defendant to a lawsuit. The notion appeared incongruous, for if the states were truly sovereign and voluntarily yielded certain enumerated authorities to a centralized, federal government, then who was the federal government to order a sovereign to appear before one of its courts? (So much for state sovereignty!)

By all accounts, it appears that the Framers never foresaw the legal wrangling that would take place in Georgia in 1793, events that actually dated back to a time preceding the signing of the Treaty of Paris.

In 1777, amid the Revolutionary War and before the drafting of the United States Constitution, Captain Robert Farquhar, a South Carolina businessman, sold supplies to the State of Georgia. Georgia never rendered payment for the supplies, claiming its obligation to pay the captain was extinguished because Captain Farquhar was a British loyalist.[142] After Farquhar's death, Alexander Chisholm, the executor of his estate, sued Georgia in federal court in an attempt to collect payment. Georgia argued it was not subject to the authority of the federal courts because Georgia was a sovereign state and therefore not vulnerable to federal courts. In 1793, the case would be heard by the Supreme Court, which would rule that Article III of the Constitution did indeed allow a citizen of one state to sue another state in federal court.[143]

The states reacted with indignation. Immediately, state legislators and regional political leaders pressured Congress to remove any language from the Constitution allowing for individuals to sue states in federal court without a state's consent. Congress's reaction was remarkably swift. The day after *Chisholm v. Georgia* was decided, the House of Representatives proposed the Eleventh Amendment to the Constitution passing it after only one day of debate in each chamber.[144] By February 7, 1795, eleven days shy of *Chisholm*'s two-year anniversary, the Eleventh Amendment to the United States Constitution was ratified. It read:

> *The Judicial power of the United States shall not be construed to extend to any suit in law or equity, commenced or prosecuted against one of the United States by Citizens of another State, or by Citizens or Subjects of any Foreign Country.*

Notice that the language of the amendment did not completely address the issue of a state's sovereign immunity. Specifically, the Eleventh Amendment prohibits any suit brought by a citizen of another state, or citizens or subjects of a foreign country, against a state in federal court. These situations deal with the federal courts' jurisdiction in cases brought to them through its diversity jurisdiction or because the parties to the suit are residents of different states. But what if the citizen was trying to bring a state to federal court over an issue dealing with federal law? Would the state still be immune from litigation?

The Eleventh Amendment was silent on this issue, and the question was not settled until 1996, in the case of *Seminole Tribe of Florida v. Florida*. In its decision, the Supreme Court held that the Eleventh Amendment did protect the state's sovereign immunity in matters arising out of federal questions, just like it did in questions of diversity, even though the language within the Eleventh Amendment did not specifically address federal question jurisdiction cases.[145, iv]

[iv] In a related matter, in *Alden v. Maine*, 527 U.S. 706 (1996), the Supreme Court held that Congress could not compel a state to subject itself to civil litigation by a private party because such a requirement violated the Eleventh Amendment protections afforded upon the states. Similarly, the Supreme Court held in *Federal*

As a result of this amendment and its associated rulings, Americans cannot generally sue a state, except where the state has consented to being a party to a case. This is generally accomplished statutorily with the state legislature passing a law describing matters to which the state may be a party. The legislature will often also pass limits to payoffs and damages in such cases. To get around this situation, many parties sue the official of the state in his or her official capacity. For example, instead of suing the state for an injury to the plaintiff, the plaintiff may sue the responsible official such as the governor or the attorney general. Relatedly, the courts have ruled that a plaintiff may not sue a judge over decisions made relating to a case, but a judge may be sued when he is acting in his administrative capacity. For example, a judge may not be sued for making what is arguably a wrong decision on a case no matter how unsubstantiated the decision may be. He may, however, be sued for sexually accosting a female employee while in his chambers, even if the offensive act took place during business hours.

4. The Matter of Choosing the President

Few constitutional issues have raised such existential questions as the matter of choosing the President of the United States. Clearly, the Framers wished to create a system conducive to the selection of the most mature, entrusted, learned, and experienced person possible; a person who is solely loyal to the people of the United States and to the states as sovereigns. This design was to stand free of partisanship and protracted obligations.

But human nature and partisanship would very quickly derail the Framers' vision and morph the process of electing the President of the United States into something quite different from what they had originally envisioned. Multiple constitutional amendments and countless debates later, consensus on the best process by which to select the nation's chief executive has still not been achieved. Questions over whether the president should

Maritime Commission v. South Carolina State Ports Authority, 535 U.S. 743 (2002), that a federal administrative agency could not adjudicate a private party's, federal-question-based complaint against the state.

be selected by popular vote or through an Electoral College still abounds. Additionally, the definition of natural born citizenship and the eligibility for candidacy remains unaddressed by Congress. There are even some who argue that presidential term limits should be rescinded.

In light of all the controversy regarding the presidential election process, it is clear that an appetite exists for further changes. However such changes, if they are to represent improvements, cannot take place without first considering how the nation arrived at the point where it is today.

The Twelfth Amendment and the Arrival of Partisan Politics

The original plan for selecting the nation's chief executive was certainly idyllic. As originally laid out in Article II of the United States Constitution, each state would create temporary committees in order to identify two persons who should serve as President, one of whom had to be a resident of another state. The membership of each committee would be equal to the number of Representatives and Senators allotted to that State. At the end of its deliberations, the state electoral committee would report the names of the two candidates and the number of votes each candidate got within that committee. The person obtaining the majority of votes would be President and the one obtaining the second most votes would serve as Vice President.

If more than one person obtained a majority, then the House of Representatives would immediately choose a President from those receiving the majority. If there was no majority, then the House would choose from the five who received the highest amount of votes, with each State having one vote regardless of how many members it had in the House of Representatives. The same process would be used for the Vice President, except the Senate would decide when the states could not.

The initial method worked wonderfully with the election of George Washington during the first and second presidential elections, but idealism and individual considerations quickly gave way to party politics. By the nation's third presidential election in 1796, the first signs of partisanship began to show as a result of Washington's decision not to seek a third term of office. Subsequently, the nation elected a Federalist president, John Adams, and a

Republican vice president, Thomas Jefferson. The result was a strained executive replete with tensions between the two rivals.

But the strife separating rival factions in government ran deeper than mere personality conflicts. The debates over the establishment of a national bank revealed the philosophical differences separating the groups. The Federalists, with members including Alexander Hamilton, John Jay, and John Adams, were more comfortable with a more centralized distribution of power. Their views, heralded by Alexander Hamilton's efforts as Secretary of the Treasury, resulted in the creation of a national bank, to which the Democratic-Republicans objected. This latter group consisted of men like Thomas Jefferson, Aaron Burr, and James Madison. These were stricter adherents to the concept of decentralized power. Theirs was a view that more zealously observed the rights of the states as sovereigns.

The differences between the two groups spilled into the arena of religious freedoms with John Adams and George Washington being comfortable with a more direct relationship between government and Christianity so long as no sect or particular church gained advantage over another. For the Republicans, even Christianity was not to be given an advantage over other religions.

The foundational differences with regard to foreign affairs were just as stark. Following the conclusion of the Revolutionary War, France and England continued their bickering, each country harassing the other and confiscating ships aligned with their opponents. These hostilities had direct consequences upon the safety of American vessels and their goods, particularly in the Mediterranean where the Barbary Pirates emanating from places such as Algiers, Tunis, Tripoli, and Morocco were actively capturing American vessels and either imprisoning their passengers or selling them to slavery.

Predictably, American traders and the seafaring community exerted pressure upon national leaders to align the United States with one side or the other, as doing so would potentially secure the protections of one of these great navies. Interestingly, like in domestic issues, the Federalists and the Democratic-Republicans disagreed over with whom to align.

Following the Revolutionary War, American ships were becoming increasingly subject to attacks by French vessels. Moreover, the Federalists feared that France would foment instability and even rebellion through the infusion of free blacks from Haiti.[146] On the other hand, the Democratic-Republicans feared that the Federalists' overtures to England would only increase the possibility of the young country being reabsorbed into the British monarchy.

Sensitive to these challenges, George Washington, while still President, settled upon a treaty with England. The treaty, approved by Hamilton and negotiated by Jay, established American trade rights in India and the Caribbean, formalized the withdrawal of British troops from American forts in the Northwest Territory, and defined compensations to the United States for mercantile ships captured by the British. As part of the treaty, the United States promised to honor its prewar debt to the British while agreeing not to seek reparations for the costs of American slaves freed by the British during the Revolutionary War.

Although Washington blessed the treaty, it earned the stern opposition from many. Madison and Jefferson needed no other reason to oppose the treaty than its favorable treatment of the British. The two quickly went to work to establish allies against the emerging Federalists and their treaty. Astutely, they secured the support of the southern members of Congress who were angered by Jay's dismissal of the effort to obtain reparations from the British for the freed slaves. These alliances would morph into the Democratic-Republican Party.

Then there was the Sedition Acts of 1798 passed under the Adams Administration. Among other provisions, the Act criminalized seditious speech. The Federalists defended the law as being necessary for the promotion of the nation's security at a time when the United States was engaged in open hostilities against France. The Act, however, was applied primarily against the Federalist's political enemies,[147] providing fodder for Jefferson and his allies in opposing John Adams.

In 1800, sensing a vulnerable president, the Democratic-Republicans mobilized to influence the various state electorates[v] into selecting their candidates. Uniting over their common battles against the proponents of the Jay Treaty and the Sedition Act, the followers of Jefferson and Madison cemented a coalition strong enough to take down a sitting president.[148] Together, they thought, they would have enough votes to win the presidency for Jefferson and place Aaron Burr as the next Vice President.

But although they were united against Adams, Jay, and Hamilton, their ranks were not without fissures of their own. Aaron Burr saw an opportunity in the unhappy Federalists to peel votes away from Jefferson and potentially end up with the presidency for himself. The political wrangling that ensued led to what is still the most hotly contest, most sordid, and most divisive presidential election in American history, one that almost led to the dissolution of the new county.

To its credit, The House of Representatives detected the fervor within its ranks and on February 9, 1801, resolved that in the event the electorate were unable to choose a candidate, it would immediately conduct a ballot to choose the new president and would continue to hold votes, uninterruptedly, until a new President would be chosen.[149]

It was therefore with great apprehension and anxiety for the future of the young country that Congress, on February 11, 1801, gathered to witness the nation's Vice President and presidential candidate, Thomas Jefferson, open the sealed envelopes containing the votes of the electors from the various states. When the counting was completed, the Federalists had amassed 65 votes for Adams and 64 for General Charles Cotesworth Pinckney, their vice presidential candidate, and one vote for John Jay. The Democratic-Republicans garnered 73 votes each for Thomas Jefferson and 73 votes for Aaron Burr.

The Democratic-Republicans had successfully defeated a sitting president, but had failed to decide who the president would actually be!

[V] State legislators in some states, qualified members of the citizenry in others.

In compliance with their resolution, the members of the House immediately left to their chambers and began the arduous process of selecting a president. For any of the men to prevail, with eighteen states in the Union, the winner needed to garner nine votes.

By 1 P.M. on February 11, 1801, the House conducted its first vote. Eight states voted for Jefferson, six for Burr, and two abstained, but no candidate obtained the necessary majority vote. The House would then conduct another vote, and another, each with similar results.

With the House at a stalemate, many wondered whether the body could select a new president. It took six days and 35 votes for a break to occur. As tensions grew, Delaware Representative James Bayard, a Federalist, voted for Jefferson to avoid risking disunion.[150] Through pre-vote negotiations, delegates from Maryland and Vermont followed Bayard's lead. The final and 35th vote was ten states to four in favor of Jefferson, with Delaware and South Carolina abstaining.[151]

America's first experience with hyper-partisan politics had come to an end, but the events of 1801 demonstrated potentially fatal flaws in the Constitution. Not only had partisanship surpassed regional allegiance, but the ambiguity in defining who the president and the vice president would be within a ticket allowed for discordance within the executive branch and for rifts within a ticket as two members of the same party jockeyed for the top position.

Recognizing the threat and motivated to prevent a repetition of the events of the 1801 presidential election, Congress drafted a correction on December 9, 1803, which was ratified by three fourths of the states by June 15, 1804. The Twelfth Amendment now required that the ballots indicate which candidate was being offered as president and which as vice president. Like in the original process, the requirement that at least one of the candidates be from another state was maintained.[vi] The House, in the case of a lack

[vi] This provision caused a small controversy in the 2000 presidential election since George W. Bush, the governor of Texas, and Dick Cheney, a Dallas resident, were both from the same state. As the race approached however, Chaney switched his driver's license and voter's registration to Wyoming and placed his Dallas home for sale . Although the validity of the candidacy was contested as offensive to the twelfth amendment's "Habitation Clause," the court found Chaney satisfied the requirements for candidacy and dismissed the case.

of a majority among the presidential candidates, would then select from the three who received the greatest amount of votes in the specific category. If the House was unable to choose a president by March 4th, then the Vice-President would act as President. In the case of a vice presidential election where the electors did not provide a majority candidate, the Senate would choose from the top two vice-presidential candidates.

The Twelfth Amendment has governed presidential elections since its adoption with only one instance where the House decided the outcome of the election; the presidential election of 1824 where the House selected John Quincy Adams to be the sixth President of the United States.

The Twentieth Amendment: Laming the Duck

The date when power was to change hands was never constitutionally prescribed. Article I simply stated that the Congress was to convene on the first Monday in December, unless the date was changed by law.[152] With the Constitution's successful ratification, the Congress set March 4, 1789, as the date in which the new government would assemble. Subsequently, March 4th was the date that the new officers took office, both in the legislature and in the executive branch.

In 1792, Congress passed a law requiring that elections be held some time in November or December. This was followed on December 2, 1844, by a law setting the Tuesday following the first Monday in November as the day when the states were to appoint the electors for the office of President and Vice President.[153] The result was problematic since the executive would have a four-months lame duck session, while for Congress, occasionally an elected official did not take office until a year following the election in cases where new members were selected after the Constitutionally prescribed congressional meeting in December.

With the increasing speed of national and international events, a four-months period from election to assumption was too long for the Office of the Presidency, a problem that became apparent with Abraham Lincoln's election and Virginia's subsequent secession.

The solution was the passage of the Twentieth Amendment shortening the lame duck period for the Chief Executive to less than two months by moving the beginning of the Presidential and Vice Presidential terms to January 20 and that of the Congress to January 3. The Twentieth Amendment also clarified that the Vice President would be the new President in cases where the sworn president either died or failed to qualify for the Office. It also assigned to Congress the responsibility of selecting the President and the Vice President if both the President and the Vice President failed to qualify in time for them to assume office.

How Long Is Too Long?

The issue of term limits for the president was extensively debated during the Constitutional Convention. For the Framers the idea held little benefit as, in the words of Alexander Hamilton, "Nothing appears more plausible at first sight, nor more ill-founded upon close inspection than a scheme. . . of continuing the chief magistrate in office for a certain time, and then excluding him from it, either for a limited period or forever afterward."[154] According to Hamilton, invoking term limits would diminish the inducement for the President to act appropriately, as the reward of earning another term in office would be erased, and the temptations of usurping power by fiat would be too great. And finally, there was the issue of depriving the community of the opportunity of selecting the person with the greatest experience.

These concerns notwithstanding, George Washington famously established the precedent of not seeking a third term of office; a precedent that was followed either voluntarily or by the will of the people until the four-term presidency of Franklin Delano Roosevelt that began on March 4, 1933, and ended with his death on April 12, 1945. Roosevelt's protracted tenure brought great concern, leading Thomas Dewey, Roosevelt's opponent in 1944 to exclaim, "Four terms, or sixteen years, is the most dangerous threat to our freedom ever proposed."[155] His position on term limits, although not powerful enough to propel his victory over the three-time incumbent, was nevertheless adopted by the Republican Congress and proposed as an amendment to the Constitution. The Twenty-Second Amendment was ratified on April 27, 1951, and gave the power of law to the precedent established by George Washington.

The debate over the prudence of a two-term limit continues with advocates extolling the weakening of the presidency during the second term of office as a fatal drawback and proponents pointing to the dangers surrounding an excessively protracted presidential tenure. Regardless of which side prevails, perhaps the single most important consequence of a protracted presidential tenure is the long-lasting effects it will have on the composition of the nation's courts.

Taxation With Representation

One final accommodation in the Constitution to the presidential election process is the inclusion of residents of Washington D.C in the Electoral College. Through the Twenty-Third Amendment, the District of Columbia receives the same number of electors it would receive if it was a state, but no less than the number of electors received by the least populous state. The change gave the District of Columbia some small say in the election of the President of the United States.

Natural Born Citizens and the Curious Case of Senator Ted Cruz

The definition of a "natural born citizen" is one issue that has not been settled. This is an important consideration as it speaks directly to ensuring the secure, unbridled allegiance of the leader of the nation to the country.

In the eighteenth century, there were two theories regarding naturalization that predated the formation of the Republic. One was the concept of *jus sanguinis*, or citizenship through blood or birthright. Under this principle an individual assumes the citizenship of his parents.[156] The other, *jus solis*, assumes the person gains his or her citizenship from the place where he or she was born.[157] The Framers did not define which of these would govern the United States. However, English common law and the tradition at the time of the Declaration of Independence followed the latter.

The predilection for *jus solis* is understandable, particularly as it applies to the Chief Executive, as assuming the citizenship of the place where one is born would better ensure the allegiance to the country. William Blackstone, the greatest authority on British law in the eighteenth century and the legal resource most relied upon by the Founders and Framers, described the philosophical foundation for a rigorous citizenship requirement thusly, "[The] maxim of the law proceeded upon a general principle, that every man owes natural allegiance where he is born, and cannot owe two such allegiances, or serve two masters, at once."[158] For him, "Natural-born subjects are such as are born within the dominions of the crown of England, that is, within the ligeance, or as it is generally called, the allegiance of the king; and aliens, such as are born out of it."[159]

The assurance of the candidate's natural allegiance to the American Republic was first brought up by John Jay during the time of the Constitutional Convention when he wrote a note to the Convention's Chair, General George Washington, regarding the matter of the qualifications for the Presidency of the United States. Jay wrote, "Permit me to hint, whether it would not be wise & seasonable to provide a strong check to the admission of Foreigners into the administration of our national Government, and to declare expressly that the Command in chief of the American army shall not be given to, nor devolved on, any but a natural born Citizen."[160]

The timing of Jay's note is significant because it predated the creation of a Committee of Eleven by the Convention that was assigned the task of making recommendations regarding qualifications for President of the United States. On August 22, 1787, the Committee proposed the following, "[The president] shall be of the age of thirty five years, and a citizen of the United States, and shall have been an inhabitant thereof for Twenty one years."[161] These recommendations were delivered to the Convention on September 4, 1787. Two days later, the Convention kept the age requirement, but without debate, changed the residency requirement to fourteen years and the citizenship to that of "a natural-born citizen."[162]

The absence of any discussion robs us of insights regarding the logic behind the changes. However, it is reasonable to believe that Jay's note to

Washington regarding the importance of the Commander in Chief to the nation played a role in the imposition of the stricter requirement for citizenship.

It is indeed a shame that the Framers did not define the exact meaning of "natural-born." However, Justice Joseph Story, one of the great strict constructionist members of the Supreme Court, emphasized the concerns regarding an unfettered allegiance to the nation by the President when he wrote,

> *[Being a natural born citizen] cuts off all chances for ambitious foreigners, who might otherwise be intriguing for the office; and interposes a barrier against those corrupt interferences of foreign governments in executive elections, which have inflicted the most serious evils upon the elective monarchies of Europe. Germany, Poland, and even the pontificate of Rome, are sad, but instructive examples of the enduring mischiefs arising from this source.*
>
> [Joseph Story, *Commentaries on the Constitution,* vol. 3. (Cambridge: Billiard, Gray, and Co., 1833): § 1473]

Congress did temporarily address the issue of defining citizenship in the Naturalization Act of 1790. In addition to considering any white alien living in the United States for at least two years eligible for naturalization by applying to the courts, Congress held that "children of citizens of the of the United States that may be born beyond Sea, or out of the limits of the United States, shall be considered as natural born Citizens: Provided, that the right of citizenship shall not descend to persons whose fathers have never been resident in the United States," and also that, except by an act of Congress, no person would be offered citizenship if a state had proscribed it.[163] However, by 1795, Congress repealed the Naturalization Act of 1790 and, with it, whatever definition it had previously provided for a natural born citizen.[164]

Historical precedent has also not been helpful at further refining the citizenship qualifications for the Commander in Chief since all presidents thus far having been born within the Untied States. However, there have been some minor variations in the source of citizenship among the presidential candidates. Some, like John McCain, were born in American possessions or within territories of the United States.[vii] However, recent questions regarding the citizenship qualifications of various presidential candidates have arisen, most notably that of President Barrack Obama who was alleged to have been born in Kenya. Belatedly, President Obama released duplicates of his birth certificate demonstrating that he was born in Hawaii after the area had achieved statehood. Prior to the release of President Obama's birth certificate, controversy brewed about whether a person born in a foreign country to an American mother was eligible to be president.

More recently arguments have been made regarding the qualifications of Presidential Candidates Marco Rubio, Bobby Jindal, and Ted Cruz. In the cases of Rubio and Jindal, the argument was made that neither was eligible to run for president, as they were the products of non-citizens at the time of their births within the continental United States. Neither case has been held to have any legal merit.

Senator Cruz's situation is more nebulous in that he was born in Canada to an American mother and a foreign father. Making the matter more problematic, Cruz possessed dual citizenship until 2014, the year before he ran for president.

Although the matter was raised by some of his opponents during the presidential election, no court ruled on his participation in the election process. Clearly, allowing someone with a recent citizenship status other than American in such chronological proximity to serving as Commander in Chief and the nation's Chief Executive could represent a source of significant personal conflict. The increasing variety of backgrounds of those seeking to be President begs the question of the legal definition of natural born citizen— a question that must soon be expressly addressed either statutorily, by amendment, or both.

---

vii John McCain was born in the Panama Canal Zone, a territory in the possession of the United States, to an active duty military family stationed in Panama. Barry Goldwater was born in Arizona when it was a territory of the United States. George Romney, the product of a Mormon family, was born in Mexico when his American father left the United States with his three wives in response to the prohibitions of polygamy within the United States. He did not renounce his American citizenship and eventually returned to the United States.

5. The Bloody End to Slavery

A Nation Born in a Sea of Missed Opportunities

The existence of slavery within the United States was a momentous travesty of justice irreconcilably inconsistent with the principles of dignity giving rise to her system of government. It is a dreadful stain that still mars her history and continues to negatively impact her people. How men so committed to the equality of persons and to the eradication of oppressive regimes tolerated that vile institution's existence in a society that was held to standards previously unknown in the history of man defies comprehension. And although this treatise will never excuse the unpardonable hypocrisy of accepting slavery into the societal fiber of a nation that honored the independence of man and his subservience to none other than his Creator, any honest effort to understand the present state of the Republic and at attempting to charter a course for the nation's future, must first evaluate how such a calamitous error came to be.

The injustice of forced servitude long predated the collective knowledge of the continent that would someday house the last great hope for humanity. Prior to European colonization of the western hemisphere, slavery was extensively practiced in Africa and the Middle East. In these lands, the conquered were stripped of their tribes and turned into commodities for the conqueror.[165] Indeed, the very word "slave" takes origin from the widespread practice in the Holy Roman Empire of making slaves of the conquered Slavs.[166] With the Christianization of Europe, the practice of taking slaves among Europeans was largely extinguished. Not until the Portuguese ventured into Africa, the Azores, and the western coast of South America in the 15th century did the practice resurface.[167]

The early British colonies employed indentured servants as a manner of securing cheap labor. Many without means would sign agreements to serve as laborers for a defined period of time in exchange for passage to the colonies. These contracts promised to release the servant as a freeman once the obligations of the contract were fulfilled. In this way, Europeans would find passage to the New World on the promise of their own work.

The first documentation of African slaves in North America is found in a letter from John Rolfe to Sir Edward Sandys, a member of the House of Commons and Treasurer of the Virginia Company of London.[168] In his report to Sandys, apparently written in January, 1620, Rolfe describes the arrival of a Dutch war vessel in August, 1619, bringing with it "20. and od Negroes, wch the Governor and Cape Merchant bought for victualle (whereof he was in greate need as he p'tended) at the best and easyest rate they could."[169] Although it is likely these men were purchased as indentured servants, it is unclear whether any of them were ever elevated to the status of freemen.[170]

The demand for indentured servants was high after John Rolfe developed an innovative strain of tobacco able to withstand the Virginia climate. Quickly, the practice of purchasing Africans as indentured servants would give way to the custom of purchasing them as chattel slaves, or humans designated as property of the master, with no observable rights or recognition of their humanity.

By the time of the American Revolution, the colonies had developed extensive experience with slavery. The Southern colonies of Virginia, North Carolina, South Carolina, and Georgia, with their more temperate climates and their large plantations, required ample hands for their maintenance and cultivation leading to a strong dependence on the slave industry.

With the American Revolution, the first opportunity for America to rid itself of slaves arrived. On June 11, 1776, the Continental Congress assigned John Adams, Benjamin Franklin, Roger Sherman, Robert Livingston, and Thomas Jefferson to draft a declaration of colonial independence from England. These men were great proponents of the philosophies of John Locke.[171] Locke's libertarian principles of natural law and the equality of the legal status of man are major components of his political writings. In fact, in his *Second Treatise of Civil Government*, Locke wrote,

> *The natural liberty of man is to be free from any superior power on earth, and not to be under the will or legislative authority of man, but to have only the law of nature for his rule. . . . Freedom then is not . . . a liberty for every one to do what he lists, to live as he pleases, and*

not to be tied by any laws, but freedom of men under government is, to have a standing rule to live by, common to every one of that society, and made by the legislative power erected in it; a liberty to follow my own will in all things, where the rule prescribes not; and not to be subject to the inconstant, uncertain, unknown, arbitrary will of another man: as freedom of nature is, to be under no other restraint but the law of nature.

[John Locke, "Of Slavery" in *The Second Treatise of Civil Government* (1690)]

It was only natural, then, for these five men to want to outlaw slavery in a society boasting of the equality of man as one of its foundational truisms. Indeed, Jefferson's draft of the Declaration of Independence proposed to the Continental Congress included a slavery provision within the list of grievances. Referring to King George III, the charge declared,

He has waged cruel war against human nature itself, violating its most sacred rights of life and liberty in the persons of a distant people who never offended him, captivating & carrying them into slavery in another hemisphere, or to incur miserable death in their transportation thither. This piratical warfare, the opprobrium of INFIDEL Powers, is the warfare of the CHRISTIAN king of Great Britain. Determined to keep open a market where MEN should be bought & sold, he has prostituted his negative for suppressing every legislative attempt to prohibit or to restrain this execrable commerce. And that this assemblage of horrors might want no fact of distinguished die, he is now exciting those very people to rise in arms among us, and to purchase that liberty of which he has deprived them, by murdering the people on whom he also obtruded them: thus paying off former crimes committed against the LIBERTIES of one people, with crimes which he urges them to commit against the LIVES of another."

(Thomas Jefferson, "Rough Draft of the Declaration of Independence," 1776.)

However, the Continental Congress contained a large faction of slave owners. The anti-slavery provision, apparently too much for the southern contingent of the Continental Congress to stomach, was amended out of that otherwise austere document.

The next opportunity to rid the emerging society of slavery came with the creation of its new government. Having declared its independence from England, the Second Continental Congress busied itself with fashioning a new form of government for their new country. It assigned a committee "to prepare and digest the form of confederation."[172, viii] However, the issue of manumission was never seriously discussed as part of the deliberations relating to the Articles of Confederation, and so, slavery continued with the Confederation.

At the end of the Revolutionary War, neither the United States nor England abolished slavery, so in turn, no efforts were made to eradicate that pernicious institution with the Treaty of Paris. Indeed, during the negotiations of the War's resolution, the topic of slavery laid dormant until Henry Laurens, a South Carolinian and the only negotiator proceeding from a southern state, injected language that would require the British to return runaway or confiscated slaves that had fallen into its possession during the war.[173]

The Constitutional Convention afforded Americans the fourth and final opportunity to peacefully eradicate slavery. By May 1787, the forces of abolition grew markedly, both in the United States and in England. Particularly in the northern states, many had mobilized, intent on ending the practice. Pennsylvania and Rhode Island, for example, passed gradual emancipation laws in 1780 and 1784 respectively. However, in the southern states, with their plantation-based economies, slave labor was viewed as an elemental component to the area's continued economic subsistence.

But the efforts of the emancipators would not be enough in Philadelphia. Tragically, the Framers were unable to prohibit the practice of slavery within the Republic, making the Constitutional Convention, magnificent as it was, a colossal failure in the effort at eradicating slavery, and by extension,

---

[viii] The committee members numbered thirteen, with one member chosen from each colony . They were: Samuel Adams, Josiah Bartlett, John Dickinson (chairman), Button Gwinnett, Joseph Hewes, Stephen Hopkins, Robert R. Livingston, Thomas McKean, Thomas Nelson, Edward Rutledge, Roger Sherman, and Thomas Stone. Francis Hopkinson was added on June 28, 1776 . (Tuesday, June 12, 1776, *Journals. of the Cont. Congress, 1774-1789*, ed. Worthington C. Ford et al. (Washington, D.C.: 1904-37) 433; Tuesday, June 28, 1776, *Journals. of the Cont. Congress*, 491.

in the efforts of truly achieving equality amongst men. The great movers of the Convention, men like Madison, Hamilton, Mason, Washington, and Franklin, felt slavery should be eradicated. Off in Paris, Thomas Jefferson, himself a slave owner, had publicly absconded slavery and noted its inconsistency with the natural law concepts that gave rise to the American Republic. In fact, in his "Notes on the State of Virginia," he wrote:

> *There must doubtless be an unhappy influence on the manners of our people produced by the existence of slavery among us. The whole commerce between master and slave is a perpetual exercise of the most boisterous passions, the most unremitting despotism on the one part, and degrading submissions on the other. Our children see this, and learn to imitate it; for man is an imitative animal. This quality is the germ of all education in him. From his cradle to his grave he is learning to do what he sees others do. If a parent could find no motive either in his philanthropy or his self-love, for restraining the intemperance of passion towards his slave, it should always be a sufficient one that his child is present. But generally it is not sufficient. The parent storms, the child looks on, catches the lineaments of wrath, puts on the same airs in the circle of smaller slaves, gives a loose to his worst of passions, and thus nursed, educated, and daily exercised in tyranny, cannot but be stamped by it with odious peculiarities. The man must be a prodigy who can retain his manners and morals undepraved by such circumstances. And with what execration should the statesman be loaded, who permitting one half the citizens thus to trample on the rights of the other, transforms those into despots, and these into enemies, destroys the morals of the one part, and the amor patriae of the other. For if a slave can have a country in this world, it must be any other in preference to that in which he is born to live and labour for another: in which he must lock up the faculties of his nature, contribute as far as depends on his individual endeavours to the evanishment of the human race, or entail his own miserable condition on the endless generations proceeding from him. With the morals of the people, their industry also is destroyed. For in a warm climate, no man will labour for himself who can make another labour for him. This is so true, that of the proprietors of slaves a very small proportion indeed are ever seen to labour. And can the liberties of a nation be thought secure when we*

have removed their only firm basis, a conviction in the minds of the people that these liberties are of the gift of God? That they are not to be violated but with his wrath? Indeed I tremble for my country when I reflect that God is just: that his justice cannot sleep for ever: that considering numbers, nature and natural means only, a revolution of the wheel of fortune, an exchange of situation, is among possible events: that it may become probable by supernatural interference! The Almighty has no attribute which can take side with us in such a contest– But it is impossible to be temperate and to pursue this subject through the various considerations of policy, of morals, of history natural and civil. We must be contented to hope they will force their way into every one's mind. I think a change already perceptible, since the origin of the present revolution. The spirit of the master is abating, that of the slave rising from the dust, his condition mollifying, the way I hope preparing, under the auspices of heaven, for a total emancipation, and that this is disposed, in the order of events, to be with the consent of the masters, rather than by their extirpation.

[Thomas Jefferson, "Notes on the State of Virginia: Query XVIII" (1781).]

Despite Jefferson's lofty ideals, a great part of the country, including him, remained invested in the perpetuation of slavery as an institution. Moreover, in the face of the country's impending failure, the Framers' primary objective was maintaining the Union. For them, in the face of the strong and increasingly hostile British and Spanish powers, saving the Union and keeping all the states as members of one unified, centralized republic was a matter of life and death. Although slavery was morally reprehensible, disunion was an immediate and existential threat.

But the threats to the peace and safety of the American people were not exclusively external. Although quieted through unification, discordance still existed among the various states regarding border controversies and land rights. Without a single unifying government, Hamilton would argue, ". . . we shall have good ground to apprehend, that the sword would sometimes be appealed to as the arbiter of their differences,"[174] resulting, in his words, in "frequent war and constant apprehension. . ."[175]

But to the southern states, there were greater threats than some mere hypothetical concern regarding boarder disputes and foreign invaders. The South worried about the disruption of their way of life. Without slaves, the southern states feared they would be unable to sustain their plantations, and their economies would collapse. Moreover, the fact that the northern states would move in a coordinated fashion to abolish slavery was a testament, in the collective mind of the South, to the tendency of the richer, more powerful states to impose their wills upon the weaker, economically poorer states. To the South, this threat was palpable, and one which its representatives would do anything to countervail, even if it meant secession.

Nor was the issue of slavery the top priority for the Northern states. For them, the most important matter to be achieved, as previously discussed, was union, particularly at a time when it appeared that slavery in America was on its way to being eradicated through individual state efforts.[ix]

That is not to say that those Framers who were willing to be more patient with the process of eradicating slavery found the institution any less morally reprehensible or inconsistent with the young nation's ideals.[176] James Madison, who accepted the eventual compromises allowing for the continued existence of slavery, called it, ". . . the most oppressive dominion ever exercised by man."[177] John Jay, in a letter to Lushington, observed, "It is much to be wished that slavery may be abolished. The honour of the States, as well as justice and humanity, in my opinion, loudly call upon them to emancipate these unhappy people. To contend for our own liberty, and to deny that blessing to others, involves an inconsistency not to be excused."[178] Even George Washington, "America's most prominent slave owner" at the time of the Constitutional Convention[179] wanted to see slavery eradicated, stating in a letter to Robert Morris in 1786, "I hope it will not be conceived. . . that it is my wish to hold

---

[ix] Although only Massachusetts had abolished slavery by 1787, the year of the Convention, efforts towards eradicating slavery were already under way in New York, New Jersey, Rhode Island, and Connecticut. In the meantime, Pennsylvania, Maryland, and Virginia (yes, Virginia) had already passed laws prohibiting the importation of slaves. (George Mason, Aug. 22, 1787, in Madison, "Notes on the Debates in the Federal Convention.")

the unhappy people, who are the subject of this letter, in slavery. I can only say that there is not a man living who wishes more sincerely than I do, to see a plan adopted for the abolition of it; but there is only one proper and effectual mode by which it can be accomplished, and that is by Legislative authority; and this, as far as my suffrage will go, shall never be wanting."[180, x]

The resulting dynamic was one favoring compromise. As Madison contended on June 15, 1788, during the Virginia Ratifying Convention, "Great as the evil is, a dismemberment of the Union would be worse."[181]

The slave dependent states, had brightly drawn their battle line within the Constitutional Convention. South Carolina, in particular, made it clear they would not be making any concessions regarding slavery. "South Carolina can never receive the plan [for a new government] if it prohibits the slave trade," averred Major Charles Pinckney, one of the state's delegates, during the August 21 session of the Constitutional Convention,[182] and Major General Charles Cotesworth Pinckney, his cousin and fellow South Carolina delegate agreed, saying, "South Carolina and Georgia cannot do without slaves,"[183] on the very next day.

This unyielding position caused great turbulence with staunch abolitionists, like George Mason, who felt the punishment for the failure to rid society of such an evil would be cataclysmic. "Every master of slaves is born a petty tyrant," he observed. "They bring the judgment of heaven on a country! As nations can not be rewarded or punished in the next world they must be in this."[184]

His words proved prophetic, but in the end, the abolitionists yielded, overwhelmed by the concerns of fragmentation coupled with the impression that slavery was doomed regardless of their actions.[xi] The Framers then turned to

[x] Interestingly, Washington's letter to Morris dealt with Washington's objections to a lawsuit brought forth by a Society of Quakers seeking to emancipate a Philadelphia slave. Washington explained that his objection was not based on his approval of slavery as an institution, but because he thought this was an issue for the legislatures to decide, not the courts.

[xi] Even Georgia Delegate Abraham Baldwin, while zealously advocating against prohibiting slavery in the union was quoted by Madison as saying, "If left to herself, [Georgia] may probably put a stop to the evil." (Abraham Baldwin, Aug. 21, 1787, in Madison, "Notes on the Debates in the Federal Convention.")

the next best goal at their disposal and the only one they felt achievable while preserving the Union, paving the road for slavery's eventual eradication.

In this regard, three compromises were made. First, Congress would be given the power to outlaw the importation of slaves beginning in 1808, twenty years after the projected ratification of the new Constitution.

Second was the implementation of the very disturbing three-fifths rule. In assessing the representation and taxation duties of the various states, the members of the nation's slave population would not be fully counted as the southern states had discordantly argued should be done. Neither would they be completely discounted as the advocates of a pure chattel property model argued should be done. Instead, "all other persons" than "free persons" and "Indians not taxed" would be given the weight of three fifths of a person for the purposes of determining the state's population.[185] This approach, it was hoped, would serve as an incentive for the southern states to emancipate the slaves because, although doing so would increase a state's taxation burden, it would immediately increase the state's representation in Congress and in the selection of the President.

Finally, as a further concession to the southern states, a fugitive slave clause was included, requiring slaves who fled to a non-slave state be returned to his or her state of origin.[186]

With their compromises in place, the abolitionist Framers were so sure of the certain death of slavery that Madison would write in *The Federalist Papers*,

> *It ought to be considered a great point gained in favor of humanity, that a period of twenty years may terminate for ever within these States, a traffic which has so long and so loudly unbraided the barbarism of modern policy; that within that period, it will receive a considerable discouragement from the federal government, and may be totally abolished, by a concurrence of the few States which continue the unnatural traffic, in the prohibitory example which has been given so great a majority of the Union. Happy would it be for the unfortunate Africans, if an equal prospect lay before them of being redeemed from the oppressions of their European brethren!*
>
> (Madison, No. 40.)

Despite their misplaced confidence, it appears the Framers generally reviled the concession they had made. The mere absence of the words "slavery" or "slaves" is a tacit acknowledgment of the ideological conflict between their concessions and the ideals they were trying to uphold for the new nation. James Madison, during the Constitutional Convention, actually acknowledged the inconsistency of staining the Constitution with the presence of language referring to slaves when he said, "[It would be] . . . wrong to admit in the Constitution the idea that there could be property in men."[187]

Tragically, the Framers' decision to gradually eradicate slavery was misbegotten. True, the Framers could have no idea that less than a decade after the drafting of the Constitution, Eli Whitney would submit his patent for a machine designed to mechanically separate cottonseeds from cotton fibers, thus adding an intoxicating and incurable financial component to the South's addiction to slavery. But the evil the Framers tolerated for the sake of unity, and which denigrated the Constitution and the principles serving as her foundation, sealed not only the fate of countless victims to lives of oppression, but a nation to a sentence of racial inequality and intolerance from which it has yet to recover.

The Road to Civil War

The road that ended in Civil War was convoluted, filled with trials, tribulations, and failures. A road initially paved with the mortars of idealistic visions for humanity and individual liberties, was instead covered with economic considerations and greed.

The economic impact of the Revolutionary War upon the nation was devastating, particularly upon the agrarian southern states. The obstructive British duties on rice produced in South Carolina and Georgia following the Treaty of Paris essentially closed that market to American agricultural producers. Predictably, the price of rice plummeted, decimating southern farmers.[188] However, at about this time, a great interest in the use of cotton fiber arose in England.[189] Detecting the increasing demand, planters in South Carolina and Georgia who had been growing indigo and rice turned to cotton. It was at this time that Ely Whitney's cotton gin would make its inroads upon the agricultural industry. Whereas a slave would have previously produced a pound of cotton each day, with the cotton gin, each was able to produce 50 pounds.[190] The sudden increased value of slave labor stifled any chance there may have been for its eradication. Instead of witnessing the continued disintegration of slavery as an institution, the South saw only the expansion of its reliance on forced labor. Supported by technological innovations and the beleaguered hands of slaves, cotton became the largest and most important exportable American product. Slavery became so inculcated into its culture that white churchmen began defending the institution through the use of biblical references.[191] By 1819, the United States had developed into what was essentially two countries: one consisting of eleven, slave-dependent states and another eleven that viewed the institution with abhorrence.

And then came the petition in 1817, by Missouri, to become America's twenty-third state.

Missouri's petition to enter the Union would not have been so significant were it not for the threat by abolitionists to repeal the Constitution's fugitive slave provision. Southern states realized that in the absence of a fugitive slave clause, slaves would be eager to flee to neighboring free states. The threat of such a change in the Constitution resulted in tensions within the halls of Congress until 1820 when Henry Clay, a lawyer from Kentucky and Speaker of the House of Representatives, orchestrated one of the great compromises in American history.

Known as the Missouri Compromise of 1820, the plan not only allowed for Missouri's admission as a slave state, but also created the free state of Maine from within the boarders of Massachusetts, thus preserving the Union's numerical balance. Additionally, the compromise mandated that slavery not be allowed north of the 36° 30" line, a latitude line separating Pennsylvania from Maryland, the Mason-Dixon line.

But the Missouri Compromise only delayed the impending violence. The issue would arise once again in 1848 with the procurement of southwestern lands from Mexico and the resolution of the Mexican-American War. With the new territory, came the petition for other states to enter the Union, once again threatening the mathematical balance between the slave states and free states. Once again, Senator Henry Clay, the Great Compromiser, negotiated another historic agreement. Under this second plan, California was admitted as a free state, and a prohibition of slave trade within the District of Columbia was enacted. Concurrently, Utah and New Mexico would be organized as territories with the agreement that each territory's citizens would ultimately decide the issue of slavery within its borders. Additionally, Congress would renounce its authority to interfere with the interstate slave trade, and would more actively enforce fugitive slave laws (to the tune of a $1,000 fine).

In 1854, events would require yet another compromise. Introduced by Illinois Senator Stephen A. Douglas, the legislation, named the Kansas-Nebraska Act, would essentially nullify the Missouri Compromise of 1820 by organizing Kansas and Nebraska into territories and opening up their lands for settlement. Once again, the white male inhabitants of each territory would determine the status of slavery within each region.

Although considered a compromise, the effect of the Kansas-Nebraska Act was anything but calming. Immediately, pro-slavery settlers immigrated into Kansas from Missouri with the intent of influencing any elections in the direction of slavery. Simultaneously, "Jayhawkers," abolitionists from Missouri, flooded Kansas with the opposite intent. The result was not only political tension, but also violent confrontation, amounting to a state of civil war within Bleeding Kansas.[192]

Perhaps more significantly, the issue of slavery and the Kansas-Nebraska Act would become the centerpiece for an election showdown between Stephen A. Douglas and an up and coming state senator from Illinois named Abraham Lincoln as each vied for that state's senate seat in Washington. The debates between the two men are among the most famous in American history and catapulted State Senator Lincoln to national prominence.

As fate would have it, the people of Illinois would select Douglas to be their Senator, but in so doing, they allowed Lincoln to become President of the United States at the most vulnerable time in American history.

With the three slave compromises enacted, the Union continued its trek into the future. In the 1850s, the United States was truly a divided house with an irreparable fissure running deeply through its foundation. With abolitionists to the north yearning to permanently end the travesty of forced bondage and slave owners to the South defending their right to own slaves, the country careened to a colossally violent confrontation.

In 1854, the final opportunity to avert a disaster presented itself. Around 1830, a United States Army physician named John Emerson, who resided in Missouri, a slave state, purchased a slave named Dred Scott. Subsequent to the purchase, Dr. Emerson was transferred to Illinois, a free state whose anti-slave status had been predetermined through the provisions in the Northwest Ordinance. Dr. Emerson, upon relocating to Illinois, took his slave with him. From there, the Army relocated the doctor to the Wisconsin Territory, where he again moved with his slave. Like in Illinois, slavery was prohibited in Wisconsin, and while there, Dr. Emerson allowed Dred Scott to marry a slave named Harriet Robinson. As a result, Harriet too became property of Dr. Emerson.

From Wisconsin, Dr. Emerson was ordered to Missouri, to which he would depart while leaving his slaves behind in Wisconsin so that their services could be leased out to third parties.

When Dr. Emerson was assigned to Louisiana, he took a wife and called for his slaves to be sent to Louisiana. Thus began Dred Scott's journey down the Mississippi with his pregnant wife. During the trip, Harriet would deliver her baby girl aboard a steamboat floating on the Mississippi River somewhere between Iowa, a free territory, and Illinois, a free state. The family eventually arrived in Louisiana where they continued in service to the Emersons.

Dr. Emerson would eventually be transferred back to the Wisconsin Territory to fight in the Seminole War, and Mrs. Emerson would move to

St. Louis. In 1843, Dr. Emerson, after retiring from the Army and moving to Iowa, died, leaving his estate, including his slaves, to his widow. Three years later, Dred Scott attempted to purchase his family's freedom. Unsuccessful at privately negotiating the end to his slave status, Scott then turned to the Missouri courts for help, arguing that his wife's and his residence in a free state had resulted in their emancipation. Moreover, the argument continued, their daughter should not be a slave since she was born on a riverboat between a free territory and a free state.

The case reached the U.S. Supreme Court in 1854 and it fell upon the Chief Justice, Roger B. Taney to author the court's opinion. To that point, Taney had been a highly esteemed Justice appointed by President Andrew Jackson to replace Chief Justice John Marshall. He was a native of Maryland who married Francis Scott Key's sister[xii] and an ardent defender of state rights and individual liberties.

Writing for the overwhelming majority of the Court in the *Dred Scott* case, Taney took the position that Scott never had standing to sue in federal court.[xiii] According to Taney, people who arrived to American shores as slaves did not come voluntarily. As a result, averred Taney, ". . . they are not intended to be included, under the word 'citizens' in the Constitution, and can therefore claim none of the rights and privileges which that instrument provides and secures to citizens of the United States."[193] According to Taney, because a slave came to the United States or the colonies involuntarily, he or she was not a citizen of this country, could never be a citizen of this country, would never be entitled to the benefits of citizenship, and would therefore

xii Francis Scott Key, of course, was a Maryland lawyer who famously penned "The Defence of Fort M'Henry," which would eventually serve as the lyrics for "The Star-Spangled Banner." He was also a staunch anti-abolitionist.

xiii Standing is the principle of being in a legal position to bring an argument before the judge. Because American courts are only authorized to hear cases or controversies in law, standing is based on the supposition that only a person who is actually involved or affected by the controversy or the matter in question may deliver an argument before a judge. Standing also requires that the person bringing the case to the court have legal access to the court. This latter requirement is extremely permissive as practically all citizens, residents, and even undocumented persons have access to American courts. As we shall see, Taney had a different opinion regarding access to the courts by slaves or even former slaves.

not have the privilege of accessing the country's courts. "On the contrary," he wrote, "they were at that time considered as a subordinate and inferior class of beings who had been subjugated by the dominant race, and, whether emancipated or not, yet remained subject to their authority, and had no rights or privileges but such as those who held the power and the Government might choose to grant them."[194] In Chief Justice Taney's view of the relationship between the state and the individual, there were no inalienable rights. According to Taney, the rights of the defeated are merely those granted to them by the benevolence or convenience of the victors.

Taney's opinion was also laced with commentary regarding state rights and sovereignty apparently in an effort to reconcile its inconsistencies between the rights afforded for African Americans in free states versus those observed in slave states. A state had the right to invoke citizenship upon former slaves, but in so doing, the state was only invoking *state* citizenship upon the individual, not *American* citizenship, because it was untenable to think that a state could invoke its will regarding citizenship upon all the other states of the union.[195]

Taney then went on to discuss the unconstitutionality of the Missouri Compromise, a matter not in question before the Court, averring that the law of each state was supreme regarding the subject of slavery and that the federal government was not given the authority or the jurisdiction to infringe upon it. [xiii]

The *Dred Scott* decision had a profound effect on the United States and on American history. Constitutionally, the effects were immense. *Dred Scott* marked the first time the Supreme Court had blocked access to the federal courts and due process to a complete segment of American society, namely, anyone who arrived to the country involuntarily. Additionally, it monumentally strengthened state rights and sovereignty by carving out an exclusive domain to the states relating to slavery and property rights. And awkwardly, it allowed

[xiii] This too is very unorthodox since judges, knowing that theirs is to decide only the legal matter in question, overwhelmingly refrain from commenting on matters outside of the legal question before them.

states to create citizen-status for some of its inhabitants so that it would be legally possible to be a citizen of the state of Maryland and not be an American!

Taken to its logical conclusion, *Dred Scott* created a country made up of loosely held states without a common identity for its citizens nor a common nationality. To say that the *Dred Scott* decision, if allowed to stand, would eventually lead to the fragmentation and disruption of the Union is no more prophetic than predicting rainfall around a hurricane.

Politically, *Dred Scott* was equally devastating. To the slave states, the decision served as welcomed reinforcement for their state sovereignty arguments. For them, the decision authenticated their position in the defense of slavery and solidified their precious fugitive slave acts. Essentially, *Dred Scott* served as the judicial precedent to validate slave states' slavery laws and emasculate any federal authority on the issue. Although clearly delivered as dicta[xiv] and non-binding, the slave states knew there was a case to be made to nullify the Missouri Compromise and the Nebraska-Kansas Act.[xv]

For the abolitionists, the *Dred Scott* decision was a source of outrage and a rallying cry, reinvigorating their efforts to completely eliminate slavery. If it was unconstitutional for Congress to pass legislation restricting or eliminating slavery, then it was time to ratify an amendment, or if necessary, to engage in armed confrontation to eradicate the perverse infestation of an otherwise free country.

And attack the abolitionists would, the most stunning of which was John Brown's raid on Harpers Ferry in Virginia in 1859, pitting an abolitionist father of twenty against a contingency of U.S. Marines.[196] Brown, supported by a small group of financiers and 21 men, stormed and seized the federal arsenal at Harper's Ferry on October 16, 1859. Ultimately, he was no match for the American military and was subdued by a small contingency of men

---

xiv Dicta is a portion of a reviewing court's opinion that does not directly apply to the question before it, but serves as a signal as to how it would rule should the matter come before it. Although not binding on the lower courts, a statement delivered as dicta can have an immense influence.

xv Interestingly, not addressed in the Court's opinion is whether its position would also invalidate the slave prohibitions within the Northwest Ordinance imposed by Congress through the Articles of Confederation.

led by Colonel Robert E. Lee who handed the "rebel" to American authorities for a trial that would inevitably end in Brown's hanging.

Brown's story, stirred up abolitionist sentiments. To them, the prospect of a continued existence in a house divided now looked untenable. The stage was set for the last and most important effect of the *Dred Scott* decision: the election of an anti-slavery President intent on keeping the Union intact and resolved to end the unforgivable sin of slavery.

That man was Abraham Lincoln.

Lincoln was truly a man destined for history. He was an ardent protector of the Union believing that no state had the right to secede from the country, and he abhorred slavery. As so many other things in American history, it was fitting that it would be he who would lead the nation through its greatest crisis.

The Consequences of the Civil War

Over six hundred forty thousand Americans would die as a result of the Civil War.[197] Their sacrifices would resolve two peacefully irreconcilable questions: 1) whether the federal government really did reign supreme over the states (to an extent); and 2) whether the institution of slavery in America would be forever eradicated.

But there were many other consequences. First, the domestic powers of the President of the United States grew. President Lincoln's broad use of executive powers as Commander in Chief eventually enhanced the power of the President at the expense of the states and of Congress. And amongst the first of these power expansions was his unilateral violation of the citizenry's habeas corpus rights.

By the time of Lincoln's inauguration on March 4, 1861, seven states had already seceded from the Union, and on April 17, 1861, Virginia voted to secede, leaving Maryland as the only conduit for supplies to the nation's capital.[198]

On April 27, 1861, President Lincoln ordered General Winfield Scott to suspend the writ of habeas corpus along a troop transportation route stretching from Pennsylvania to Washington. Under this action, and in contradiction to one of the nation's founding principles, a citizen held against his or her will within the predefined corridor would not be eligible to seek an opinion from a judge or magistrate as to the appropriateness of his or her detention.

Lincoln's Constitutional premise for the measure stemmed from Article I, Section 9, which stated, "the privilege of habeas corpus shall not be suspended, unless when in cases of rebellion and invasion the public safety may require it." After witnessing an active rebellion that threatened the lives of American troops and caused frequent unrest within Maryland, Lincoln reasoned that the suspension of the writ of habeas corpus was both appropriate and necessary in order to conduct the war and maintain order within the Union.

A few days later, Maryland State Representative John Merriman, acting in his capacity as First Lieutenant in the Baltimore County Horse Guards[199] and under orders from Maryland Governor Thomas Hicks, led a group of men on a mission to destroy railroad lines within the state. On May 25, federal officers captured and detained Merriman who promptly filed a writ of habeas corpus. The writ was addressed to the Chief Justice of the Supreme Court, Roger Brooke Taney, the same Justice who had previously written the *Dred Scott* opinion.[200] In unprecedented fashion, Taney responded by traveling to Baltimore to hear Merriman's motion.

Taney quickly crafted an opinion damning the President's action. No one, he wrote, had "thrust aside the judicial authorities . . .and substituted a military government in its place."[201] He explained that although Article I, Section 9, of the United States Constitution allowed for the suspension of the writ of habeas corpus, that authority rested only with Congress and not with the President of the United States.

Lincoln disregarded the Chief Justice's order and continued to hold Merriman, essentially acting outside the bounds of his constitutional authority. Under any other circumstances, the Merriman matter would have amounted to a constitutional crisis, but during the Civil War, the Constitution's very existence was threatened. Instead of battling the President, Congress interceded on his behalf in March 1863, granting the President the authority he had already employed.[202]

The congressional intervention may have put the issue of the appropriateness of Merriman's detention to rest, but President Lincoln's precedent of ignoring a Supreme Court Justice's order remains a source of debate among constitutional scholars and professors of American history.

Lincoln's Emancipation Proclamation is another action where the Chief Executive acted in unprecedented fashion. In 1862, Lincoln made the emancipation of slaves a central issue to the nation's future. Unquestionably, one of Lincoln's aims was to permanently free all persons held in forced bondage within the United States. Some people close to the President had philosophical problems with any solution other than an immediate end to slavery. But Lincoln was cognizant of the illegality of such an act. In short, Lincoln understood that, even in a time of war, the President simply did not have the authority to negate the property rights of the people. Clearly, what was needed, he concluded, was a constitutional amendment.

But, there were other pressures upon the President pushing him to hasten the process towards emancipation. By 1862, the South's troop reserves were faltering, and slaves were increasingly enlisted in the fight against the Union. Lincoln recognized that a presidential emancipation would serve t[illegible] stem the tide of slave participation in the war. But how could that happ[illegible] without tarnishing the Constitution?

By the summer of 1862, Lincoln decided he would issue an ultim[illegible] to the rebel states, giving them a deadline to return to the Union or [illegible] permanent emancipation of their slaves. In order for his offer to [illegible] weight, however, he needed a decisive victory; one that would pl[illegible] of the hostilities squarely on the side of the Union.

That time arrived on September 19, 1862, with the Un[illegible] Antietam. On September 22, President Lincoln release[illegible] Emancipation Proclamation, which declared that if the [illegible] cease hostilities and rejoin the Union by January 1, 1[illegible] those states would be free.[203] As expected, none of th[illegible] offer, and on January 1, 1863, Lincoln issued the [illegible] tion, freeing all slaves in the ten states still in re[illegible]

States and allowing ex-slaves to join the armed forces as paid members of the military.[204]

The president's emancipation of slaves was undoubtedly an aggressive political, historical, and constitutional move that essentially changed the purpose of the Civil War.[205] From the moment of the Proclamation's issuance, the War ceased being a dispute over the relationship between the governing authorities and morphed into an existential battle no lesser in scope than the Revolutionary War. Under the influence of the President's pen, the Civil War became a confrontation that would define the relationship between the nation's races.

But did Lincoln have the legal authority to emancipate the slaves without due process or compensation to the owners? Every consideration based
n human justice and righteousness bellows approvingly. Lincoln, who felt
power of divine intervention in his actions, never had any doubt of his
ns, stating at the time of the signing of his infamous executive order, "I
in my life, felt more certain that I was doing right, than I do in signing
r."[206]

stingly, the legal argument also stands decidedly in his favor. The
owers to emancipate slaves did not merely arise because the na-
r active rebellion, but as a result of the rebel states' rejection of
ition whose protections they would have otherwise sought.
ose states seceded from the Union and organized into a
vely engaged in hostilities against the American gov-
ey renounced any protections afforded to them by
recaptured, they would be subject to whatever
ding government that the victor saw fit.

itutional standing, recognition of what the
achieve is also in order. The Emancipa-
e slave held inside the United States.
ne so had he possessed the neces-
t. As a result, his Emancipation
hin the states still in rebellion
the Union.

States and allowing ex-slaves to join the armed forces as paid members of the military.[204]

The president's emancipation of slaves was undoubtedly an aggressive political, historical, and constitutional move that essentially changed the purpose of the Civil War.[205] From the moment of the Proclamation's issuance, the War ceased being a dispute over the relationship between the governing authorities and morphed into an existential battle no lesser in scope than the Revolutionary War. Under the influence of the President's pen, the Civil War became a confrontation that would define the relationship between the nation's races.

But did Lincoln have the legal authority to emancipate the slaves without due process or compensation to the owners? Every consideration based on human justice and righteousness bellows approvingly. Lincoln, who felt the power of divine intervention in his actions, never had any doubt of his actions, stating at the time of the signing of his infamous executive order, "I never, in my life, felt more certain that I was doing right, than I do in signing this paper."[206]

Interestingly, the legal argument also stands decidedly in his favor. The president's powers to emancipate slaves did not merely arise because the nation was under active rebellion, but as a result of the rebel states' rejection of the very Constitution whose protections they would have otherwise sought. Because each of those states seceded from the Union and organized into a confederacy, they actively engaged in hostilities against the American government. In doing so, they renounced any protections afforded to them by the Constitution, and when recaptured, they would be subject to whatever organizational decisions regarding government that the victor saw fit.

But to help bolster its constitutional standing, recognition of what the Emancipation Proclamation did not achieve is also in order. The Emancipation Proclamation did not free a single slave held inside the United States. Unquestionably, Lincoln would have done so had he possessed the necessary constitutional authority, but he did not. As a result, his Emancipation Declaration only applied to slaves residing within the states still in rebellion against the United States and no longer part of the Union.

The congressional intervention may have put the issue of the appropriateness of Merriman's detention to rest, but President Lincoln's precedent of ignoring a Supreme Court Justice's order remains a source of debate among constitutional scholars and professors of American history.

Lincoln's Emancipation Proclamation is another action where the Chief Executive acted in unprecedented fashion. In 1862, Lincoln made the emancipation of slaves a central issue to the nation's future. Unquestionably, one of Lincoln's aims was to permanently free all persons held in forced bondage within the United States. Some people close to the President had philosophical problems with any solution other than an immediate end to slavery. But Lincoln was cognizant of the illegality of such an act. In short, Lincoln understood that, even in a time of war, the President simply did not have the authority to negate the property rights of the people. Clearly, what was needed, he concluded, was a constitutional amendment.

But, there were other pressures upon the President pushing him to hasten the process towards emancipation. By 1862, the South's troop reserves were faltering, and slaves were increasingly enlisted in the fight against the Union. Lincoln recognized that a presidential emancipation would serve to stem the tide of slave participation in the war. But how could that happen without tarnishing the Constitution?

By the summer of 1862, Lincoln decided he would issue an ultimatum to the rebel states, giving them a deadline to return to the Union or risk the permanent emancipation of their slaves. In order for his offer to carry any weight, however, he needed a decisive victory; one that would place the tide of the hostilities squarely on the side of the Union.

That time arrived on September 19, 1862, with the Union's victory at Antietam. On September 22, President Lincoln released his Preliminary Emancipation Proclamation, which declared that if the rebel states did not cease hostilities and rejoin the Union by January 1, 1863, all slaves within those states would be free.[203] As expected, none of the rebel states took the offer, and on January 1, 1863, Lincoln issued the Emancipation Proclamation, freeing all slaves in the ten states still in rebellion against the United

Lincoln's mission to save the Union and eradicate slavery left the South in ruins and resulted in more than 205,000 actual combat casualties and another 415,000 war-related deaths,[207]the greatest in American history. The price for the atonement of America's great sin was monumental, but no undertaking was more necessary. Although the nation and the Constitution were irreversibly morphed from their prior existence, both survived the Civil War.

On December 18, 1865, the Thirteenth Amendment was adopted, finally accomplishing what the Framers were unable to do in the late eighteenth century: end the existence of slavery within the United States.

The Fourteenth Amendment soon followed. Adopted on July 9, 1868, it was broader in scope. Section 1 declared that all persons born or naturalized in the United States were subject to its laws and were citizens of both the state they lived in and the nation, ending the controversy over the relationship of state citizenship and American citizenship. Section 2 made it clear that the representation of the States would be apportioned according to the population of each state. The shameful three-fifths rule was finally erased. Section 3 prohibited anyone who had engaged in an insurrection or rebellion against the United States from serving in public office within the United States unless allowed to do so by a two-thirds vote of each Chamber. Section 4 guaranteed the debts incurred by the United States in conducting the Civil War, but absolved it of any debts incurred by rebel states. And finally, Section 5 gave Congress the power to enforce the provisions of the Fourteenth Amendment through appropriate legislation.

The Fifteenth Amendment, the third and last of the Civil War Amendments, was ratified on February 3, 1870, and guaranteed the right to vote to all male citizens of the United States regardless of race, color, or previous condition of servitude.

With these three amendments, the Constitutional defects dealing with race and slavery were finally put to rest. But societal challenges remained, demonstrating that although a state may regulate actions, it is much less capable of prohibiting prejudice and animus among its citizens.

6. The Right to Vote

The Constitution never determined who had the right to vote. Instead, the regulation of suffrage (the right to vote) was determined by the various states.[208] Initially, only land-owning, white males were given the right to vote. However, it was only a matter of time before the right to vote expanded.

The effort at ending slavery resulted in the first, national, concerted effort at enfranchising a group other than white males. With the recognition of blacks as citizens in the Fourteenth Amendment,[209] the stage was set for the extension of the right to vote through the passage of the Fifteenth Amendment to the Constitution. Despite this, efforts quickly materialized to disenfranchise the nation's blacks through statutory interventions. Predictably, these efforts were particularly intense in the South where southern Democrats, insistent on keeping blacks from fully participating in society, passed a series of measures designed to suppress African Americans.[xvi] These laws included such measures as the implementation of poll taxes to keep the poor, the overwhelming majority of which were black, from voting.

But these suppressive laws did not stop at the polls. Legislation designed to perpetuate racism and discrimination abounded, including the prohibition of interracial marriages, criminal sanctions for unemployment, and perhaps most visibly, the requirement that commercial activities be separated by race. Just about every activity imaginable, from receiving a haircut to the acceptance of support services by the blind (who ironically were unable to assess the color of their own skin), were to be separated by skin color. This separation perpetuated the unequal standing between whites and blacks in the nation's societal, legal, educational, and financial structure.

Women were the next non-white-male group to gain suffrage. Interestingly, in 1797, New Jersey became the first state to afford women the right to vote, but that right was repealed in 1807.

---

xvi Legislation designed to infringe on black Americans' abilities to vote were called Jim Crow laws named after a caricature of a black dance performed by Thomas D. Rice, a white actor, and named "Jump Jim Crow." The term became a pejorative used in reference to African Americans.

The nineteenth century saw women's role in society change dramatically. By 1880, 2.6 million women were employed, and women had positioned themselves as a significant force within the learned professions.[210]

In 1848, the earliest steps towards women's suffrage materialized with the efforts of Elizabeth Cady Stanton, Susan B. Anthony, and Lucretia Coffin Mott through groups such as the National Women's Suffrage Association and the American Woman Suffrage Association. Their political involvement was closely tied to the Progressive, abolitionist, and temperance movements through which they gained organizational experience and strength.

The congressional effort at procuring women's suffrage began earnestly in 1872 with Senator Aaron A. Sargent's introduction of bills aimed at statutorily securing the vote for women. Frustrated in his statutory efforts, Senator Sargent changed tack in 1879 and introduced a bill that would grant women suffrage through a constitutional amendment. Early efforts to pass the bill were defeated, but with the onset of the Socialist and Progressive movements, candidates supporting women's suffrage began inhabiting congressional seats, shifting the tide in favor of the suffragists.

By the turn of the twentieth century, women had achieved suffrage in the territories of Wyoming, Utah, and Washington, and in the states of Colorado and Idaho,[211] but little progress had been made in the national arena. In 1918, the suffragist movement received a strong pillar of support when President Woodrow Wilson, in his State of the Union Address, urged the passage of a constitutional amendment granting women the right to vote.

In 1919, despite staunch opposition from Southern Democrats, the bill calling for the passage of the Nineteenth Amendment was passed, and on August 18, 1920, ratified. As with slavery, state sovereignty was used to conjure up an argument against the amendment's binding authority. In *Leser v. Garnett*,[212] Oscar Leser, a Maryland judge, argued that the Nineteenth Amendment ought not apply in his state since Maryland had not voted for the amendment's ratification, and the Maryland Constitution limited suffrage to men. By allowing the Nineteenth Amendment to dictate voting rights in Maryland, Leser argued, the state's autonomy was being destroyed.

The Supreme Court predictably ruled against Leser, basing its opinion on the identical language of the Fifteenth Amendment relating to blacks and its power over non-ratifying states, including Maryland. With that Supreme Court case, any legal resistance against women's right to vote was finally defeated.[xvii]

It would take the passage of the Twenty-Sixth Amendment in 1971 to guarantee the right to vote for all adult American citizens, adult being defined as anyone who is at least eighteen years old. The movement actually arose from the nation's discussion regarding the Vietnam War. During the 1960s, many states required persons to be at least twenty-one years old to vote. But a draft that would involuntarily send eighteen-year-olds into combat without giving them a voice at the polls seemed increasingly incoherent. Further inconsistencies arose when Congress set the voting age for federal elections, but not for state and local ones, resulting in the logistically awkward situation of citizens being able to vote on some of the questions posed to them at the voting booth but not others.[213, xviii] Under increasing public scrutiny, Congress passed a proposed constitutional amendment, and with its ratification, for the first time, the Constitution of the United States affirmatively defined who possessed the right to vote. In 1971, after 182 years of governance, universal suffrage finally graced the pages of the country's guiding document.

7. Setting Congressional Compensation; Madison Rides Again!

As we have already seen, not all of Madison's proposed constitutional amendments made it into the Bill of Rights. One that did not was the second proposed amendment. It read:

---

xvii The issue of women's rights would not conclude with the attainment of suffrage. There were still issues of equal pay and opportunity in the workplace. Those efforts would result in the passage of the Equal Pay Act in 1963 and Title VII of the Civil Rights Act of 1964, and although an effort has been made to pass an Equal Rights Amendment, its ratification never materialized. (Johnson, *A History of the American People*, 659)

xviii *Oregon v. Mitchell*, decided by the Supreme Court in 1970, asserted Congress's authority to set the voting age for federal elections.

> ***Article the second...*** *No law, varying the compensation for the services of the Senators and Representatives, shall take effect, until an election of Representatives shall have intervened.*
>
> [James Madison, Proposed Amendments to the Constitution of the United States (1789)]

Despite Congress's approval of the amendment, it did not achieve ratification since it was only accepted by six states.[214] But interestingly, Congress never set an internal time limit or expiration date upon the ratification process for the articles proposed by Madison.

Fast forward to 1982 when Congressional salaries had been increasing precipitously over the preceding three decades.[215] In that year, Gregory D. Watson, an economics major at the University of Texas-Austin was looking for a topic for a term paper. Watson thought Madison's proposed constitutional amendment was still eligible for ratification and wrote about it. His efforts earned him a C, specifically because he failed to convince his professor that the proposed amendment was still valid. Undeterred and unaware that Wyoming had recently passed the amendment in protest to the recent congressional pay raises, Watson began a solitary campaign to ratify the Compensation Amendment. He first took his battle to Maine and Colorado where he succeeded. His campaign sparked the imagination of the various state legislatures at a time when the people of the United States had grown increasingly suspicious of their elected officials and wary of congressional pay increases. By May 7, 1992, the legislatures of Michigan and New Jersey became the thirty-eighth and thirty-ninth states to ratify the Twenty-Seventh Amendment to the Constitution of the United States, completing a 202-years process from congressional proposal to final ratification.

Needless to say, Congress and constitutional scholars alike were stunned when Don W. Williams, the Archivist of the United States, certified the amendment as ratified on May 18, 1992, and published it on the following day's Federal Register.[216]

Despite Congress's befuddlement and the inauspicious resuscitation of the long dormant amendment, the amendment's enactment was a testament to the power of the individual at shaping the course of a nation.

Chapter 4

The Transformation of American Society and the Morphing of the Constitution

With the passage of the Thirteenth, Fourteenth, and Fifteenth Amendments, the United States finally corrected the one great flaw in her Constitution. The dispute over the various states' subservience to the Union also vanished. There no longer existed a realistic argument that membership within the Union was in some way voluntary or discretionary. The Civil War achieved a strong centralized government, endowing the nation with the flexibility and might to ward off its enemies, both internal and external.

The American Republic would now go on to face challenges of a more innocuous and erosive nature. Amazing and rapid changes befell the American people following the Civil War. It was an era where the country moved from a largely agrarian to an increasingly industrial one. It was a time when people, as individuals and not as family units, moved from their rural farms and ranches to much smaller abodes within cities, and where they learned to rely more on their governments and less on their families or their God.

It was also a time of immense and massive immigration. The nations of eastern Europe were to be decimated by poverty and political oppression, sending millions of their tired, their poor, and their huddled masses yearning to breathe free[i] to welcoming American shores replete with promise and opportunity.

With these changes to American culture and demographics came the temptation to discard the country's faith in the premises that had given rise to her existence. The stage was set for another Civil War, but this one was a battle to be waged with the pen and bullhorn, not the musket. For the next 150 years, a new battle for the heart of the nation would ensue, and its preeminent battlefields would be the American courts.

1. Dismantling American Exceptionalism; the People Dismiss the Union's Foundational Philosophies

America's original system of government was one that placed the individual at the core. It conceded that the will of each individual was his to determine, driven by his own personal relationship with his Creator. Unlike any other form of government, the individual provided foundational support for the greater politic. He was not viewed as a member whose purpose was to aggrandize the state. Rather, it was the government that existed for the purpose of supporting the individual. It was the government that was endowed with the responsibility of maintaining stability within the state so that individuals could peacefully engage in their pursuits of happiness. In other words, the underlying magnificence of the American system of government was that it would not view man as existing to serve itself, but ultimately, to serve God as each saw fit. And as we have demonstrated, therein lies the crux of the greatness and success of the United States of America, the Constitution, and every action undertaken by American citizens in pursuit of happiness.

With the passage of the Civil War Amendments, structurally at least, the nation stood upon a constitutional foundation that had struck a balance

[i] Of course, this famous phrase comes from Emma Lazarus's sonnet, "New Colossus" that she wrote in 1883. Lazarus wrote the sonnet in support of a fundraiser for a pedestal that would eventually support the monumental statue.

between the need for government and the respect for human independence. It was a balance that still honored the various states as the primary structures of government, although they admittedly emerged from the Civil War as much weaker entities.

How is it that this incredibly enlightened society came to abandon these exalting and liberating revolutionary principles? The answer lies in her responses to the historical challenges that befell her and her inability to free herself of the hateful consequences of slavery.

At its inception, the United States of America was largely an agrarian nation and its business model was essentially family centric. The influence of tobacco and cotton upon the national economy was paramount, and families ran the countless number of plantations and farms. Admittedly, there were many other economic influences. The Northeast housed a healthy manufacturing sector and sported a robust and growing maritime industry, while the Midwest was growing more food than any other place on earth. Other areas benefited from growing timber and iron industries. However, even among the manufacturing sectors, partnership and proprietary based organizational structures were the norm, inherently limiting the size and scope of any individual enterprise. Consequently, much of the labor within the United States remained household based, keeping individuals close to their families and within their communities of origin.

As the nation made its way to the Civil War, a number of changes took place that would favorably position it to capitalize from the industrial growth spurt of the late nineteenth and early twentieth centuries.[217] To the south, the economy flourished under the influence of King Cotton. The Midwestern states and the Northeast developed their textile, lumber, and metal industries with virtually no limits to their expansive potentials.

The nation's advancements were not merely physical in nature, as there were necessary legal changes to accommodate the rapidly evolving societal and economic developments. Chief among these was the creation of the corporate structure. The idea that an enterprise could be undertaken through something other than a proprietorship or a partnership had not been fully developed prior to the nineteenth century. But, by the early 1800s, certain businesses were tinkering with the idea of creating entities whose ownership could survive the passage of its owners. Such a structure would offer the advantages of flexibility and permanence, allowing the company to adapt to changing market pressures. The corporate model also possessed the ability to raise massive amounts of capital. For these reasons, by 1810, corporations had become a common organizational structure for banks, turnpike enterprises, and insurance companies.[218]

But for corporations to truly flourish, some hurdles had to be cleared, such as the acknowledgement of a citizen's right to create one. Initially, the creation of a corporation had to be approved by the legislature. The early parts of the nineteenth century saw the passage of laws allowing individuals or groups of individuals to create corporations.

The appearance of legislation limiting stockholders' liability risks to the amount they invested also facilitated the spread of corporate entities and allowed citizens to avoid any threat to the remainder of their holdings and property. By the 1860s, these limited liability statutes had been adopted throughout the various states.[219]

Despite these dramatic shifts, American economic progress would come to a screeching halt with the onset of the Civil War. With total expenditures of about $6.6 billion (more than twice the costs of purchasing all of the South's slaves),[220] the South was left to absorb the brunt of the War's financial impact. The Deep South was hit particularly hard, and those states dependent on cotton production suffered the greatest. The mid 1860s saw the South's plantation system reduced to virtual non-existence with little opportunity for recovery. With the emancipation of slaves, the available supply of labor was sharply reduced at a time when the supply of cotton from foreign markets like India, Brazil, and Egypt increased, driving the price of cotton down. The Deep South responded to the pressures on the cotton market by making itself even more dependent on the crop,[221] and the disparity was worsened by her absence from the early Reconstruction congresses.

But no one could foresee the shear fluidity of the nation's passage through the latter half of the nineteenth century. With startling speed, the distributions of commodities productions within the country flipped from 53% agriculture, 33% manufacturing, and 14% mining and construction in 1869 to 33% agriculture, 53% manufacturing and 14% mining and construction in 1899.[222] The shift was in no small part due to the technological changes that gripped the country.[223] Quickly, Americans moved from the farmlands to the cities, changing the characteristics of the labor force from a mostly agrarian workforce in 1860 to one evenly split between manufacturers and farmers in 1910.[224]

The pangs torturing Europe influenced and added to the nation's domestic changes. The 1840s saw Ireland gripped by the potato famine, resulting in the loss of one third of the Irish population.[225] In the nearly 20 years spanning 1841 through 1860, 1,694,000 Irish men and women relocated to the United States, establishing themselves mostly in Boston and New York.[226]

In 1848, Germany saw the failure of its revolutionary movements that prompted a wave of German migration. The arriving Germans were mostly Mennonites, Amish, and Calvinists. These were generally more skilled than their Irish counterparts and more eager to leave the big city in search for vast stretches of land.[227] In all, approximately 951,000 Germans migrated to the United States during the 1850s.[228]

Jews fleeing the Russian pogroms also came to the United States during the latter half of the nineteenth century with their numbers swelling to more than 500,000 by 1880 from a mere 30,000 just 30 years earlier.

And the waves continued. In the decades following the 1870s, America's immigration pattern radically changed from one primarily emanating out of England, Ireland, Germany, and Scandinavia to Hungary, Poland, Russia, Serbia, Greece, and Italy.[229] These new immigrants largely settled in the Northeast and mid-Atlantic states, and many relocated to cities in Ohio, Michigan, and Illinois. The influx provided American industry with an overabundant supply of inexpensive and unskilled labor, thus expanding the American economy such that, by the mid 1890s, America became the world's primary industrial power.[230]

The unprecedented influx of people into the United States not only radically expanded the size of the American workforce, but permanently changed the nation's sociopolitical and cultural makeup. With the progression of the nineteenth century, the portion of the country that traced its roots to the nation's founding and the antebellum years diminished in importance, replaced by a massive contingency that did not, directly or indirectly, experience the American Revolution or the tragedy of the Civil War. Although these recent additions to the population were equipped with a formidable work and religious ethic and were among the most resilient of America's immigrants, they were generally not the product of families and cultures that had been exposed to the principles of limited governance and American federalism. Their story was laced with a search for opportunity and security in an independent country whose political foundation had already been forged; it was not one where they would extricate themselves from an oppressive monarch to create a new nation.

The same technological and industrial changes that allowed for the continued growth of the American economy also facilitated the entrance of women and children into the workforce. The number of women in the workforce doubled between 1880 and 1900, driven largely by jobs in teaching and retail stores, and by the appearance of the typewriter, which allowed women an active role in the administrative and corporate work environment.[231]

Children were a natural source of labor for many of the nation's economic sectors including the mining industry. Yet, the zeal to recruit these politically silent and vulnerable citizens resulted in the development of harsh working conditions and oppressive working environments. Initial congressional efforts to curtail child labor were thwarted when the Supreme Court struck down federal child labor regulations as unconstitutional. But by the turn of the century, the states reversed the tide of child participation in the workforce through the enactment of compulsory child education laws. Thanks to these admittedly piecemeal, state-led efforts, children were being sent to schools instead of factories.

In short, the nation's passage out of the nineteenth century and into the twentieth irreversibly morphed it into something new and different, a fact not lost in its leaders and political thinkers. As the nation raced to a time characterized by international wars, massive economic growth, technological change, and cultural upheaval, it did so with a collective consciousness that was vastly different from the one that had produced it. By the turn of the twentieth century, the nation's primary philosophical concern centered on combating social injustice and ascertaining fairness and equity. No longer was its top priority stamping out even the hint of a tyrannical state. Instead of being a nation made up of people who turned to their families, their neighbors, and their God for the support they needed in their daily lives, the United States increasingly became a nation willing to rely on its government to address the societal problems that plagued it, even if doing so meant granting the federal government greater encroachments onto the authorities of the states and into the lives of the individual.

In America, people perceived the rise of a new despot and tyrant; the employer and owner. If these had risen to the level of despots, it was only because a system was created that allowed their ascent; a system that placed greed and self-gain ahead of the rights of others; a system that allowed the rich and powerful to abuse the meek and vulnerable.

For many, that system was capitalism.

Throughout Europe, sociopolitical philosophers rushed to find solutions to these growing threats. In England, Jeremy Bentham posited his ideas of Utilitarianism, where the appropriateness of a law or policy was not measured by the protection of one's individual freedoms, but by the utility of the policy to society as whole. Natural law as espoused by the Founding Fathers was antithetical to the views of Bentham and people who thought like him. The measure of right and wrong lay in finding the greatest happiness for the greatest number. His views of the needs of the many outweighing the needs of the individual gave rise to a new prioritization of individuals and society that was not based on the rights of the individual, but based on the needs of the collective.

Bentham's ideals of societal architecture and design were custom fit to address the perceived evils of capitalism. In the capitalistic society of the day, the needs of the worker and individual were being ignored for the sake of profit for the owner and employer. The individual existed only to serve the needs of the employer and to support his enrichment. If natural law, individualism, greed, selfishness, and its accompanying capitalistic economic system led to the oppression of the worker, then a system based on the betterment of the whole was the logical answer, and the state was the natural entity to implement the necessary corrections.

In Wales, Robert Owens envisioned a societal structure where the elements of production were not owned by the individual, but by the state. He proposed establishing communities inhabited by families responsible for their maintenance and for the execution of the common goal. In his system, even the children were raised, not by the parents, but by the communal system.

Karl Marx and Frederic Engels built upon the issue of class struggle, arguing that all societies are essentially made up of a class that controls production and a class that provides the labor for production. They believed that the internal strife that developed among the competing classes through capitalism would lead to society's destruction. For them, the answer lay in a socialist based economic model where all classes, and indeed all ownership, would cease to exist. Under these conditions, the people would be free to work for society's betterment, and strife would eventually dissolve.

Fascism espoused another premise. For the fascist, the unifying force was not the unification of all classes, but of the nation. The focus became not class warfare, but international and interracial warfare as the different nations maneuvered themselves for the domination of their inferior competitors.

Other philosophical variants arose between the nineteenth and twentieth centuries, and although they competed against each other for the hearts and minds of the people, they all shared a significant trait: the inherent distrust of the individual as society's driving force and the belief that societal designs need be fashioned by an authoritarian, autocratic ruler or government—the very opposite of the Founders' ideals.[ii]

With the infusion of societal changes neither anticipated nor addressed by the Founders, the stage was set for the morphing of the Constitution into something far different from what was originally intended. As the horrors of life in factories, particularly those afflicting children became apparent, and with the emergence of vast inequities between socioeconomic strata, community activists began espousing solutions to the problems. Increasingly, those advocating for solutions saw the Constitution not as a framework within which they were to fashion their repairs, but as an obstruction. What followed was a century's long effort of chipping away at the factors that had provided America with its greatness, and whether purposefully or not, would lead to the weakening of the country's moral and cultural fabric.

In the United States, the Progressive Movement was one of the most politically influential forms of collectivism. The ideas of progressivism borrowed from the various collectivistic and utilitarian philosophies of the day. Generally, progressives believed that the human condition needed to be promoted through reason and scientific design. Through his intellectual powers, man ought to design societal and economic structures that would allow for an ideal distribution of wealth, fairness, justice, and opportunity. In reality, Progressivism ran counter to natural law because it substituted the primacy of the individual's freedom with the will of a designing body determining the proper conduits for productivity and achievement.

Unwittingly, one of the primary influences on American and European progressivism was Charles Darwin. His work on evolution and the corollary doctrine of the survival of the fittest within ecological populations was applied by sociological philosophers and political reformers to society; a concept known as Social Darwinism. At its purest, the concept held that the

---

[ii] Anarchism offered an exception to this rule since it held the state to be an unnecessary encroachment upon man's natural existence. Where one went from that conclusion was problematic with some strains of anarchism advocating for complete individualism even to the point of advocating for violence against authorities while others ascribed for a collectivist state.

strong amongst society would naturally dominate the weak. Quickly, Social Darwinism morphed with nationalistic strains into ideas of racial superiority, imperialism, fascism, and Nazism. This is also the time that saw the rise of eugenics whose aim it was to improve the human gene pool and promote a higher social order through the manipulation of reproductive patterns within society. The result was a movement calling for the educated elite to fashion societal policy. The super-educated would be the guardians of the people[232] and responsible for implementing reforms that would enhance human existence even at the expense of human liberty.

Although the progenies of Social Darwinism and its cousin, the Progressive Movement, would eventually result in the rise of nationalism and two world wars, in the United States, the philosophy would sprout political movements, shape elections, and dramatically change the Constitution.

The Sixteenth Amendment: Taxing People's Income

The effort to pass the Sixteenth Amendment to the Constitution was the first successful legislative effort stemming from the Progressive Movement. Unlike all prior amendments, the Sixteenth Amendment did not aim to either define the rights of the people or correct a previously identified problem within the Constitution. Instead, it was the product of a policy decision on the federal government's taxation authority.

The Framers categorized taxes as internal and external. External taxes were those imposed upon anything existing outside the taxing jurisdiction; in this case, the United States of America. These included things such as imports, properties outside of the United States, and tariffs. Internal taxes were those levied from properties within the United States and were divided into direct and indirect taxes. Direct taxes related to real property, and indirect taxes related to goods.[233]

The Framers were well aware of the ominous power of taxation and the great potential for its abuse—after all, "taxation without representation" was a rallying cry toward independence. Recognizing that "the power to tax involves the power to destroy,"[234] the Framers were very much preoccupied with the potential for abuse and oppression on the part of the federal government. Consequently, they sought to restrict and define the new government's scope of taxation powers. These limitations were laid out in three references in the Constitution.

First, Article I, Section 8, clause 1, allowed Congress to levy and collect taxes, duties, imposts, and excises to pay debts and provide for the common defense and general welfare, but the same clause limited these powers by requiring that all duties, imposts, and excises be uniform throughout the United States. Second, Article I, Section 2, Clause 3 required that direct taxes be apportioned among the several states in proportion to the population. Another provision, Article I, Section 9 also allowed Congress to lay taxes for the importation of slaves not exceeding ten dollars, and finally, that same section prohibited the imposition of taxes upon exports from any state.

In addition, the Framers made external taxing authority exclusive to the federal government.[235, iii] Alternatively, the power to impose internal taxes was shared between the federal and state governments.

Most importantly, under the Constitution's original drafting, Congress could only impose direct taxes upon the states and not directly upon the people. This is consistent with the concept of the states being organized as independent sovereigns. Since only the states had direct jurisdiction over its citizens, Congress was not given the authority to directly tax the people living within the various states. The federal government was, therefore, limited in how it could obtain its revenues through 1) taxes on consumable items, particularly those imported from places outside of the United States; and 2) taxes on the states themselves, which would provide money in proportion to their populations by raising funds within their jurisdictions.

It was a brilliant system. Being that the federal government quickly grew beyond what it could afford through tariffs alone, America's original tax design forced the federal government to become dependent on the states for its financial subsistence. Each year, the federal government would have to bill

[iii] There was one exception that allowed for the collection of external taxes by the states as would be necessary to execute the federal taxation requirements.

the states for its services. The states, in turn, would have to raise the money and deliver it to the federal government. As it was essentially charging the states for its services, the federal government, each year, had to account for its activities, explain its plans to the states, and then collect on it. Under this scheme, the states, and not the federal government, were the masters of the purse and its chief purveyors. Perhaps more than any other provision, this taxation methodology served as the strongest guarantee for the decentralization of power and for the protection of the rights of the varies states.[iv]

Great as the original taxation scheme may have been, the unforeseeable tolls of government and their strain on its resources would overwhelm the government's abilities to remain fiscally sound. The War of 1812, for example, was likely the first of the unforeseen tolls of running a nation, costing the United States about $3 million dollars. Even so, the nation was able to largely finance the war through increases in excise and direct taxes.[236]

Over time, as the financial drains on various states grew, the apportionment scheme was increasingly viewed with hostility because of the disparities in its application. The Framers had made an error in assuming that each state's ability to pay was proportional to its population when each state's ability to pay its taxes was, in reality, proportional to its wealth and its money-generating capacity.

As was becoming increasingly apparent, the northern states, with their robust manufacturing sectors, were more easily able to pay a tax based purely on the size of its populations because the wealth per capita was greater than those of the agrarian southern states. As such, southern states, even though they were asked to pay a proportional amount based on their populations, were actually shouldering an arguably unfair, per capita, economic burden in support of the nation's finances.[237] These inequities became even more apparent during the Civil War when, devoid of the Confederate states, the poorer western states would be left to shoulder an overwhelming portion of the war's financial burden when taxed proportionate to their population.[238]

[iv] Another integral provision is the role of the senate, which will be discussed in the section dealing with the Seventeenth Amendment.

Congress first turned to personal income as a source of cash in 1862 with the passage of the Internal Revenue Act. The income tax stood without a legal challenge until 1872 when Congress allowed the law to expire.[239] Even so, the Supreme Court did consider the constitutionality of an income tax in *Springer v. U.S.* In this case, William M. Springer's income tax return for the year 1865 showed he owed $4,799.80 in taxes. Springer returned his income tax forms to the deputy tax collector along with a statement of protest questioning the authority to even demand the requested information.[240] When the federal government attempted to collect, Springer refused to pay. The government responded by seizing his property and selling it in order to offset his alleged debt.

Springer argued that an income tax was a direct tax. As such, the Constitution required each state's tax liability to be apportioned in a manner that was proportionate to its population. An income tax failed to do that and was consequently prohibited by the Constitution.

The Supreme Court responded by lamenting that the Framers had never defined a direct tax. "It is a matter of regret," the Court quoted Hamilton, "that terms so uncertain and vague in so important a point are to be found in the Constitution."[241] Consequently, the Court would be forced to rely on case precedent in determining whether or not an income tax was a direct tax.

The Court first observed that, to that day, direct taxes had described taxes imposed on real property and slaves.[242] But the Court also recognized the excess burden placed on some communities by the equal apportionment requirement. It concluded that if the tax on incomes were to be considered a direct one, it would be "intolerably oppressive."[243] As a result, the Court reasoned "that *direct taxes,* within the meaning of the Constitution, are only capitation taxes, . . . and taxes on real estate, . . ."[244] and called a tax on income as being "within the category of an excise or duty."[245]

The income tax, according to the *Springer* Court, was an indirect tax, not subject to the Constitution's proportional apportionment provision, and henceforth, Constitutional. Mr. Springer would have to pay the allocated taxes. And even though Congress had long since repealed the income tax, it remained an option for the nation to employ in its future.

Following the *Springer* decision, America slumbered through Reconstruction. Although there were some signs of recovery in the 1880s, the 1890s was a time of great economic hardship in the United States, bringing labor unrest, a stock market collapse, and countless business failures.[246] Predictably, with a southern region still reeling from the effects of the Civil War, the economic hardship led to disproportionate regional economic deflations and even greater inequalities in the distribution of taxation burdens.

Congress once again turned to the income tax and passed a 2% tax for incomes of over $4,000.00, including those incomes obtained from land.

Without delay, the tax was challenged on Constitutional grounds. Once again, the argument centered on the tax's non-compliance with the constitutionally prescribed apportionment provision. The argument reached the Supreme Court in 1895 in two cases known as *Pollock I* and *Pollock II*.[247] In *Pollock I*, the Court took a different approach from the *Springer* Court, stating that a tax on income stood in the same category as the product from which the income was obtained.[248] Thus, if the income was obtained from land, then such a tax would be considered a direct tax and subject to apportionment. But the *Pollock I* case did not address other sources of income.

The Court ultimately had the opportunity to determine the status of taxes imposed on other sources of income in *Pollock II*, concluding that a tax upon a person's entire income was direct and subject to the constitutional apportionment requirement.[249] The income tax, said the Court, was therefore unconstitutional!

The repercussions of the *Pollock II* decision were immense. At a time when the federal government found itself in need of generating greater revenue, the prohibition of an income tax dealt a major blow to its fiscal policy and to the federal government's efforts at greater revenue generation. Moreover, the decision was a virtual death knell to the populist efforts of restructuring the tax burden. Economists like Edwin R. A. Seligman demonstrated the inherent unfairness of the then existing tax structure and vociferously called for a tax on income in an effort to rectify the financial inequities they saw.[250]

As William Howard Taft assumed the presidency, a battle brewed within Congress between the more liberal ranks, who favored an income tax, and the conservatives, mostly Republicans, who opposed it. The conservatives were finding it increasingly difficult to ward off attacks from the more progressive wing of the Republican Congress and from the public that was convinced of the unfairness of tariffs. Taft, initially hoping to avert an income tax, worked to implement a 1% corporate tax for the privilege of doing business in the United States.[251] As part of his dealings regarding the implementation of a corporate tax, Taft supported the passage of an amendment to the Constitution that clarified the legality of an income tax. The process proceeded quickly, and by February 1913, the Sixteenth Amendment to the Constitution had been ratified:

> *The Congress shall have power to lay and collect taxes on incomes, from whatever source derived, without apportionment among the several States, and without regard to any census or enumeration.*
>
> (U.S. Constitution, Amend. XVI)

And with those words, the federal government was given the power to tax every American's income. It was then left to President Woodrow Wilson to sign the bill invoking a federal, personal, income tax into law in October, 1913. Although the original manifestation of the personal income tax called for a 1% tax on incomes greater than $3,000.00 for individuals and $4,000.00 for married couples, a surtax taking the rate to a maximum of 6% for the highest incomer earners was also implemented.[252]

Moving forward, it would not be long before the costs of two successive world wars, a stronger international American presence, and a growing social benefits program would catapult the nation's income tax drain to much greater levels.

The Seventeenth Amendment

The controversy regarding the manner in which the members of the Senate are selected dates back to the country's inception. For the Framers, the Senate was a carefully crafted chamber serving multiple purposes. For one, the Senate was to serve as the great stabilizer to the whims of the people represented in the House of Representative. With its one-third turn over rate, equality of representation, and longer terms of its officeholders, the Framers ensured the Senate would provide stability and wisdom to the political process.

The Senate also decentralized power. The manner in which its members were selected was crucial to this function and to the vital role the state legislatures played in the selection process.[253] In requiring that each senator be elected directly by the state legislature, the Framers aimed to ascertain the allegiance of the Senators to the states. It was a fundamental component of ensuring that the federal government remained at the mercy of the states. In the words of James Madison:

> *The house of representatives will derive its powers from the people of America, and the people will be represented in the same proportion, and on the same principle, as they are in the Legislature of a particular State. So far the Government is* national *not* federal. *The Senate on the other hand will derive its powers from the States, as political and co-equal societies; and these will be represented on the principle of equality in the Senate, as they now are in the existing Congress. So far the government is* federal, *not* national.
>
> (Madison, *The Federalist Papers*, No. 39)

The concept that the Senate was supposed to follow the commands and directives of the state legislatures stemmed from the arrangements made in the Articles of Confederation and stood unquestioned during the Republic's early decades. Initially, the state legislatures would instruct their senators,[254] and woe to the senator who dared disobey its state legislature's directives. This design helped guarantee that federal powers would be checked, not only through the enumeration of powers, but by the direct stronghold the legislatures of the various states would have on at least one of the two legislative chambers. This was all part of the layers of decentralization and tension the Framers built into the governing system in order to keep an overpowering central government from forming.

Despite the effort, the allegiance in the design of the constitutional republic was imperfect. Whereas the states had the power to recall their representatives under the Articles,[v] the Constitution did not maintain that authority.

The dissolution of the recall power greatly weakened the states' influence over their senators, affording the latter greater leeway in voting. The only recourses available to the states in controlling their senators were the threat of withholding a senator's reelection and the power of the censure.

John Quincy Adams was apparently the first senator subject to the state's wrath. When he voted in favor of the Embargo Act, the Federalist Massachusetts legislature opted to hold his reelection early, ensuring Adams's defeat. The blow was so severe that Adams chose to resign his position in response.[255]

However, the effectiveness of censures and sanctions is only as strong as the sense of honor of the recipient. As more senators became emboldened against rebuke, the sanctions lost their effectiveness, and the power of state governments over their senators continued to fade. By 1860, the Senators viewed the directives sent to them from the states as recommendations rather than instructions.[256]

Eventually, even the threat of not being reelected lacked effectiveness. Although the Framers envisioned a senatorial election environment where the state legislatures would reign supreme, by the 1830s, the relationship between the senators and the state legislators flipped as senators discovered the power of supporting the election of favorable state legislators.[257] By 1900, the process had morphed such that political observers viewed the results of the state legislative elections under the light of the victorious senator. By this point, the election of state legislative members merely represented a porous

v Articles of Confederation; Article V: "For the most convenient management of the general interests of the United States, delegates shall be annually appointed in such manner as the legislatures of each State shall direct, to meet in Congress on the first Monday in November, in every year, with a power reserved to each State to recall its delegates, or any of them, at any time within the year, and to send others in their stead for the remainder of the year."

and passive membrane between the will of the people and the election of their senator. The selective and scrupulous role the state legislature was initially intended to serve of vetting out the senatorial candidate and of making sure that the elected senator was an esteemed and loyal servant of the state had dissolved, replaced by the essentially direct determination of the senator by the people through the election of the senator's allies.

The matter of senatorial election consumed some of the legislatures so much that the issues of running the state became of secondary importance. In effect, the passage of an amendment allowing for the direct election of the senators by the people merely served to codify a process already in existence.[258]

Efforts to change the election process for senators date back to the 1820s when Representative Henry Randolph Storrs from New York proposed the direct elections of senators. The motion was tabled, but Representative Edward A. Hannegan resurrected the issue in 1835 when he introduced a similar resolution, which again was tabled. During the 1850s, five more resolutions calling for the direct election of senators were introduced, all of which were unsuccessful.[259] Interestingly, then Representative and eventual President Andrew Johnson, was involved in at least two of those resolutions, and even though he continued to work for the direct democratization of the Senate chamber as Senator and President, his efforts never succeeded.[vi]

It was not until Reconstruction that the question of direct election of senators was heatedly debated in Congress. By the 1890s, the pattern of deadlocks and delays in the election of certain senators by state legislatures had reached a sufficient magnitude to force the question upon the people. In 1892, California held the question up for a vote, finding 92% of voters in favor of the popular election of senators. In 1893, a similar election in Nevada found 88% in favor, and one in Illinois, held in 1902, had 85% of the voters voting in favor of the measure.[260]

[vi] Andrew Johnson was a staunch advocate for the democratization of the Constitution, even calling for the repeal of the electoral college. [John William Perrin. "Popular Election of United States Senators." *The North American Review*. vol 192. no. 661. (Dec 1910), 801]

As it turns out, the concept of direct elections of senators was in line with the anti-establishment views of the populist movement, which had gained strength during the 1890s. From their standpoint, the election of the senate by the state legislatures was a model ripe for corruption and political favors among the elites.

The newspaper publisher and congressman, William Randolph Hearst, added fuel to the fires of electoral reform with his many writings on the topic. Attorney and Representative William Jennings Bryan was another ardent proponent of direct senatorial elections. Their cases were helped by the few but shining examples of state underrepresentation. For example, in Indiana during the 1850s, the legislature allowed a Senate seat to remain vacant for two years because of political infighting within the state's legislature. In Oregon, one third of its state legislators refused to take their oaths of office in 1897 to prevent the election of its federal senatorial candidate, not only preempting the state's presence in the federal chamber, but shutting down its legislative process as well.[261] Added to these difficulties was the election of Montana mining magnate William A. Clark; an election so riddled with corruption and payments to state legislators that the elected Senator resigned rather than allow the Senate to refuse him his seat. Rather than end with his resignation, the matter continued as the acting Montana governor assigned Clark back to the seat three days later, only to replace him days after that. Clark was re-elected to the senate during the next state electoral term in 1901, allowing the beleaguered magnate to finally assume his seat without interruption.[262]

Despite the relative rarity of such events, they provided reporters and populist advocates the fodder needed to make the case for reforming the senatorial electoral process. In 1912, Congress approved the language of the Seventeenth Amendment, sending it to the states for approval. By April 8, 1913, the Seventeenth Amendment received its 36th state ratification from Connecticut and was certified on May 31, 1913, by then Secretary of State, William Jennings Bryan.

The Seventeenth Amendment affected America profoundly. With the state legislatures throughout the nation dominated by rural interests, the passage of the Seventeenth Amendment represented a power play by urban interests in taking control of the Senate from rural ones.[263] Had the Seventeenth Amendment not been passed, the 1914 Senate would have been deadlocked at 48 seats for each party. As it was, the election saw a number of seats go to the party that was not in control within the state legislature, thus giving the Democrats, a 52-42 majority.[264] By 1917, the distributions of senatorial seats would have likely been 53-42 in favor of the Republicans. Under the Seventeenth Amendment, the 54-42 distribution actually favored the Democrats.[265]

Additionally, the passage of the Seventeenth Amendment represented a major score for the House of Representatives as it increased the degree of congruence in the make-up and opinions of the bodies.[266] By making the people directly decide the composition of both houses, the bodies became more similar in their loyalties, their thoughts, and ultimately, their actions. But one final effect may have been even more profound than any other, and with far greater consequence. Once the state legislatures were extracted from the senatorial election process, the courts were left as the sole guardians of the Tenth Amendment and of the rights of the states. The states' abilities to protect their sovereignties became insufficient to resist the centralization of power that was being assembled by the liberal progressives.

Prohibition

The Eighteenth Amendment was the direct result of the Progressive Movement. Ratified in 1919, the amendment prohibited the manufacture, sale, transportation, and importation of intoxicating liquors within the United States.[viii]

Although technically promoted by the Women's Christian Temperance Progressive Union and the Anti-Saloon League, many of these organizations' members were actually self-proclaimed Progressives. Although their arguments centered around a national effort to curtail domestic violence and other

[viii] Interestingly, the Eighteenth Amendment did not prohibit the private possession, purchase, or consumption of alcohol.

saloon-related activities, they subscribed to the classic progressive notion that society's ills (in this case, the evils and immoralities associated with alcohol consumption) could be addressed by the application of "science and professional solutions."[267]

Like many other progressive efforts, the move towards temperance was rooted in moralistic, class, ethnic, racist, and sexist precepts. The lower, morally weaker class, in this case, was made up of poor male immigrants from Ireland, Italy, and Poland. The morally superior class consisted of educated women from higher economic, Anglican backgrounds. The solution was the Anglification of the poor, morally deficient immigrants through government action concocted by the superior, educated class.[268]

It is telling that the issue of curbing alcohol use was never discussed at the Constitutional Convention, particularly when men like Thomas Jefferson and James Madison publicly stated their concern for the role of alcohol as a societal evil.[269] The reason for this is simple: The concept of regulating alcohol at the federal level, and particularly by constitutional fiat, was wholly inconsistent with the principles of natural law. Prohibition would have been a concept totally foreign to the Framers, and not because they were ignorant of the dangers associated with alcohol. It was not discussed because these men did not conceive such an immensely intrusive dictum in a world where the consolidation of a national government's power was overtly feared. The concept of prohibition had to wait for a time when Americans became receptive to a totally different philosophy of governance; one that allowed for the federal government to directly meddle in peoples' lives. For these reasons, laws such as the Eighteenth Amendment represent a "characteristically 20th-century exercise in social engineering."[270]

The result of the Eighteenth Amendment was, in many ways, devastating. Although it did result in the reduction of alcohol consumption, within months the prisons filled, the court system was overwhelmed, and the United States' large urban centers were overrun with organized crime and corruption. More than any other law, Prohibition allowed for the rise of organized crime in a manner the country had never seen. The futility of law enforcement efforts in stemming the demand for alcohol quickly became evident. America's most powerful crime families appeared during this time with the sole purpose of filling the economic gap created for them by government fiat. And throughout America's greatest cities, mayors, commissioners, and police officials quietly celebrated the appearance of these great crime families with a wink, a nod, and an encouraging toast delivered from beneath their raised whiskey glasses.

After less than fifteen years, the country had enough of the Progressive's social engineering experiment on alcohol. The passage of the Twenty-First Amendment repealed the Eighteenth Amendment in 1933, an open admission to the error of embracing the centralization of power, particularly when it imposed harsh dictums on peoples' lives.[ix]

The March of the Agencies

One of the great threats to a truly republican form of government lies in the enforcement and application of its laws. In theory, in a republic, a select few democratically elected members of society are responsible for making the regulatory decisions for the rest of the citizenry. Also in theory (but arguably not so in practice), these members are to possess certain skills, knowledge, or experiences that endow them with a degree of wisdom and insight not shared by the general population.

These assets are supposed to allow them to make better decisions regarding the manner in which the state is to regulate itself, and if they are found wanting in these areas, the electorate takes action and replaces them. Absent from this discussion, though, is the question of regulation and enforcement. How is the republic supposed to enforce the conduct of affected citizens? How is it to police itself?

The problem with the idealized discussion of a republican government is that it generally stops with the consideration of the process through which laws

ix For the record, Section 2 of the Twenty-First Amendment affirmed the authority of the states, territories, and possessions to regulate the transportation and importation of intoxicating liquors within their jurisdictions.

are created and does not address a concurrent evaluation of how laws are to be applied. It is within the enforcement arm of the republican form of government where the greatest threat for tyranny lies. In a small, decentralized, non-intrusive government arrangement, this is a minor omission. The larger and more involved a government becomes in the affairs of the individual, the more this shortcoming grows into a tyrannical threat.

The laws enacted by the republican legislature can never contain enough detail to answer all the enforcement questions that may arise. Moreover, the generally informed members of the legislature do not possess the detailed training and understanding of the technical nature of the various specific facets in society and governmental operations to be able to apply the law.

It is unclear to what extent the Framers recognized this dilemma. They centered much of their attention on the workings of the legislature and granted to the President the broadly construed responsibility of administering the congressionally passed laws. However, the initial members of Congress recognized the need to give the government some oversight structure and framework through which it could carry out the affairs of the nation.

For the Framers, the construction of some administering capacity began with the establishment of a limited number of agencies responsible for conducting the affairs of the federal government. These were the Department of State, the Department of War, the Department of the Treasury, and the office of the Attorney General. For a while, these four relatively small agencies that often reported directly to Congress were sufficient to run the affairs of the state. But with the progression of the nineteenth century and the appearance of interstate corporations and monopolies, the federal government found it necessary to take on a more robust regulatory role, prompting the creation of more agencies.

The onslaught of regulatory agencies really began when states employed them in efforts to regulate the booming railroad industry. In 1887, the federal government, using its powers in the Interstate Commerce Clause, created the Interstate Commerce Commission (ICC).[271] Although initially placed within the Department of the Interior, the ICC was made an independent body in 1890.[272] The ICC was initially weak, but over time, particularly with the emergence of the Progressive Movement, was strengthened and cloaked with rate-making authority.[273]

Indeed, the Progressive Movement, with its distrust of the free market and corporations, was an essential force in increasing the size and power of the administrative arm of the federal government.[274] Its vision called for strict oversight by the so-called "experts" of the affected industry, but ignored the tendencies for these experts to become corrupted and the role political favoritism would surely play in their internal dealings. Seemingly with untiring resolve, the administrative branch of government would grow such that today, it is not clear how many agencies actually exist. Consider that in 1790, the whole federal government employed 1,000 non-military personnel. Presently, there are over 2.84 million civilian employees in the federal government.[275]

A small list of the largest active federal agencies would include the Commodities Futures Trading Commission, the Federal Trade Commission, the Consumer Product Safety Commission, the ICC, the Internal Revenue Service, the Federal Communications Commission, the National Labor Relations Board, the Federal Deposit Insurance Corporation, the Nuclear Regulatory Commission, the Federal Mine Safety and Health Review Commission, the Federal Energy Regulatory Commission, the Occupational Safety and Health Review Commission, the Board of Governors of the Federal Reserve System, the Federal Maritime Commission, and the Security and Exchange Commission.[276]

These agencies all share certain traits. They are made up of appointed members with specific tenures who may only be removed as a result of misconduct. They all have regulatory authorities equal in force to the power of law on those they regulate. These powers, although broadly construed, are limited to the regulation of a specific area of industry or society, and each is supposed to be designed in such a manner as to protect it from the influence of the legislature or the executive.

By their very structure, the agencies represent an affront to the vision of a republic. Yes, the people within it are somewhat removed from the general population in that they possess certain intellectual traits or experiences placing them in a more insightful position to regulate, but this is where the parallels to republicanism end. They are not elected. They are not directly accountable to their constituents. Their constituents are poorly defined, if at all. They not only create the regulations, but apply them and judge those who fall under their jurisdiction, thus ignoring the concept of separation of powers. Indeed, the administrative branch of government, more than any other predesigned component, carries with it the potential of breaking the binds of checks and balances that would keep it from governing in a manner constrained by the people. With this degree of independence and unbridled authority over its subjects, the only opportunities of checking the administrative system lies with a scrupulous legislature and a frugal finance policy.

Indisputably, the measures needed to control a runaway administrative branch have not been implemented. Even more threatening, the idealized view that agencies cannot be created without congressional consent no longer holds true. The twentieth century saw the creation of more than 240 administrative agencies through the unilateral actions of presidents.[277] Among others, these included the National Security Agency, the Defense Intelligence Agency, the Peace Corps, and the Bureau of Alcohol, Tobacco, and Firearms. Unable to get congressional approval for these agencies, presidents created them using executive orders, departmental orders, and reorganizational plans.[278]

Not only are these agencies arguably created in a manner outside of the agreed governmental design, but they are overseen less scrupulously by Congress than legislatively-created agencies, do not observe political balance structures within their memberships, tend to report directly to the president, and do not have well-defined terms on their appointees.[279] The end result is that the president, armed with his legion of bureaucrats, can make policy with a stroke of the pen and act largely unencumbered by Congress.[280] This tilts the original balance of powers strongly in favor of the executive—wholly inconsistent with the design of a federal republic and with the doctrine of separation of powers. Small wonder Americans hear the constant clamor of the restrictive and cumbersome role regulatory policies play in their daily lives!

2. The Judiciary Rewrites the Constitution

More than any other, the Framers underestimated the power of the judiciary. For them, and particularly for Alexander Hamilton, the judiciary, with no police, no lawmaking powers, and no authority to allocate funds to itself, was predicted to be the weakest branch of government as it merely possessed the power of opinion. However, through those opinions and through its interpretations of key phrases in the Constitution, the judiciary has been able to singlehandedly revamp America's legal foundations and society itself.

Expansion of Powers Through the Interstate Commerce Clause

Under the Articles of Confederation, the states were free to engage in a virtually unlimited degree of competitive business activities. These included coining their own money, not accepting each other's currency, taxing imports from other states, and even impeding the passage of vessels and goods from their neighbors. These practices were extremely disruptive to the young nation's economic stability, and Congress was powerless to stop it. The Framers recognized that such economically disruptive policies could not continue unhindered. Consequently, during the Constitutional Convention, they included the Interstate Commerce Clause within the substance of the Constitution:

> *to regulate Commerce with foreign Nations, and among the several States, and within the Indian Tribes.*
>
> (U.S. Const. art. I, § 8, cl. 3.)

The Framers originally intended for the Interstate Commerce Clause to allow Congress the power to normalize trade between the states and to develop certain standards that would apply evenly throughout the new country so that trade could proceed unimpeded. *Gibbons v. Ogden,*[281] the first case argued before the Supreme Court regarding the Interstate Commerce Clause and the events leading up to it, provide great insight as to the original workings of the third clause within Article I, Section 8 of the Constitution.

Thomas Gibbons owned at least two steamboats in New Jersey, which he routinely ran between Elizabethtown, New Jersey, and New York City. However, the State of New York had granted Robert Livingston and Robert Fulton, two steamboat magnates, exclusive rights to navigate self-propelled boats within the state.

Aaron Ogden was a former governor of New York who had purchased the exclusive rights assigned Livingston and Fulton and was in a position to control all the navigation business within the State of New York. Seeing Gibbons's activities as an obvious affront to his exclusive rights and, ultimately, to his business, Ogden sued Gibbons in New York State to enforce his exclusivity rights and force Gibbons to stop operating his self-propelled ships within the state.

Gibbons defended his actions by claiming that the New York laws were illegal since they conflicted with federal laws passed by Congress under the powers afforded to it by the Interstate Commerce Clause. Predictably, the New York courts agreed with Ogden, so Gibbons appealed to the Supreme Court of the United States where Chief Justice John Marshall presided.

Stating, "Commerce cannot stop at the external boundary line of each State,"[282] Chief Justice Marshall agreed with Gibbons. Congress has the power to regulate business conducted across state lines. However, congressional authority does not extend into those commercial matters "which are completely within a particular State, which do not affect other States, and with which it is not necessary to interfere for the purpose of executing some of the general powers of the government."[283] In other words, "The completely internal commerce of a State, then may be considered as reserved for the State itself."[284]

Consequently, in its original interpretation, the Interstate Commerce Clause played a permissive role. First, it permitted Congress to pass laws that would help ensure the uninhibited commercial intercourse between the states, and second, it upheld the notion that commerce among the various states ought to be free and unimpeded.

Over the remainder of the nineteenth century and into the twentieth, the posture regarding the limitations of the Interstate Commerce Clause remained fairly static. While Congress was perceived as being afforded certain authorities to promote the free intercourse of commerce among the various states, the states were perceived as being prohibited from interfering with the free flow of commerce between their borders.

The twentieth century brought with it new challenges. The time leading up to World War II was marred by great economic hardship. At the peak of the Great Depression, the White House was inhabited by Franklin Delano Roosevelt who believed in a Keynesian model of economics where government was called to directly intercede in economic activity and to promote it.

With that philosophy arose numerous governmental interventions and innovations designed to spur the economy. Among these were the creation of the Federal Housing Administration, the Tennessee Valley Authority, the National Recovery Administration, and the Works Project Administration as well as the passage of the Social Security Act, the National Labor Relations Act, the Housing Act, the Food Stamp Act, the Farm Security Act, and the Agricultural Adjustment Act. But these federal interventions upon the economy had been previously untried, and standing before them was the Supreme Court of the United States.

At the time of Roosevelt's election, the Court was relatively conservative, buoyed by four members: Pierce Butler, James McReynolds, George Sutherland, and Willis Van Devanter. These men, known as "the Four Horsemen," strictly interpreted the Constitution and the limits upon the federal government. They also had a great deal of influence upon the youngest and most critical member of the Court, Justice Owen Roberts.

Having experienced a number of disappointments at the hands of the Supreme Court and aware that many of his signature programs would be coming up for a review before a hostile bench, President Roosevelt proposed the Judicial Procedure Reform Bill of 1937 that would allow him the authority to appoint an additional member to the Court for each member who had reached the age of 70 and had not retired. Regarded by many as unconstitutional and perhaps fearful that such a weapon could be used against Congress, legislators did not pass the measure. Nevertheless, the controversy that ensued was massive, dominating the newspapers and the nation's political discussion.[285]

Perhaps in response to the pressures of a progressive administration, when the opportunity came to review the constitutionality of the Social Security Act of 1935, Justice Owens sided with the Court's liberal faction in declaring it constitutional.[286, x] Although Roosevelt's bill ultimately failed within the halls of Congress, its presumed effects of staving off the hostility of the bench was enough to result in the largest reinterpretation of the Constitution in history.[287]

Other changes guaranteed the Court's receptiveness to Roosevelt's New Deal. In 1935, Justice Van Devanter announced his retirement, allowing Roosevelt to replace one of the four conservative Horsemen with a more liberal member, Justice Hugo Black. The balance within the Court was now solidly changed in favor of the president and the preservation of his policies. In 1938, another conservative member, Justice Sutherland, retired, replaced by another liberal, Justice Stanley Reed. When one of the great judicial thinkers of his time, Justice Benjamin Cardozo, died later that year, he was replaced by Justice Felix Frankfurter. The following year saw the resignation of Justice Louis Brandeis and the death of Justice Pierce Butler who were replaced by Justices William O. Douglas and Frank Murphy. By 1941, Roosevelt would also appoint Justices Harlan Fiske Stone, James F. Byrne, and Robert H. Jackson. As a result, a court that had once been hostile to the president was now firmly under his control.[xi]

---

[x] The case upholding the constitutionality of the Social Security Act, *West Coast Hotel Co. v Parrish*, 300 U.S. 379 (1937), was actually adjudicated slightly prior to Roosevelt's introduction of the Judicial Procedures Reform Bill and accompanying fireside chat, thus casting doubts as to the President's influence upon Justice Owens' switch.

[xi] In 1943, after the *Wickard v. Filburn* decision, Roosevelt was able to replace one of his own appointees, James F. Byrnes, with Wiley Blount Rutledge. Justice Byrnes left the bench so he could head the Office of Economic Stabilization.

It is likely that Roscoe Filburn was not aware of the full implications the Supreme Court changes would have on him when he planted his crop of wheat in Ohio in 1941. Filburn owned a farm where he tended to livestock, sold milk, raised poultry, and grew wheat. Although he would sell a small portion of the wheat, the crops he grew were used primarily for self-consumption, including nourishment for his livestock.[288] Regardless, he did not engage in any interstate commerce.

In July 1940, the Agricultural Adjustment Act was amended by Congress to impose maximum wheat quotas on farms of 11.1 acres of production with a yield of no more than 20.1 bushels per acre. Later that year and prior to the beginning of the planting season for wheat, Filburn received notice of his quotas and was again informed of them in 1941 before harvesting. Regardless, Filburn planted 23 acres, and produced an excess of 239 bushels from 11.9 excess acres of land, making him subject to $117.11 of penalties.[289]

When fined, Filburn filed suit in federal court against Claude R. Wickard, the Secretary of Agriculture, making two arguments. First, he claimed the fine should be nullified based on a Due Process argument because he had received inappropriate notice of the amended quotas and penalties. Second, he made a jurisdictional argument, averring that the law should not be applicable to him since he did not engage in any interstate commerce and, therefore, was not subject to federal government scrutiny.

Although the due process argument that Filburn made is debatable as a matter of fact, the constitutional argument he waged regarding the Interstate Commerce Clause was valid as a matter of law. Recall Chief Justice Marshall's words affirming that if a business activity was conducted only within the territory of a single state, then the federal government was powerless to regulate that activity, and its regulation would fall squarely upon the state.[290]

At trial, the district court agreed with Filburn based on what it opined was inadequate notice. Because the court found in favor of the plaintiff in the factual aspects of the case, it did not need to address the constitutionality of a law, as the point had already been made moot prior to having reached the constitutional question. Consequently, as is the legal custom, the trial court left unaddressed the issue of the constitutionality of the federal government's actions.

But, the Secretary of Agriculture appealed the case all the way to the Roosevelt-packed Supreme Court, which overruled the district court's decision regarding its perceived Due Process shortcomings and inadequate notice opinion. With the actions of the Secretary of Agriculture now validated, the district court would have to hear the case again and address the issue of the constitutionality of the quota scheme.

Clearly, under the interpretation of the powers afforded the federal government in *Gibbons*, such federal intervention into intrastate commerce would not have been tolerated. However, the Court's membership had drastically changed by 1942, the year the *Wickard* case was decided. In a decision delivered by Justice Robert H. Jackson, one of the many Roosevelt appointees, the Court affirmed the actions of the federal government while providing a new and radically different interpretation of the Interstate Commerce Clause.

According to Jackson, the federal government's unprecedented foray into intrastate commerce was completely appropriate because of the aggregate effect of Filburn's commercial activity. Under the new interpretation developed by the Court, the federal government's authority to meddle with *intrastate* commerce was acceptable if the activity it was regulating, in its aggregate, would have an effect on interstate commerce. So when an activity, even if it was intrastate in nature, was such that it could permeate the interstate economy if engaged by many within a state, then the federal government was justified in regulating the activity, even if it occurred purely within the borders of a single state. As a matter of fact, the activity didn't even need to be commercial in nature to fall under the ambit of congressional authority. To quote Justice Jackson, "But even if appellee's activity be local, and though it may not be regarded as commerce, it may still, whatever its nature, be reached by Congress if it exerts a substantial economic effect on interstate commerce. . ."[291]

The effects of the *Wickard* ruling and its implications upon the extent of federal power are enormous. The *Wickard* ruling essentially allowed for an unlimited reach of federal authority into the lives of everyday Americans. Following this case, the federal government could openly and confidently regulate the services its citizens provide, the wages they earn, the conditions under which they work, the types of products they purchase or produce, the drugs they consume, and the educations they receive; all activities previously regulated only by the various states. It is safe to say that the Constitution would never have been adopted if the delegates had envisioned a federal government with the breadth of powers afforded to it by the *Wickard* decision. And it is worth highlighting that this dramatic expansion was done, not by the people, but by the judiciary with power it was never constitutionally afforded.

Yet, in 1942, under the specter of the overwhelming influence of the Roosevelt administration, the Supreme Court was able to erase more than a century of legal jurisprudence to allow for the survival of a program promoted by the one person responsible for appointing most of the Supreme Court members.

America's experience with the Roosevelt administration and his effects upon the Supreme Court also serve to validate the importance of presidential term limits. When Roosevelt took office, there were no presidential term limits. Consequently, Roosevelt was able to serve into his fourth term before his sudden death on April 12, 1945. In his twelve years as president, Roosevelt spent sufficient time in the White House to appoint nine justices with little resistance from a senate that saw no fixed end to the president's reign. His overwhelming number of appointments to the Court radically changed its character and in turn, the character of the nation and of the Constitution.

Interestingly, had Roosevelt been term limited, he would have made only four appointments to the Court, perhaps fewer, with the next five falling under the auspices of his successor. What differences, if any, a two-term limit would have made upon the Supreme Court's rulings is conjecture. However, the danger of having a President who, because of an unlimited time in office, is in a position to control two of the three branches of government through his appointments to the bench, is unbearable as he would essentially be able to rewrite the Constitution to his liking through the works of his appointees to the Supreme Court.

The leeway granted to Congress in regulating commercial activity through the Interstate Commerce Clause was so great that legal scholars debated whether there would be any limit to its reach. But eventually, questions regarding potential limitations to congressional action arose. In 1995, the Supreme Court shot down the federal Gun-Free Zone Act of 1990 where Congress made it a federal offense to carry a firearm in any school zone. When challenged, the government argued it was allowed to engage in this kind of regulatory activity because of the powers afforded it by the Interstate Commerce Clause. For the first time, the Supreme Court held that the government's reach into a regulatory activity was improper, concluding that the carrying of a firearm in a school zone "had nothing to do with 'commerce' or any sort of economic enterprise," and, in turn, was not within the powers afforded to Congress to regulate under the Interstate Commerce Clause.[292] Similarly, in *Morrison*, the Supreme Court struck down the portion of the Violence Against Women Act of 1994 that provided victims of sexual violence a civil remedy in federal courts, stating that "Gender-motivated crimes of violence are not, in any sense of the phrase, economic activity."[293]

With those limitations in mind, the country entered the twenty-first century with a debate on health care and health care reform. That debate spurred an interesting discussion about the extent of federal powers under the Intestate Commerce Clause. In the Patient Protection and Affordable Care Act of 2010 (PPACA), Congress fashioned a federal health care scheme that required individuals to purchase health insurance. Failure to do so was punishable by a fine collected by the Internal Revenue Service.

For Congress to force a person to purchase insurance under the Interstate Commerce Act meant another expansion of federal authority. Up until that point, using its interstate commerce powers, Congress had regulated persons engaged in certain activities (serving customers regardless of race; maintaining certain minimum safety standards), or required those who were participating in the marketplace to refrain from certain activities (not growing more than a certain amount of crops). Never before had the federal government required someone who had chosen not to participate in the marketplace (not buy health insurance) to participate in the marketplace (buy health insurance) under pain of a penalty for not doing so. Allowing the federal government to engage in such a coercive form of regulatory activity would certainly represent an expansion of federal powers with all sorts of unknown legal ramifications.

Predictably, the PPACA was immediately challenged in federal court on the basis of its constitutionality, soliciting great national attention. Many worried that if the Supreme Court upheld this new twist on congressional power, there would be virtually no limitation to what the Congress could force its citizens to do in the name of interstate commerce. The case appeared before the Supreme Court as *National Federation of Independent Businesses v. Sebelius*.[294] Surprisingly, however, the court chose to handle the case, not as an Interstate Commerce Clause controversy, but as a taxing and spending authority issue.

In an opinion written by Chief Justice John G. Roberts, the Court held that the penalty imposed upon those who did not purchase health insurance was in fact a tax. Consequently, Congress, in enacting the PPACA, had relied not on its interstate commerce authorities, but in its power to tax a person who did not purchase health insurance. And because the federal government's power to tax is virtually unlimited, the kind of tax imposed upon the people under the PPACA was certainly constitutional. The controversy over any congressional authority under the Interstate Commerce Clause had been avoided, and the PPACA preserved.

Flipping the Balance Between the Federal and State Governments

As previously discussed, the Bill of Rights was passed by Congress and adopted by the people to serve as added protections against the federal government. It lists and affirms certain rights so fundamental and central to our existence as human beings that government ought never infringe upon them.

The interesting paradox in the ratification of the Bill of Rights is that those rights, although generally considered to be pivotal to an appropriate relationship between the government and the individual, were not originally applied to the states. The reason centers on the differences between the federal government, the various state governments, and the people they represent.

As the theory goes, the federal government was created by the states from nothing. In so doing, it was given only the powers and authorities the states had endowed upon it. This explains why the federal government is one of *limited* authorities: the so-called enumerated powers.

The states, by contrast, possess *unlimited* powers, except as restricted by their respective constitutions and laws. In other words, each state was seen as possessing all the powers of a king. It is each state's constitution alone that restricted these unlimited powers to those that the people within each state felt appropriate to yield. Seen under the light leading to its creation, the Bill of Rights could *only* apply to the federal government, as it would be illogical for the restrictions applied by the states upon their creature, the federal government, to be applied by that same federal government upon the states.

Even though some rights contained within the Bill of Rights were considered essential to maintaining a proper relationship between any democratically elected government and its citizens (such as the freedom to freely worship, the freedom of assembly, and the freedom of speech), the stipulations to preserve and honor those rights within the federal constitution would not apply to the states. Moreover, whether those limitations would apply to a particular state was a matter to be decided solely by the people residing within that state and not by some outside power like the federal government.

The Civil War, with its three amendments, changed all that. Specifically, Section 2 of the Fourteenth Amendment, which spoke directly to the States, altered the relationship between the States and the federal government with three Clauses: the Privileges and Immunities Clause, the Due Process Clause, and the Equal Protection Clause.

The first of these, the Privileges and Immunities Clause has been deemed by the Court to contain very limited effects. It reads, "No state shall make or enforce any law which shall abridge the privileges or immunities of citizens of the United States."

In order to decipher the exact significance of that clause, one would have to know exactly what the Privileges and Immunities of the Citizens of the United States are. Some guidance to that question is gleamed from the Privileges and Immunities Clause of Article IV, Section 2 of the United States Constitution. It states, "the citizens of each state shall be entitled to all privileges and immunities of citizens in the several states."

Although still not very helpful, a particularly thorough elucidation of what those rights specifically entail is contained in a Circuit Court opinion by Bushrod Washington, George Washington's nephew:[xii]

> *The inquiry is, what are the privileges and immunities of citizens in the several States? We feel no hesitation in confining these expressions to those privileges and immunities which are, in their nature, fundamental; which belong, of right, to the citizens of all free governments; and which have, at all times, been enjoyed by the citizens of the several States which compose this Union, from the time of their becoming free, independent, and sovereign. What these fundamental principles are, it would perhaps be more tedious than difficult to enumerate. They may, however, be all comprehended under the following general heads: protection by the government; the enjoyment of life and liberty, with the right to acquire and possess property of every kind, and to pursue and obtain happiness and safety; subject nevertheless to such restraints as the government may justly prescribe for the general good of the whole. The right of a citizen of one State to pass through, or to reside in any other State, for purposes of trade, agriculture, professional pursuits, or otherwise; to claim the benefit of the writ of habeas corpus; to institute and maintain actions of any kind in the courts of the State; to take, hold and dispose of property, either real or personal; and an exemption from higher taxes or impositions than are paid by the other citizens of*

[xii] Bushrod Washington sat on the Supreme Court of the United States. In those days, Supreme Court justices would travel throughout the country to decide lower cases, a function referred to as "riding circuit." *Corfield v. Coryell* was one such case that ended up being decided by Justice Washington.

the State; may be mentioned as some of the particular privileges and immunities of citizens, which are clearly embraced by the general description of privileges deemed to be fundamental; to which may be added, the elective franchise, as regulated and established by the laws or constitution of the State in which it is to be exercised. These, and many others which might be mentioned, are, strictly speaking, privileges and immunities, and the enjoyment of them by the citizens of each State, in every other State, was manifestly calculated (to use the expressions of the preamble of the corresponding provision in the old Articles of Confederation) "the better to secure and perpetuate mutual friendship and intercourse among the people of the different States of the Union."

[*Corfield v. Coryell*, 4 Wash. C.C. 371 (Pa Circ. Ct. 1825)]

Later, in the *Slaughterhouse Cases*, the Supreme Court interpreted the protections of the Privileges and Immunities Clause of the Fourteenth Amendment to apply to those rights "which owe their existence to the Federal government, its National character, its Constitution, or its laws."[295] In other words, the privileges and immunities afforded to the citizens of the United States exist because the American people, through their representatives, decided that those rights are ones that specifically define or restrict their relationship with the federal government, and by extension, with the states. They may not directly be those inalienable rights imparted upon us by our Creator, but they are nevertheless ones the people have imparted upon themselves through their laws and system of government.

The Equal Protection Clause has a much broader reach. A detailed analysis of how this plays out in legal practice will not be explored here, but will be addressed in the Civil Rights section of this book where it had its greatest impact. Suffice it to say here that the interpretation of the Equal Protection Clause has been construed to allow the federal government to impose its will upon the states and directly upon the people; a very different hierarchical power arrangement than was originally construed when the states created the federal government, or passed the Fourteenth Amendment later on.

The Due Process Clause similarly resulted in the reversal of the original relationship between the federal and state governments. In its first reading, the Due Process Clause would seem to have a fairly straightforward application. It speaks only to the guarantee of equal access to governmental safeguards and equal limitations upon governmental powers by an individual.

However, a broader interpretation would allow for the application of the Bill of Rights not just to the federal government, but to the states as well. The concept dates back to the dissenting opinion by Justice Hugo L. Black in *Adamson v. California.* in (1947).[296] *Adamson* was a Fifth Amendment case regarding the prohibition against self-incrimination. Adamson argued that because of a nuance in California law, the court proceedings were stacked in such a manner that, to properly defend himself, he would have been forced to risk incriminating himself in other crimes about which he was not presently being accused. Being faced with such a Hobson's choice, he argued, was unconstitutional and counter to the prohibitions of self-incrimination contained within the Fifth Amendment.

However, the court that had convicted Adamson and whose procedures the Supreme Court of the United States was scrutinizing was not a federal court. It was a state court, and in order for the constitutional prohibition against self-incrimination to apply to the courts of California, the Fifth Amendment, a federal constitutional requirement designed to apply only to federal courts, would have to restrict the state courts as well, a concept that had previously been foreign in constitutional law. Ultimately, the United States Supreme Court in the *Adamson* case refused to apply the Fifth Amendment upon the nation's state courts and upheld the California's conviction.

But Justice Black saw the matter differently and wrote a dissent to that effect. He believed the framers of the Fourteenth Amendment intended for the Bill of Rights (all of it) to henceforth apply to the states as well as the federal government. Consequently, in Justice Black's view, the California courts were required to uphold the Fifth Amendment through the power of the Fourteenth Amendment, and its actions should have been found to be unsound.

Although Justice Black lost the battle in *Adamson*, the concept was to be reargued in other cases. As the arguments were made, the Court eventually decided that if a right is so essential that it represents a "fundamental principle of liberty and justice which lie[s] at the base of our civil and political institutions,"[297] then it must be applied to the states under the Fourteenth Amendment.[298]

There are several freedoms and liberties the Court believes must be applied to the states despite the original intent and purpose of the Bill of Rights. These include freedom of speech, freedom of the press, the free exercise of religion, freedom to peaceably assemble, the right to own property, the right to be justly compensated for property taken from you, the right to counsel, due process protections, protections against cruel and unusual punishment, the right to a jury trial for certain crimes, double jeopardy protections, the right against self-incrimination, and most recently, the right to own and bear arms for the purposes of self defense. As a matter of fact, about the only rights within the Bill of Rights not yet applied by the Supreme Court upon the states are the protections against quartering soldiers, requirement that a grand jury indictment be obtained prior to initiating a trial, the right to a jury trial in civil cases, and the prohibition on excessive fines.[299]

The consequences of the selective application of the Bill of Rights upon the states have generally been favorable. It would be a travesty of justice to not require all governments within the United States to observe property rights, double jeopardy prohibitions, or restrictions against cruel and unusual punishments. But in some areas, the results have not been as productive. Chief among these have been the restrictions placed upon the federal government regarding religion and interference with public worship, as will be discussed below.

The Misapplication of the Religious Clause of the First Amendment

The demise of religion's standing in the Constitution and the legal corpus is purely the result of the meddling of the judicial branch. No legislature ever voted to remove religious symbols from public buildings, or prohibited prayer at any educational institution except under the coercive effects of the judiciary. Admittedly, religion has been used on countless occasions to deny rights with the effect of not only diminishing the sacredness of worship, but also of opening the door to liberally trained attorneys, some cloaked with judicial robes, who wished to extricate religious worship and Christianity from the public forum. The chronology of how this took place is both disheartening and insightful, particularly for those who understand the importance of restoring religious freedom and worship to its rightful place.

Slavery, Catholicism, Political Expediency, and the Extrication of Worship from Public Schools

The close relationship between church and state (a purposely porous wall) continued after the passage of the Constitution into the antebellum period. In few places was this relationship stronger than in the nation's schools. America's public schools, originally known as "common schools," were largely Protestant institutions where prayer and hymn singing abounded. In these schools, the King James Bible was studied with fervor,[300]and The New England Primer, a schoolbook replete with religious sayings and Bible passages, was the primary reading and writing source.

However, the rifts among the various sects of the 1600s and 1700s continued. With the increase of immigration by Southern European Catholics during the nineteenth century, hostility toward them grew. This was the time of the rise of the Know Nothing Party, which embraced, among other priorities, the goal of suppressing Catholics within the United States.[xiii] To a large degree, their efforts were aimed at the common schools where they worked to ensure that the Protestant Bibles were read, and Protestant values were faithfully taught.

In response, Catholics, faced with increasing resistance at having their faith taught in the common schools, established their own, parallel school system and began seeking tax exemptions and public funding for their schools.[301]

---

xiii The name "Know Nothing" derived from the agreement amongst the group's earliest members to answer, "I know nothing," when asked about their activities.

In 1875, when the Republicans, under President Ulysses S. Grant, found themselves needing to rally support for the Presidential election, they resurrected anti-Catholic sentiment for their benefit. Former House Speaker, James Blaine, a Republican, ran against Grant for the party's nomination, and in an effort to win the support of the Know Nothing wing of the party, attacked Catholics by submitting an amendment to the Constitution designed to prevent the funding of Catholic schools. Blaine's proposed amendment was interesting in that it spoke directly to the states, just like the Fourteenth Amendment, enacting restrictions on how states employed money and lands in support of religious schools. Designed as an addition to the First Amendment, the Blaine Amendment read:

> *No State shall make any law respecting an establishment of religion, or prohibiting the free exercise thereof; and no money raised by taxation in any State for the support of public schools, or derived from any public fund therefor, nor any public lands devoted thereto, shall ever be under the control of any religious sect; nor shall any money so raised or lands so devoted be divided between religious sects or denominations.*
>
> (Blaine Amendment, 1875)

As can be seen, the Blaine Amendment would not have prohibited religious education within the common school system. Instead, it would have prohibited public money or capital from being "under the control of any religious sect." Specifically, the amendment was crafted to allow funding of religious education in public schools where Protestantism was openly taught and to prohibit any government support of religious education outside of public schools where the teaching of Catholicism and other religious sects took place.

The amendment would pass in the House of Representatives, but after not passing in the Senate, it was not ratified. Blaine also did not win the presidency. Although some states objected to the passage of his amendment because of its intrusive effects upon state sovereignty, similar amendments would pass throughout the established states and would become part of the constitutions of many of the newly admitted states.

But if anti-Catholicism fomented the genesis of prohibitions against government support for religious education, racism and bigotry expanded it. During Reconstruction, Republicans led the effort at expanding public education specifically in the hopes of educating freed blacks, and since school buildings were uncommon, children generally met in churches with church ministers as their public school teachers.[302]

Predictably, southern, white Democrats resisted the push towards public education, and as the members of the various Catholic communities became involved in educating freed blacks, the legislative war against Catholics became tangled up with the prejudicial war against blacks, giving the effort to discontinue support for religious education within particularly southern states the dual purpose of disadvantaging blacks as well as Catholics.

The conclusion to be drawn from these trends is that the concept of separation of church and state related to funding religious education did not result from some lofty aspirational concept by the national designers wanting to separate churches from the tarnish of politics, nor did it arise out of a concern over the potential of tyranny and oppression of one religious sect over another, nor even because of some intellectually contrived offense of teaching religion in front of non-believers. Rather, the case against religious education in public schools arose from a discriminatory assault to disadvantage Catholics and blacks even at the risk of negatively impacting the opportunity for religious education for all.

The Courts' Misguided Role in the Extrication of Religion from Public Life

The trend to suppress religion did not end with the interventions in the nation's schools. Concurrent with the efforts to block public support for religious education came the efforts to make it more difficult for Americans to freely practice their religion. These efforts would not be focused on the state legislatures or on the passage of some discriminatory amendment to a state constitution. Instead, the battle would play out in the nation's courts.

In 1874, Mr. George Reynolds was convicted of polygamy in a Utah Court. At that time, Utah was a territory with a burgeoning anti-polygamy legislative posture. Reynolds appealed the conviction, under various legal theories, one of which was the infringement upon his religious freedoms.[303] Ultimately, the Supreme Court heard the case and ruled against Reynolds, asserting that although Congress and the state did not have the authority to regulate religious beliefs, they were able to prohibit certain religious practices, such as polygamy. In its analysis, the Court entered a discussion regarding the meaning of religious freedom and the proper role of government in regulating religious-based conduct. As part of its analysis, the Court quoted the entire paragraph of Jefferson's letter to the Danbury Baptist Association regarding the separation of church and state,[xiv] marking the phrase's first entry into the legal corpus.

Admittedly, the Court's foray into the realm of regulating religious-based conduct within a territory did not equate to the same judicial oversight over a state. After all, a territory of the United States is not sovereign and, accordingly, is subject to the direct authority of the federal government. A state, however, is sovereign and subject to greater protections against legal intrusions by federal courts.

Enter the Fourteenth Amendment.

The opportunity to extend the same regulatory oversight regarding religious freedom into the states presented itself in 1940 with *Cantwell v. Connecticut.*[304] The controversy arose from Newton Cantwell's actions, as a Jehovah's Witness minister, of door knocking with the intent of proselytizing his faith to the residents of New Haven, Connecticut. His routine was to approach a home, and if the homeowner listened, he would ask permission to play a phonographic recording of his church's message. If the homeowner listened to

---

[xiv] The Court cited the letter in its attempt to define religion and religious freedom, which it correctly observed had no definitions within the Constitution. The Court in *Reynolds* did not specifically define "religion" or "religious freedom," but used the Danbury Baptist Association letter, Madison's "Memorial and Remonstrance," and sections of the Jefferson's Bill for Establishing Religious Freedom in defining the proper relationship between government and religious worship.

the message, then he would ask the homeowner to purchase a book teaching the Jehovah's Witness faith or to make a contribution to his church. Mr. Cantwell was eventually arrested for violating a state statute prohibiting the solicitation of "... any valuable thing for any religious, charitable, or philanthropic cause, ..."[305, xv]

In Court, Cantwell argued that the statute was unconstitutional because it inhibited his freedom of worship and his freedom of speech in contradiction to the due process rights afforded to him by the Fourteenth Amendment of the Constitution. The Court agreed, stating that whereas the First Amendment to the Constitution has prohibited Congress from making any law establishing a religion or prohibiting the free exercise thereof, "[t]he Fourteenth Amendment has rendered the legislatures of the states as incompetent as Congress to enact such laws."[306]

In its ruling reversing Cantwell's convictions, the Court acted to protect Cantwell's freedom of speech and his right to freely exercise his religion. However, the ruling was based on authority borrowed from the Fourteenth Amendment, not from those original given to it by the Constitution.

This new power the Court employed would give it authority to accomplish many positive things against the encroachments of an overzealous state. In *Everson v. Board of Education*,[307] for example, the Court, in an opinion authored by Hugo Black, upheld a New Jersey tax law calling for the collection of money to support school transportation for all children regardless of whether the children were being transported to secular or religious schools. *Everson* marked the first time the Court applied the freedom of religion clause in the First Amendment to a state. In his opinion, Justice Black again employed Jefferson's wall of separation analogy stating,

> *The "establishment of religion" clause of the First Amendment means at least this: neither a state nor the Federal Government can set up a church. Neither can pass laws which aid one religion, aid all religions, or prefer one religion over another. [Footnote 6] Neither can force or influence a person to*

xv Although the law included a few exceptions to the prohibition of exchanging valuable items or money for solicitations, the Cantwells did not qualify for them.

go to or to remain away from church against his will, or force him to profess a belief or disbelief in any religion. No person can be punished for entertaining or professing religious beliefs or disbeliefs, for church attendance or nonattendance. No tax in any amount, large or small, can be levied to support any religious activities or institutions, whatever they may be called or whatever form they may adopt to teach or practice religion. [Footnote 7] Neither a state nor the Federal Government can, openly or secretly, participate in the affairs of any religious organizations or groups, and vice versa. In the words of Jefferson, the clause against establishment of religion by law was intended to erect "a wall of separation between church and State."

[*Everson v. Board of Education*, 330 U.S. 1, 15-16 (1947)]

And with that, the character of the Constitution changed in a manner never intended by the legislature, or the people, and it was changed by an unelected and a virtually un-checkable subgroup of government. Although the Court's actions in these two cases promoted religious freedom and liberty, the unfortunate and longer lasting result of its actions were to divine a new function for the Courts; the role of arbiter of the constitutionality of state laws relating to religion, something the courts had never previously possessed. So, although the Courts in *Cantwell* and *Everson* prevented infringements, they also opened the door for later judicial activists to erode the rights to publicly worship and publicly acknowledge the supremacy of God.

And relentlessly chisel away at religious rights they did.

In *McCollum v. Board of Education*,[308] in 1948, an atheist mother of a student sued to discontinue the religious education program in his school because her child was being criticized for not attending religious education classes. The Supreme Court upheld the mother's complaint, effectively ending religious education in American schools.

Suddenly, and without a vote or a congressional debate, America's children enrolled in public schools were no longer able to recite Bible verses in class as part of their education despite the fact that such activity had taken place continuously since before the country's inception. No longer were teachers able to employ excerpts from the Bible as teaching aids in writing exercises. And no longer were books such as the New England Primer, a staple of American education for the first fifty years of America's history, allowed as a textbook in American education.

The *McCollum* decision was only the beginning of the concerted effort to extricate worship and religious observance from public life. In 1962, the Court struck down prayer in school, using the same logic it did in *McCollum*.[309] In *Lee v. Wiesman*, in 1992, the Court said that the prohibition against school prayer extends to the commencement ceremony.[310, xvi] In 2000, the prohibition was also extended to prayers led via the public address system prior to the start of varsity football games in public schools.[311] And in *Wallace v. Jaffree*, in 1985, the Court said that even a moment of silence was not acceptable.[312]

Religious symbols in celebration of religious events would also take a similar hit. Following a victory in *Lynch v. Donnelly* where the Court upheld a city's display of religious symbols in celebration of Christmas,[313] in *Alleghany v. ACLU*, the Court struck down a crèche placed inside a courthouse with the words "Glory to God for the birth of Jesus Christ." [314] The Court spared the display in *Lynch* because it sat on private property and, in the Court's opinion, served more as a depiction of the historical origin of the holiday than a promotion of a particular religion. The display in *Alleghany* was struck down because it was too prominent and, according to the Court, represented displays designed to promote religion.

And just like in the arena of prayer, the assault on the public display of religious symbols would not stop at the crèche. The Ten Commandments would be brought down from public school classrooms in *Stone v. Graham*.[315]

[xvi] This is a particularly fascinating case with regard to the hostility displayed by the Supreme Court towards public prayer when one considers the action was brought by a Jewish student complaining about a non-denominational prayer led by a Jewish Rabbi in a predominantly Christian community. The Court averred that because students felt compelled to attend a commencement ceremony, the fact that the school was asking these non-faith students to quietly stand while the invocation took place constituted coercion on the part of the state. Equally as offensive to the Court, the fact that the rabbi had been asked to keep his comments non-denominational represented the state's attempt at invoking a state religion. [*Lee v. Weisman*, 505 U.S. 577 (1992)]

And although in *Van Orden v. Perry*[316] the Court would rule that the Ten Commandments could continue to grace the Texas state capitol building, in *McCreary County v. ACLU*,[317] just one year later, it would order them down from courthouses and public schools.[xvii]

The issue of government support for sectarian schools would also succumb to the relentless attacks from judges. When New York enacted a grant program to, among other things, assist schools serving low-income areas and provide tuition assistance for low-income parents, the Court struck down the program, calling it unconstitutional because practically all the schools that qualified were Roman Catholic. The Court said the grants would enhance opportunities for the poor to choose non-public education, which would enhance religion, and this was unacceptable.[318] Since then, the Court has been all over the map in its position regarding tax relief for participants in private schools.

No discussion of the First Amendment's establishment clause is complete without noting what is arguably the most famous trial in American history—the Scopes Monkey Trial in Tennessee.

In 1925, John Thomas Scopes, a teacher at Rhea County High School in Dayton, Tennessee, was teaching the theory of evolution, and he was soon arrested for his actions. His teachings violated the Butler Act, a Tennessee statute prohibiting the teaching of any theory that denied the Biblical story of creation. The events marked a wonderful opportunity for the ACLU, which was looking for a case it could use to challenge the Tennessee law.

The trial took place in Dayton, Tennessee, and became a national sensation when the media learned that Clarence Darrow, one of the country's preeminent criminal defense attorneys, would be pitted against former presidential candidate, William Jennings Bryan.[319] The public's interests especially

---

[xvii] Worthy of observation is an unusual turn of events in Oklahoma, where a complaint to have the Ten Commandments removed from the statehouse grounds was successfully prosecuted before the Oklahoma Supreme Court. Here, however, the governor has refused to abide by the Court's order to remove the statue. What happens next in this controversy, if anything, and what precedent this will set is of great interest in the ongoing debate regarding the proper place for the Ten Commandments. (Abby Phillip, "Commandments Statue Isn't Going Anywhere, Governor Says," *The Washington Post*, Jul. 7, 2015.)

piqued when Bryan, the prosecuting attorney, agreed to take the stand and be cross-examined by Darrow. What resulted was one of the most contentious displays of courtroom behavior in any high-profile case.

In the end, Bryan's reputation sat discredited, and Darrow lost the case for his client.

Although the Scopes Monkey Trial failed to reach any great jurisprudential significance, it did herald the presence of yet another challenge in deciphering the extent and reach of the First Amendment. Could the courts interfere with the states' abilities to craft the substance of non-sectarian lessons taught in public schools? The Scopes Monkey Trial represented palpable evidence that they could, and a stark predictor that they soon would.

Indeed, in 2007, in a case where a school was teaching intelligent design alongside evolution as alternative explanations for man's creation and development, the court struck down the curriculum as unconstitutional. Even though the curriculum did not mention any particular religion, the court still disallowed the class as not based on science, placing itself in the position of defining what science is. According to the circuit court, the teachings constituted proselytization and were offensive to Jefferson's divined wall of separation between church and state.[320]

Tragically, however, the Courts' invocation of Jefferson's wall did not tell a balanced story behind its intent. Although Jefferson irrefutably did profess a very strict separation in the Dansbury letter, he was referring only to the role of the federal government. Of note, he did *not* refute the Association's view that the federal government could not alter state laws. And although Jefferson did make similar assertions in the Virginia General Assembly, he never implied, nor would he, that Virginians would have the authority to directly define the relationship between church and state in any other state.

As we have seen, the Fourteenth Amendment allowed the courts to play a pivotal role in redefining the relationship between the federal government, the people, and the states. These judicial interventions served not only to flip the normal balance of power between the states and the federal government, but also to restrict many of the people's rights in ways contrary to the nation's initial governmental design. As a result, every law, every statute, and even every ordinance has been made subject to the review of a relatively few appointees, leaving the people with little permanence to their voice and their laws. Indeed, Washington, in his Farewell Address, warned of the irreparable harm such reliance on court opinion to accomplish policies could have. He said:

> *The spirit of encroachment tends to consolidate the powers of all the departments in one, and thus to create, whatever the form of government, a real despotism. . . If in the opinion of the people the distribution or modification of the constitutional powers be in any particular wrong, let it be corrected by an amendment in the way which the Constitution designates. But let there be no change by usurpation; for though this in one instance may be the instrument of good, it is the customary weapon by which free governments are destroyed.*
>
> (George Washington, Farewell Address, Sept. 16, 1796)

Unquestionably, the actions of the courts—not the American people—have served as a tsunami of change upon American society and upon the critical elements of its foundations. The concern regarding this proclivity is not merely relating to the usurpation of power. Truly, the results of these judicially enacted changes have led to the secularization of the American people, and the erosion of their ties to God. No transformation has been more instrumental in causing Americans to stop asking what they can do for their country and instead demanding what their country can do for them than the abandonment of the central role of a Creator who imparts upon man certain unalienable rights and demands that individuals love those around them as they do themselves. As John Adams presciently observed in his letter to his cousin, Zabdiel Adams,

> *Statesmen my dear Sir, may plan and speculate for Liberty, but it is Religion and Morality alone, which can establish the Principles upon which Freedom can securely stand. . . The only foundation of a free Constitution, is pure Virtue, and if this cannot be inspired into our People, in a great Measure, than they have it now, they may change their Rulers, and the forms of Government, but they will not obtain a lasting Liberty. (suspension points included by Adams)*
>
> (John Adams Letter to Zabdiel Adams, Jun. 21, 1776)

Clearly, the philosophy portrayed by the courts is in conflict with the nation's foundation. The presence of a greater and more destructive agenda by twentieth-century jurists in adopting this secular approach is made even more stark by their capricious dismissal of another body of case-specific precedents that could easily steer them to an interpretation of the First Amendment that is much more accommodating to religion and public worship.

In Chapter 2, we already saw a few examples of authoritarian opinions the courts could have used to support alternative conclusions to those expressed in Jefferson's letter to the Danbury Baptist Church. These included the proposals of Patrick Henry and the writings of George Washington and John Adams to name a few. And there are more, very compelling examples.

Jasper Adams, the President of the College of Charleston, asked James Madison, Chief Justice John Marshall, and Justice Joseph Story for their impressions of a pamphlet he sent them entitled, "The Relations of Christianity to Civil Government." In large measure, the pamphlet dealt with the question of whether non-denominational Christianity could be considered America's national religion.[321] Madison predictably stated that government could not favor any religion, including Christianity, and that public funds, in his view, ought not be used to support Christian education at the expense of education regarding other religions.[322]

Chief Justice Marshall's view was quite different. We have already seen where he wrote, "The American population. . . is entirely Christian, and with us, Christianity and religion are identified. It would be strange indeed, if with such a people, our institution did not presuppose Christianity."[323] This prose was Marshall's response to the question posed by Adams.

Justice Story's response was equally as insightful, "My own private judgment has long been (and every day's experience more and more confirms me in it) that government can not long exist without an alliance with religion to *some extent;* and that Christianity is indispensable to the true interests and solid foundations of free government."[324]

Based on these authoritative precedents, courts could have easily crafted phrases vastly different from "a wall of separation of church and state." With equal intellectual credibility, they could have said, "American governance presupposes Christianity" (based on Marshall); "Christianity stands as indispensible to the true interests and solid foundations of a free government" (based on Story); and "no lasting liberty can exist without moral and religious virtue" (based on Adams). Had they done so, America would be a much different nation, one where children still prayed or stood silently and respectfully while others did, and adults publicly and comfortably revered the many blessings mercifully given to them by their Creator. The fact that they didn't speaks volumes about the biases and agendas of the various judges and justices giving rise to these more secular legal tenets.

3. Equal Protection and the Persistent Problem of Race Relations

Without question or parallel, the greatest error the United States has ever made is its tolerance of slavery. The consequences of this decision began a chain of events ending in civil war and disrupting the fiber of the nation while destroying the backbone of the American economy. Although the Civil War served to end slavery in the United States, it did not end the poisonous consequences of that dreadful institution. The effects of the protracted tolerance of such evil continued to eat away at America's soul, staining the purity of its purpose and eviscerating it of the promise of its goals. These injustices needed to be erased at all cost, but like in the treatment of cancer, the cleansing process inflicted at least as much pain upon the host as it did upon the target.

The Issue of Race Relations and Ingrained Discrimination Comes to a Head

With the procurement of their constitutional freedoms through the ratification of the Civil War Amendments, black Americans quickly worked toward the improvement of their condition. Although some early progress was made in what was very clearly a white man's world, these early and fragile steps were short lived. During Reconstruction, the Democratic-controlled southern state legislatures passed laws designed specifically to disadvantage blacks, and segregation was their most insidious. Under these laws, blacks were forced to use separate lavatories, separate neighborhoods, and separate restaurants. The restrictions bled into the governmental arena with requirements that blacks attend separate schools, separate beaches, separate public pools, and separate secondary educational institutions. In addition, these governmental facilities were not equal to those accessible by whites. They were universally underfunded, understaffed, and inferior to comparable facilities available to whites because they existed, not to provide equality to black citizens, but to guarantee that blacks would never be able to compete on equal footing with whites.

The demeaning acts against blacks did not end with segregation. In 1887, when 10,000 mostly black sugar workers went on strike in Louisiana, Governor Samuel Douglas McEnery purposefully and maliciously withdrew the militia, allowing lynch mobs to kill scores of black men. In 1917, St. Louis saw rioting that killed more than 100 black men. And in 1919, when a black youngster entered a white beach near Chicago, he was stoned and killed while in the water. A white police officer refused to arrest the killer, sparking mob violence that left 23 blacks and 5 whites dead. Despite the escalating violence and discrimination, neither the nation's legislatures nor its governmental executives moved to rectify the situation.

In 1890, Louisiana presented pre-Civil-Rights-Movement advocates with one of the first opportunities to combat these racially demeaning laws. The Louisiana legislature had just passed the Separate Car Act, designating the front section of passenger trains within the state to whites and the back to blacks.[xviii] The law was immediately targeted by concerned citizens of New Orleans who formed the *Comité des Citoyens* (Committee of Citizens) to fight the legislation. In a move foretelling of the techniques to be employed by the Civil Rights Movement, the *Comité* chose to initiate a legal challenge.

They found Mr. Homer Plessy, a man who was of seven-eighths European descent, one-eighth African, and the son of a free man. On June 7, 1892,

---

[xviii] Interestingly, the railroad companies opposed the measure because of the costs they would incur in having to supply more railroad cars, but the law was nevertheless passed and given the full effect by the state of Louisiana.

Mr. Plessy bought a ticket in New Orleans for a train bound to Covington, Louisiana, boarded the train, and sat in the whites only section of the train.[325]

The *Comité* had previously informed the train of Mr. Plessy's mixed race status to which train attendants responded by asking Plessy to remove himself from the white section of the train. When Plessy refused, he was arrested and escorted off the train. Plessy's trial took place before Judge John Howard Ferguson who found Plessy guilty of disobeying Louisiana's Separate Car Act and sentenced him to a $25 fine.

The case was appealed, reaching the Supreme Court of the United States in 1896 as *Plessy v. Ferguson.* Plessy's team argued the capricious nature of the law and how it established a precedent for discrimination not just based on race, but on hair color and nationality, among other characteristics. Ultimately, the Court disagreed, stating that the exercise of police power to separate different classes of people based on skin color was indeed reasonable. Additionally, the Court rejected the argument that the establishment of separate but equal facilities represented an unequal distribution. On the contrary, such a separation was, on its face, entirely equal and only deemed inferior if a particular group deemed itself to be inferior.

And so, the venomous dogma of segregation was judicially adopted as a sound legislative dogma within the United States.

But *Plessy* was not unanimously decided. Justice Harlan, writing for the dissent, presciently wrote, "In my opinion the judgment this day will, in time, prove to be quite as pernicious as the decision made by this tribunal in the *Dred Scott* case."[326]

It would take another fifty years and the loss of countless more black American lives to partially undo the effects of this disgraceful ruling and public policy.

But progress sometimes comes from the most unexpected sources, and in interracial relations, such a source was war. With World War I, many blacks saw an opportunity to end racial discrimination through military service. In their eyes, demonstrations of valor in battle would prove their worth to the country and eventually lead to the opening of doors in American society.

At the beginning of World War I, blacks were prohibited from serving in the Armed Forces. However, in need of troops, Congress passed the Selective Service Act of 1917, authorizing a mandatory military draft that included blacks despite the protestations from white supremacists. The military created black enlisted and officer training programs. The 369th Regiment, the first African American regiment to serve with the American Expeditionary Force, was organized in 1916 and assigned to train in South Carolina where its members were predictably subjected to overt acts of racism by the locals.

The Regiment was eventually deployed to France and assigned labor duties. Because American soldiers refused to serve alongside their black countrymen, black troops had to be placed under French command. The black American soldiers wore French helmets, carried French weapons, and eventually were to shore up the depleted French ranks in combat. Their valor shone in the battlefields of Europe where these black military members saw 191 days of combat, more than any other American unit in the war.[327]

The black soldiers earned the respect from friends and foes alike as they won 171 individual commendations.[328] But their achievements did not stop the profound lack of respect and appreciation from the citizens of the very country whose wellbeing they shed blood to preserve. The doors they were hoping to pry open seemed to close even tighter. Black veterans were increasingly subject to lynchings (sometimes while wearing their military uniforms) between 1918 and 1919, spurred by the fear that they would demand equality under the law.[329]

World War I had another impact on race relations. With the demand for labor growing in the northern states, hostilities in Europe essentially choked the supply of cheap labor. Perceiving a lack of economic opportunity in the South and persistent socioeconomic oppression, blacks began migrating to the north as early as 1910, initiating the largest demographic movement in American history: the Great Migration. The newly expanded presence of blacks within major cities, including Chicago, Philadelphia, New York, and Washington, D.C., saw an intensification of white supremacy and segregation in those areas.

World War II offered another opportunity for blacks to integrate into American society. Although the military was still segregated at the beginning of World War II, the number of black personnel serving in the nation's military swelled from less than 4,000 to 1.2 million.[330] Like in World War I, blacks were initially assigned non-combat duties, but a depletion of forces resulted in their entering the line of fire.[xix] For the first time, black Americans took to the air to fight for their country. The Tuskegee Airmen of the 332nd Fighter Group flew over 15,000 missions between May 1943 and June 1945, where they served with great distinction.

But the first major breakthrough in the black soldier's position in the military occurred during the Battle of the Bulge. American losses from the engagements in Ardennes between December 1944 and January 1945 were staggering. The critical depletion in American forces led General Dwight D. Eisenhower to desegregate his personnel. For the first time since the Civil War, black Americans served alongside white Americans in combat. Once again, black Americans would serve heroically under the pressures of war, and once again their bravery would not result in the dissolution of the segregationist lines back home. Indeed, it was not until July 26, 1948, when President Harry S. Truman finally signed Executive Order 9981 that segregation would finally end within America's military ranks.

For whites, the post-War period was a time of celebration, prosperity, and reproduction. The same cannot be said for blacks. For the millions of Americans of African descent, the oppression continued. The divisive dogma of separate but equal upheld in *Plessy* had now thickly invested itself within the nation's societal and legal framework, cloaked with a shroud of hatred that rapidly grew into death sentences for many black men and women. If a black man flirted with a white woman in the South, the punishment was violence to the point of lynching by men cowardly dressed in white hoods. If a black man

---

xix The D-Day invasion included the participation of about 1,700 black personnel. ("African Americans in World War II Fighting for a Double Victory," *Nationalww2museum.org* accessed Mar. 26, 2015, *http://www.nationalww2museum.org/assets/pdfs/african-americans-in-world.pdf*)

was able to rise beyond his circumstances to a position of prominence, he was rewarded by his exclusion from some of America's finest neighborhoods. And if that black man was somehow able to transcend racial barriers and seek homestead within a white neighborhood, his welcome was the torching of the letters "KKK" upon his front yard.

The Ku Klux Klan became increasingly active during this period. Essentially, the militant arm of the Democratic Party in the South, the KKK saw its inception in Pulaski, Tennessee, in 1866, under the leadership of the Confederate General, Nathan Bedford Forrest. Although it had been in existence for nearly 80 years by the 1950s, the maliciousness of the KKK following World War II was unparalleled in its history. Particularly, Klansmen in Alabama, Mississippi, and Georgia behaved ruthlessly, a fact made even worse as its membership infested themselves in those states' police departments and governors' offices.

However, the data on the number of lynchings tells a different story. The Tuskegee Institute has maintained a tally of the number of lynchings in the United States dating back to 1882. The 1890s saw a high level of activity with 161 black Americans lynched in 1891. The numbers diminished slowly through the ensuing decades, but did not reach single digit status until 1929. Oddly, despite the racism and intense segregation, 1952 is the first year where no lynchings were recorded in the United States. Indeed, the 1950s saw six years with no recorded lynchings.[331]

Despite the decline in lynchings, the social and legal environment was ripe with discrimination, disenfranchisement, and oppression of the black race in America.

But all of that was about to change under the steadfast influence of an attorney named Thurgood Marshall. Born in Baltimore, Maryland, Marshall was the grandson of slaves. Because of its segregationist policies, Marshall would be unable to attend the University of Maryland Law School. Instead, he graduated from Howard University School of Law before returning to Maryland to practice law. In 1934, Marshall represented Donald Gaines Murray against the same University of Maryland School of Law that had not allowed him admission years earlier, thus beginning his long affiliation with the National Association for the Advancement of Colored People (NAACP). The case went to the Maryland Court of Appeals, where the court ruled in favor of Murray, handing Marshall a defining victory in Civil Rights litigation.[332]

By age 32, Marshall had established the NAACP's Legal Defense and Education Fund. Marshall would argue and win a slew of Civil Rights cases on behalf of black men and women.[xx]

And then came the *Brown* series of cases.

Brown represented the compilation of five cases filed in 1951 stemming from petitions by black parents to various school boards who sought admission of their black children to segregated white schools. If the courts were to agree with the parents, the doctrine of separate but equal would essentially be overturned.

The Supreme Court first heard the case in 1953, but was unable to come to a consensus. Instead, it agreed to rehear arguments the following year. In the interim, one of the justices who had opposed overturning *Plessy*, Chief Justice Fred M. Vinson, passed away. His death allowed President Dwight D. Eisenhower to appoint Earl Warren, the Republican governor of California and a staunch supporter of the President's, to head the bench. The appointment, in many regards, was odd since Mr. Warren never previously served on the bench. Chief Justice Warren made it his priority not only to overturn the constitutionality of the separate but equal doctrine, but to do it through a unanimous opinion.

[xx] *Chambers v. Florida*, 309 U.S. 227 (1940) finding that the compelled admissions of black defendants by white police officers was inadmissible evidence; *Smith v. Allwright*, 321 U.S. 659 (1944) overturning a Texas law requiring all voters in a Democratic primary election be white; *Shelley v. Kraemer*, 334 U.S. 1 (1948) disavowing courts from their power to enforce restrictive covenants barring Negros or Asians from occupying property (although the covenants were not necessarily illegal, without the backing of a court order, they could no longer be enforced, rendering them powerless); *Sweatt v. Painter*, 321 U.S. 629 (1950) holding that the separate but equal doctrine was inapplicable to law schools because of the inequality of the facilities and the inequality of other the intangible factors such as the types of relationships the students would be able to foster under the different roofs; and *McLaurin V. Oklahoma State Regents*, 339 U.S. 637 (1950) striking down a state law that required blacks to obtain segregated graduate education.

Using his political skills, Warren employed a very aggressive and dynamic stance in formulating the Court's opinion, essentially brokering a deal among justices. The opinion was carefully crafted to maintain consensus but still affirm that the separate but equal doctrine was inherently harmful to black children and could consequently not withstand the scrutiny of the Fourteenth Amendment's Equal Protection Clause.

With one swoop, the Warren Court did what the legislature and prior courts had been unable to accomplish over scores of years. For the first time, all children stood on equal footing before the law. The time had arrived, at least in the eyes of the courts, for black children and white children to go to school together, be educated together, and play together.[xxi] But merely because the law called for a set of circumstances to exist did not necessarily mean that change would swiftly happen.

The following year, an event instigating the great awakening of the Civil Rights Movement took place, but this time, it was under much more tragic circumstances. Emmitt Till, a 14-year-old black teenager from Chicago, Illinois, traveled to Mississippi to visit his great uncle, Moses Wright. The trip arose as a result of a visit by Wright to Emmitt's home in Chicago where he spoke of the wonders of the Mississippi delta in the summer.

A mere three days after his arrival in Money, Mississippi, Emmitt went to Bryant's Grocery and Meat Store with his cousin and some friends to buy candy. While still outside of the store, Emmitt apparently bragged about some pictures in his wallet showing white and black children together. Emmitt told of how the white children were actually friends of his and of having a white girlfriend. During this exchange, one of the boys dared Emmitt

[xxi] The complexity and unlikelihood of the *Brown* decision make it a truly miraculous achievement, an observation that did not escape Justice Felix Frankfurter who was instrumental in delaying the disposition of the *Brown* case at the end of 1953. When speaking to his former aid, Philip Elman regarding the incredulity of the *Brown* decision Frankfurter said "Phil, this is the first solid piece of evidence I've ever had that there really is a God." Elman later validated Justice Frankfurter's statement by observing, "Without God, the Court would have remained bitterly divided, fragmented, unable to decide the issue forthrightly. . . God won *Brown v. Board of Education*, not Thurgood Marshall, or any other lawyer or any other mortal." [James E. St. Clair and Linda C. Cugin, *Chief Justice*]

to speak to the white proprietor of the store, Mrs. Carolyn Bryant. There are varying accounts relating to the events that transpired in the few minutes while Emmitt remained in the store with Mrs. Bryant. Regardless, Emmitt was guilty of the crime of speaking to a married, white woman in Mississippi during the 1950s and suggesting that they date. The incident would end with the children scurrying for an illusory safety when Bryant went to her car to fetch her pistol.

Carolyn's husband, Roy, did not hear of the events until his return from a shrimping trip on August 27. In the wee hours of August 28, Roy Bryant and his half brother, J.W. Milam, with perhaps a third, black man, went to Wright's home where they kidnapped the boy, took him to a barn, mutilated him, shot him in the head, and dumped his body in the Tallahatchie River. The body was discovered in the river three days later.

Through Emmitt's mother's unrelenting efforts, the boy's body was delivered back to Chicago, where she exposed it in an open coffin as part of a public funeral. Photographs of the youngster's mutilated face with one eye missing were published in *Jet* magazine and *The Chicago Defender*, allowing the country to view the consequences of the hatred and racial injustice pervading it. The effects of the story of a boy's horrific murder and the visual evidence of the consequences of the act sent a glaring message through black communities all over the nation, mobilizing many to action, and setting the stage for revolution.

In the meantime, Bryant and Milam were tried and acquitted. Only later, once safely outside the reach of the arms of the law, did the two admit to murdering Emmitt Till with no legal consequence.

But the spark that would ignite the Civil Rights Movement took place December 1, 1955, in Montgomery, Alabama, when a young black woman named Rosa Parks refused the order of a white bus driver to give up her seat in the front of the bus for white riders.[xxii] Her insubordination led to her arrest

[xxii] In an amazing historical twist, Rosa Parks had previously encountered the bus driver of that fateful day. In 1943, Ms. Parks boarded a Montgomery bus. Mr. James Blake, the same bus driver that had asked her to give up her seat in 1955, was the bus driver that day. After accepting her toll, Mr. Blake asked Parks to depart the bus and enter through the rear entrance. Ms. Parks did indeed step off the bus, but did not reenter, vowing

and subsequent conviction for disorderly conduct the very next day. Parks appealed, but more importantly, the indignation regarding her experience caught the attention of the Women's Political Council, which distributed leaflets calling for a boycott of the city's buses on December 5, 1955.

The day after Parks' arrest, a meeting of black ministers and leaders was held at the Dexter Avenue Baptist Church to publicize the December 5 boycott; a meeting that included the presence of a young black minister who was relatively new to Montgomery and unknown to its citizens, Martin Luther King Jr.

The one-day boycott on December 5, 1955, saw the participation of over 90% of the black population in Montgomery, Alabama, sending a resounding message to the community and to a watching nation.

Motivated by the great success of the one-day boycott, black leaders met on the evening of December 5 to consider its continuation. The members created the Montgomery Improvement Association (MIA) and named King its president.[333]

That evening, before a crowd of thousands, King delivered a rousing speech where he said, in a prelude to the greatness he would achieve,

> *My friends, I want it to be known that we're going to work with grim and bold determination to gain justice on the buses in this city. And we are not wrong; we are not wrong in what we are doing. If we are wrong, the Supreme Court of this nation is wrong. If we are wrong, the Constitution of the United States is wrong. If we are wrong, God Almighty is wrong. If we are wrong, Jesus of Nazareth was merely a utopian dreamer that never came down to Earth. If we are wrong, justice is a lie, love has no meaning. And we are determined here in Montgomery to work and fight until justice runs down like water and righteousness like a mighty stream.*[xxiii]

---

never to ride a bus driven by Blake. Rosa Parks failed to check whether Blake was driving the bus on December 1, 1955, allowing their lives to intersect once again; this time with historically altering circumstances. [Elaine Woo, "Rosa Parks/1913-2005 She Set Wheels of Justice in Motion," *Los Angeles Times*, Oct. 25, 2005, accessed Apr. 4, 2015, *http://articles.latimes.com/2005/oct/25/nation/na-parks25.]*

xxiii ["5 December 1955 Address to the First Montgomery Improvement Association (MIA) Mass Meeting" "Martin Luther King and the Global Freedom Struggle," *King Encyclopedia* (Stanford University).]

The Rosa Parks experience led to a protracted boycott and community mobilization effort of an unexpected magnitude. For 381 days, the black community of Montgomery resolved to not ride a bus. Neighbors and complete strangers alike volunteered to provide private transportation to black citizens while others walked to their destinations. The resulting financial strain on the Montgomery transit company was crippling.

Not until America's bus ridership segregation laws were overturned in *Browder v. Gayle,*[334] did Montgomery eventually change its ordinance, ending the boycott. But the events in Montgomery gave rise to a national movement bent on correcting centuries of wrongs perpetrated on American blacks.

After 1956, the issue of race relations and equal rights for America's black citizens came to life with a fervor, and with the advent of television and its penetrating visual effects upon the nation's psyche, America got the opportunity to see the images of a government undertaking unjust and oppressive actions. Americans saw black individuals, who minutes earlier had been engaged in deep prayer, beaten with sticks by men cloaked in the garments of state authority. They witnessed black men and women beaten down merely because they wanted to peaceably cross a bridge in Selma, Alabama. They saw armed police officers open fire into black men and women's homes, killing its inhabitants in cold blood. And they witnessed the hatred unleashed merely because schools and their buses were about to be shared with students of a different race.

Undoubtedly, the Civil Rights Movement became a very painful process for peace-loving Americans outside the South who were being exposed to a side of their country they had never seen before and perhaps did not even know existed. But however painful this process was for Americans, it was also necessary and ultimately cleansing. The process itself gave rise to some incredible figures who confronted injustice and hatred with dignity and civility. Chief among these, of course, was Dr. Martin Luther King, Jr. And while King worked to win the hearts and minds of Americans, Thurgood Marshall worked to win the body corpus.

Time and time again, Marshall fought in the courtroom with the same vigor that King displayed in the streets. Marshall took his legal arguments in favor of equal rights and human decency to America's courts and won, changing the legislative environment for black Americans with each victory. He would eventually be appointed to the bench of the Second Circuit by John F. Kennedy, and in 1967 would become the first black American to serve as Justice in the Supreme Court of the United States.

But the efforts at promoting and defending Civil Rights in America were not all positive. While King and his followers advocated for peaceful demonstrations, and Marshall worked the legal process, other voices calling for violent resistance gained strength in response to the persistent and relentless atrocities perpetrated against blacks. Ironically, the genesis of the transition may be traced back to one of the most famous and peaceful events of the Civil Rights Movement; the Woolworth lunch-counter sit-in, in Greensboro, North Carolina.

On February 1, 1960, four black students from North Carolina A&T University sat at the white counter in the Greensboro Woolworth. Their actions were essentially spontaneous, spawning from their private dorm conversations regarding their disdain towards racism and segregation. Predictably, the students were refused service. Despite being shunned, they remained at the counter until the store closed about an hour after their arrival to the counter. However, they returned the next day armed with books to read and accompanied by other black students. The Greensboro four sat from 11 am to 3 pm, receiving attention from the press and heckles from white customers.

For the next five days, the sit-ins continued as hundreds assembled at the store (including members of the KKK). Quickly, similar protests appeared in Tennessee, Virginia, and Kentucky.

By Saturday, February 6, the Greensboro Woolworth temporarily closed its doors. However, on April 1, 1960, the store would reopen, still refusing to integrate.

And the students would resume their protests.

With the issue unresolved and protests occurring throughout the country, the Southern Christian Leadership Conference (SCLC) called for a meeting at Shaw University in Raleigh, North Carolina. Under the leadership of Ella Baker, it formed the Student Nonviolent Coordinating Committee (SNCC) to organize the effort at coordinating sit-ins.

On July 25, 1960, the Greensboro Woolworth would integrate, but for the SCLC the fight was not over, and its political activities designed to end racial injustice continued. The sit-ins and variants such as wade-ins at segregated beaches, kneel-ins at segregated churches, and sleep-ins at segregated hotels, spread throughout the nation. But the racism that pervaded the country was unyielding.

These mostly peaceful demonstrations were consistently met with aggressive police resistance, harassment by onlookers, and violence against unarmed innocents, causing many to wonder whether purely peaceful demonstrations were sufficient to the cause. In the face of continued violence against peaceful protestors, some black activists began conceiving a role for violent resistance. The arguments were becoming increasingly difficult to refute in light of the too often fatal attacks on black demonstrators and the overt refusal of authorities to act. A short list reminds us of the violence and lack of justice:

- In 1955, Reverend George Lee was killed in Mississippi for urging blacks to vote. Local officials did not charge anyone for the crime, and the Governor refused to investigate.[335]
- That same year, again in Mississippi, Lamar Smith was killed by white assailants for urging blacks to vote. Although the murder was witnessed, no one was charged.
- On October 22, 1955, John Earl Reese was killed in a cafe in Mayflower Texas, as part of a ploy to intimidate blacks into abandoning hopes for a new school. Two white men were eventually charged with the crime. Although the first was found guilty, he was given a five-year suspended sentence for the crime. The charges were dropped on the other.[336]

- On January 23, 1957, in Montgomery, Alabama, Willie Edwards, Jr., a truck driver, was forced to jump off a bridge to his death because Klansmen thought he was dating a white woman. His murderers, identified as three members of the KKK, were never tried.[337]
- In 1961, Herbert Lee was murdered in Liberty, Mississippi, by E.H. Hurst, a state legislator, because Lee had been working for a voter registration campaign. Hurst was acquitted after black witnesses were pressured into providing false testimony.[338]
- On June 12, 1963, Medgar Evers, a Civil Rights activist and WWII veteran, was shot to death in his driveway in Mississippi by Byron De La Beckwith, a member of the White Citizens' Council and of the KKK, for working to end segregation at the University of Mississippi. Evers was buried with full military honors at Arlington.[339]
- On September 15, 1963, the Sixteenth Street Baptist Church, the site of many Civil Rights meetings, was bombed, killing four girls: Addie Mae Collins (14), Denise McNair (11), Carole Robertson (14), and Cynthia Wesley (14).[340]

Particularly disturbing were the events leading to the deaths of the civil rights workers, James Chaney, Andrew Goodman, and Michael Schwerner, on June 21, 1964. The three men had gone to Meridian, Mississippi, to investigate the burning of a Mount Zion Church by the Klu Klux Klan. While in Neshoba County, they were arrested by Sheriff Cecil Price who initially released them, but subsequently re-arrested them and turned them over to local Klansmen. The Klansmen took them to the woods, beat them, and killed them.[341] Although Chaney was black, Goodman and Schwerner were white, prompting a somewhat more serious interrogation by the FBI. As part of their investigation, dozens of bodies were found in the Mississippi woods along with those of the missing civil rights workers. Ultimately, seven Klansmen were tried in state court, and all seven were acquitted of murder charges, prompting the federal government to prosecute the alleged murderers for Civil Rights violations.[342]

As these vile, violent, and unchecked events continued throughout the 1950s and 1960s, black families and neighborhoods responded by arming themselves. Throughout the South, armed black men took turns protecting their neighborhoods.

In North Carolina, Robert F. Williams became particularly active in preparing for armed confrontation. Williams had moved to Monroe, North Carolina, shortly after returning from his service in the United States Marine Corps and joined the local chapter of the NAACP. There he worked with Dr. Albert Perry. Together, they actively engaged in efforts aimed at integrating Monroe. In 1957, rumors swirled that the KKK was preparing a violent attack on Dr. Perry's home. Williams prepared for an armed defense, and when a group of white men in a motorcade did attack, they were met with gunfire and successfully repelled.[343]

Williams' advocacy for armed resistance did not end with the defense of Dr. Perry's home. In 1959, at the failed conclusion of a months-long legal effort to bring justice to a black woman who had brought sexual assault charges against a white man, Williams was quoted as saying, "I made a statement that if the law, if the United States Constitution, cannot be enforced in this social jungle called Dixie, it is time that Negroes must defend themselves even if it is necessary to resort to violence."[344] Williams would become the first Civil Rights Movement leader to advocate violence and would eventually move to Cuba to call for armed insurrection through newsletters and a program called Radio Free Dixie.

Williams' call for violence would have a profound influence on the Civil Rights Movement. With the continued presence of race-based violent crimes by white thugs and the ensuing absence of legal justice, the frustration among blacks mounted. Increasingly, the peaceful approach to political and social change was viewed as futile by those most directly affected by the success of the Civil Rights efforts. Organizations such as the Black Panthers and the Nation of Islam attracted young black Americans who adhered to the mantras of self-defense, violence, and insurrection. By 1964, the manner in which demonstrators interacted with police rapidly deteriorated.

On March 24, 1964, an attempted sit-in in Jacksonville, Florida, turned violent when black demonstrators began throwing Molotov cocktails. Malcolm X, the national representative of the Nation of Islam at the time, publicly offered to help any Civil Rights organization accepting the right to self-defense and the philosophy of black nationalism, and openly advocated for militant activity. "It'll be Molotov cocktails this month, hand grenades next month, and something else next month," he proclaimed. "It'll be ballots, or it'll be bullets."[345]

Congress had to act. On July 2, 1964, Congress passed Public Law 88-352, the Civil Rights Act of 1964, forbidding discrimination based on sex and race. The bill also created the Equal Employment Opportunity Commission (EEOC) for the implementation of the law.

The effect of the Civil Rights Act was immense. With this one law, Congress acted to end segregation in public places and to ban discrimination on the basis of race, color, religion, sex, or national origin.

But, whether Congress had the authority to engage in such expansive regulation was a valid constitutional question, one to be tested by the Heart of Atlanta Hotel, a Georgia based establishment that wished to continue the practice of segregation within its doors. The hotel sued the federal government shortly after the Civil Rights Act became law, and the case quickly reached the highest court in the land. For the Supreme Court, the question was whether Congress, through Title II of the Civil Rights Act of 1964, exceeded its constitutional authority by interfering with the right of a business to choose its customers. The hotel argued that it was a private enterprise conducting business exclusively within the state of Georgia, and therefore, Congress was unable to directly regulate its commercial activities.

Countering the allegations, the government argued that Congress was within its authority to regulate commerce of this nature under the powers afforded to it by the Interstate Commerce Clause. The government noted that the hotel was situated close to Interstates 75 and 85, and state highways 41 and 23, making its target interstate travelers. Additionally, 75% of the hotel's guests were from outside Georgia, and the hotel spent a significant amount on advertising outside of the state.

Ultimately, the Court would find that the hotel's commercial activities were largely interstate in nature. Consequently, even though the hotel conducted business only within the state of Georgia, its business was sufficiently interstate in nature to allow Congress to have authority over its activities.[346]

But the question remained regarding Congress's power to impose the prohibitions within the Civil Rights Act on enterprises conducting business solely within a single state. The Supreme Court would address this controversy in a companion case to *Heart of Atlanta*, published on the same day, and dealing with Ollie's Barbecue, a family run restaurant in Birmingham, Alabama.

Ollie's did not tailor to out-of-state customers. Nearly all of its customers were locals. Consequently, the government could not reasonably argue that Ollie's engaged in interstate commerce. However, the Court found that discrimination placed a significant burden on the flow of foods and products. For this reason, the Court held that Congress acted well within its authorities in prohibiting civil discrimination by commercial entities operating within the United States, in this case restaurants, even if the enterprise was conducting all of its business within a state's borders.[347] These two cases, like the *Filburn* case during the Great Depression, served to expand congressional powers to a level the Constitution had not previously been construed to allow. Although the construction was undertaken in the name of civil justice, the implications of the expansions of congressional powers would have significant consequences in weakening the position of the various states in numerous other areas not dealing with Civil Rights.

With the affirmation of Congress's authority to pass the Civil Rights Act, the federal government was now in a position to directly intervene on discriminatory activities within the various states. However, the Civil Rights Act was insufficient at curbing the wave of race-based violence that gripped the nation. On July 16, 1964, Thomas Gilligan, an off-duty police officer, shot and killed James Powell, a black 15 year-old. The officer was responding to an incident he had witnessed involving Patrick Lynch, a white man who apparently insulted black students in the neighborhood on a daily basis. As Gilligan chased Lynch into a building, he encountered Powell and thought the child was charging him with a knife. Gilligan shot Powell twice, killing him.

No proof was ever found of Powell having charged Gilligan with a knife, but the officer was nevertheless cleared of wrongdoing, inciting a riot. The unrest spanned six days and left at least 118 persons injured and one dead.[348]

Within months, similar riots broke out in Philadelphia following the arrest of Ms. Odessa Bradford who was falsely rumored to have been beaten and killed by a white police officer.[349] In 1965, another riot erupted in Los Angeles as a result of a police officer's actions during a police stop. By the time the Los Angeles riot was over, 34 people lay dead, 4,000 were arrested, and millions of dollars of property were destroyed.[350] Another riot in Detroit in 1967 left 43 people dead, 700 injured, and thousands without homes.[351]

Then there were the myriad voting rights violations. Throughout the nation, and particularly in the South, blacks were either being disenfranchised by discriminatory laws and regulations keeping them from voting, or were being overtly intimidated into staying away from the voting booth. Ensuring black Americans' abilities to vote became the next goal of Civil Rights Movement.

In January 1965, members of the Southern Christian Leadership Conference and the Student Nonviolent Coordinating Committee decided to target Selma, Alabama, due to the area's particularly low black voter registration rates and the brutality of the police response.[352] A series of marches aimed at improving black voter registration led to the disgraceful shooting death of Jimmie Lee Jackson at the hands of Alabama state troopers on February 18, 1965, as he tried to protect his mother from being beaten.[353]

In response, Movement leaders organized a march from Selma to Montgomery, Alabama, for Sunday, March 7. The march would take demonstrators along Highway 80 and across the Edmund Pettus Bridge,[xxiii] spanning the Alabama River in South Selma.

On the day of the march, the demonstrators were met by an overwhelming police force as they attempted to cross the bridge. They were violently taken down by the police in front of the cameras of the national news services. The images of the peaceful, mostly black demonstrators being clubbed and turned back by overaggressive police forces, including mounted policemen, left an indelible impression, and March 7, 1965, would forever be remembered as Black Sunday.[354]

Martin Luther King Jr., who was in Atlanta at the time of the confrontation, responded forcefully. On the same day as the attack on the marchers, King began recruiting religious leaders from all over the country to participate in a second attempt at crossing the Edmund Pettus Bridge on March 9. Under a federal court order prohibiting a second march until March 11 and despite pressure from President Johnson, Dr. King assembled the marchers on March 9 and walked to the bridge where, confronted by the Alabama National Guard and local troops, he asked the participants to kneel and pray. After a tense stand off between the armed policemen and the kneeling and prayerful marchers, King would direct the participants to turn around and abort the march.

The impact was stunning. Although initially subject to intense criticism for having blinked, the stark images of police authorities in full riot gear standing unyieldingly before a group of men and women kneeling in the streets of Alabama engaged in prayerful pleadings tugged at the sense of justice throughout the nation.

On March 15, 1965, President Johnson addressed Congress, identifying with the protestors. By March 19, Johnson submitted the draft of the Voting Rights Act of 1965, and on March 21, thousands of Americans, black and white, met in Selma, Alabama, and undertook their trek over the

xxiii The Edmund Pettus Bridge was named after Brigadier General Edmund Winston Pettus, a Selma lawyer who also served as Democratic Senator to the United Senate from 1897 through his death on July 27, 1907. At one time, he was Grand Dragon of the Alabama Ku Klux Klan.

EdmundPettus Bridge to Montgomery under the watchful eyes of federalized Alabama National Guardsmen.

On August 6, President Johnson signed the Voting Rights Act of 1965. The Act prohibited any restrictions on one's right to vote based on race, culminating a massive effort to protect the rights of racial minorities to access the voting booth. The passage of the back-to-back Civil Rights acts represented a massive success for those fighting for racial justice in America.

But on April 4, 1968, the unspeakable happened. Martin Luther King Jr. was assassinated.

Dr. King had gone to Memphis, Tennessee, in support of a strike by the black sanitary public works employees. Among the many demands of the striking black workers was the desire to be paid the same amount as white workers for time lost from work as a result of inclement weather.[355] On April 1, a self-avowed racist in pursuit of a big, imaginary reward for the murder of Martin Luther King Jr. rented a room across from the Lorraine Hotel where Dr. King reportedly had been staying.[356, 357] He stalked the Lorraine until 6:01 PM on April 4, 1968, when James Earl Ray finally got a clear shot at Dr. King. Ray fired a single bullet into his victim's neck severing Martin Luther King Jr.'s spinal cord.

The sudden and tragic loss of Dr. King sent shockwaves through the nation. Americans were incensed that a believer in peaceful resistance who had essentially become the symbol of the Civil Rights Movement and non-violent protests was killed in broad daylight. The outcry was particularly stark in America's black communities where rioting ensued in 168 cities resulting in over 27,000 arrests.[358]

Martin Luther King Jr. was a mere 39 years of age when he was killed by James Earl Ray, but in that brief period of time, he did more in the name of human dignity and Civil Rights than columns of men had achieved over the span of hundreds of years. His incredible mark on America's sense of justice and the values he represented serves no less an influence today than the day he marched onto the streets of Montgomery, Alabama, intent on correcting one of America's greatest ills.

The Contentious Road To School Desegregation

While the battle raged for generalized desegregation and voting rights, another parallel campaign was waged to integrate America's schools. It was a battle like no other, demonstrating the need for strong interventions by the federal government and by its courts. But it also highlighted the dangers of allowing those same institutions to take an excessively strong role in addressing issues directly impacting homes and communities.

The *Brown* decision, although a significant victory for Civil Rights in the United States and a major turning point for the legal standing of black Americans, resulted in a firestorm of resistance from Southern Democrats intent on protecting their way of life and the region's culture against the oppressive intrusions of the federal government. The ambiguity of the Court's *Brown* opinion added to the struggle. Although the Supreme Court acted to eradicate the separate but equal doctrine as a constitutionally appropriate model for public education, it did not comment on the necessary corrections. So by 1955, the parties returned to the Supreme Court to determine how to integrate the schools. Predictably, the Court refused to decide how integration should proceed, stating that those programs should be undertaken locally and then, as questions arose, the appropriateness of the program would be decided.[359] However, the Court did opine that desegregation should proceed with "all deliberate speed."[360]

The reaction to *Brown II* was immediate. Advocates for desegregation viewed the Court's final disposition as ineffective while those against took the ruling as a rallying cry to delay and obstruct desegregation efforts. Chief among the obstructionists was the Southern wing of the Democrat Party where Senators Strom Thurmon (D-SC), Richard Russell (D-GA), and Harry Byrd (D-VA) played pivotal roles in mounting a counter-attack.

Together, they promoted a resolution named the Southern Manifesto, which was signed by more than 100 southern federal legislators and expressed their disdain at the Court's *Brown* decisions while proclaiming their resolve to resist.[361] Citing the absence of a constitutional basis for its opinion, the signors warned of the "explosive and dangerous condition created by the [*Brown*] decision," and astonishingly accused it of ". . . destroying the amicable relations between the white and Negro races that have been created through 90 years of patient effort by the good people of both races. . . plant[ing] hatred and suspicion where there has been heretofore friendship and understanding."[362] Further, the signors pledged to ". . . use all lawful means to bring about a reversal of this decision" as they sought to right the wrong that had been created.[363]

Several techniques arose to either escape the grasps of the Supreme Court's new posture or to delay the implementation of the remedies the courts were invoking. The schools in Mansfield, Texas, quickly came under a court order to desegregate. The Mansfield School Board complied, but the mayor and the chief of police remained defiant and refused to cooperate with the board's decision. On August 30, 1956, protestors gathered with the aim of preventing black children from enrolling in Mansfield High School. The protestors hung and burned an effigy of a black student, brought cars bearing racist signs, and threatened harm upon black students who attempted to enter the building. The events caught the attention of Texas Governor Allan Shivers who refused to deploy the Texas Rangers to enforce the board's decision. President Eisenhower also refused to interfere.

In Arkansas, the Little Rock School Board created a blueprint for desegregation beginning in September, 1957, with the admission of nine black students into the all-white Little Rock Central High School, but the plan was vehemently opposed by the Governor of Arkansas, Orval Faubus.

On September 4, 1957, when the Little Rock Nine were scheduled to enter the school, a crowd of protesters assembled in front of Central High School. Governor Faubus, in disobedience to the Supreme Court's order and in direct defiance of the federal government, deployed the Arkansas National Guard to maintain the peace and prevent the entry of the black students. With the School Board condemning the Governor's actions, President Eisenhower tried to diffuse the situation by meeting with Faubus in the White House. His interventions failed under the weight of the Governor's resolve to keep the federal government from changing the culture of the people of Arkansas.

With the situation at a stalemate, the mayor of Little Rock asked the President to send in federal troops, and President Eisenhower made his intention known of complying with the mayor's request in order to enforce a federal court's order.

On September 23, Governor Faubus withdrew the National Guard from the area surrounding Central High School. But agitators and demonstrators remained despite a presidential order for them to cease and desist.[364] On September 24, the President deployed the white members of the 101st Airborne Division to maintain the peace and escort the black students into the school. Concurrently, President Eisenhower federalized the Arkansas National Guard, taking it out of the hands of Governor Faubus. [xxiv]

The Little Rock Nine gained entry into the school, but the harassment and torment of the students continued to the point where one of the nine was

---

[xxiv] The events in Arkansas raise the question of whether the President of the United States can use federal troops against American citizens.

Technically, the National Guard is a unit of the United States Armed Forces Reserves stemming from the militia clauses in Article I, Section 8 of the Constitution. It has its roots within the local militias formed by the earliest American colonies. These loosely bound units were further organized into colony-wide militias beginning with Massachusetts in 1636. ("The Nation's First. *Massachusetts National Guard*." accessed Apr. 11, 2015, http://www.thenationsfirst.org/the-nation-s-first.html on April 11, 2015) Although Congress was seemingly given plenary powers to form and maintain a militia, its initial action was to pass the Militia Act of 1792 providing for the organization of state militias and authorizing the President of the United States to deploy the militias during times of imminent invasion or insurrection. ["Militia Act of 1792" (Constitution Society), accessed on Apr. 11, 2015, http://www.constitution.org/mil/mil_act_1792.htm] Due to the nation's distrust of standing armies, the state militias played critical roles in the prosecutions of the War of 1812, the Civil War, the Mexican-American War, and the Spanish-American War.

In 1903, the Dick Act was passed, essentially defining the National Guard. At least two decentralizing measures were preserved. First, the governors were charged with approving or denying entry of the state National Guard into federal service. Additionally, entry into federal service was also subject to personal discretion. [Barry M. Stentiford, *The American Home Guard: The State Militia in the Twentieth Century*, (Texas A&M University Military History Series, 2002), 12-13] The Act also stated the National Guard could be ordered for service inside or outside of the United States. However, in 1912, Attorney General George Woodward Wickersham opined that sending the National Guard outside of the United States violated the Constitution. According to Wickersham, because the National Guard is a militia, it could only be deployed outside of the United States when in pursuit of an invading army. (Stentiford, *The American Home Guard: The State Militia in the Twentieth Century*, 13.)

expelled in December, 1957, after she dumped a bowl of chili upon a white male student in response to the taunting she received from him in the cafeteria. Another black student had acid thrown at her eyes, and yet another was subjected to a burning attempt when she was locked in a bathroom stall.

Ultimately, only Ernest Green, an Eagle Scout, would finish the curriculum. Although he became the first black student to graduate from Central High School, Arkansas' first foray into high school integration was anything but successful. In the meantime, Green would make it his life's vocation to work on minority and labor relations issues, eventually serving as Assistant Secretary of Labor for President Jimmy Carter.

While Arkansas struggled with the events at Central High School, Alabama dealt with its own issues. Autherine Lucy and Pollie Anne Myers were

---

In 1916, Congress required that guardsmen take an oath to support the Governor of their state *and* the President of the United States while giving superseding authority over the guard to the President. [*Rudy Perpich v. DOD*, 496 US 334 (1990)]

After World War I, the National Guard essentially lay decimated and stood virtually non-existent until 1933 when further actions by Congress reorganized the militia into a State National Guard and the National Guard of the United States. Under the new organizational plan, Congress, during times of a national emergency, could order these troops into active national service. Of significance, during the time of active duty service, guardsmen and guardswomen are relieved of their state guard position, only to return to their state service once Congress discontinues their recruitment. (*Perpich*, 496 US 334)

In 1952, Congress removed the presence of a national emergency as a condition for federalization of the National Guard. However, it implemented a gubernatorial consent requirement, which was in place at the time of the events in Arkansas. The gubernatorial consent requirement would not be partially repealed until the Montgomery Amendment in 1987, allowing gubernatorial discretion in foreign deployments when based on objections to location, purpose, type, or schedule of such active duty. (*Perpich*, 496 US 334)

Consequently, it appears that Eisenhower clearly stood within his Constitutional bounds in mobilizing federal troops into an American city. The act of a rogue governor bent on disobeying federal law could have easily been construed as an insurrection, or near to one. Eisenhower, then, was well justified in deploying federal troops to enforce federal law against the will of a defiant state.

Fortunately, Governor Faubus, the day prior to the federal military intervention withdrew his troops from Central High School and did not officially object to the presidential action. By his actions, Governor Faubus, who clearly objected to the will the President was attempting to exercise, consented to the federalization of the Arkansas National Guard. It is an interesting question as to how differently the events at Little Rock would have progressed militarily, historically, and constitutionally if Faubus would have resisted the federalization of the state militia and, worse yet, if he would have ordered the Arkansas National Guard to stand its ground in the face of the injection of federal troops.

admitted to study at a graduate program at the University of Alabama in 1952. However, unbeknownst to the university, both young ladies were black. When the university learned of their race, it promptly rescinded their admissions, but the women retained counsel to compel their enrollment into the school. The university resisted the women's legal actions.

On June 29, 1955, after the disposition of the *Brown* case, a federal judge ordered the two young ladies be enrolled at the University of Alabama. However, Myers had a history of an extra-marital pregnancy, ostensibly allowing the university to escape the court's order. Lucy was left to continue alone.[365]

On February 1, 1956, Lucy was escorted through the enrollment process and successfully began attending her graduate classes. By February 6, her third day of class, increasingly large and hostile crowds of demonstrators greeted Lucy and her security guards, prompting the university to exclude Lucy from the university due to safety concerns and thus end her attempt at obtaining a post-graduate education there.

The University of Alabama's segregation stance would continue undaunted until James Hood and Vivian Malone attempted to register in 1963. Hood and Malone had met the academic criteria for admission to the University of Alabama. They were being refused enrollment, but presented themselves to the university's campus anyway on June 11, 1963.

George Wallace, the Democratic Governor of Alabama, who in his inauguration speech had called for "segregation now, segregation tomorrow, segregation forever," stood at the university's front door to block the two students' entrance. The stalemate would end only after Wallace was ordered to step aside by Brigadier General Henry V. Graham under orders from President John F. Kennedy.[366] In a highly publicized spectacle, General Graham arrived on campus, flanked by four sergeants, walked up to Governor Wallace, saluted him, and said, "Sir, it is my sad duty to ask you to step aside under the orders of the President of the United States." Wallace would eventually yield, and Malone and Hood would register as students at the University of Alabama.

Lucy, on the other hand, would not attend the University of Alabama until 1988, obtaining her master's degree on May 9, 1992.[367, xxv]

In Virginia, the resolve to circumvent the effects of the *Brown* decisions came quickly and culminated in a legislative effort to immunize the state from the effects of federally mandated integration; an effort known as Massive Resistance. Democratic Governor Thomas Stanley, pressured by Democratic Senator Harry F. Byrd and the Byrd Organization, developed methods through which Virginia could circumvent the *Brown* decisions. The Stanley Plan, which was adopted by the Virginia Assembly in 1956, afforded the governor the authority to close any school in danger of being desegregated.[368] Stanley never exercised his newly obtained authority, but his Democratic successor, Governor Lindsay Almond, did.

In 1958, in reaction to federal judicial orders to desegregate schools in Charlottesville, Norfolk, and Front Royal, Almond ordered the closing of the affected public schools.[369] But the effects of the plan backfired as it was the white schools that were closed, negatively impacting approximately 10,000 white students whose families scrambled for alternative ways to provide their children with an education. Ironically, the black schools remained open due to the lack of interest on the part of white families to have their white children attend black schools.[370]

The affected schools remained closed until 1959, when the federal District Court declared the school closings unconstitutional, forcing the Virginia

---

xxv Interestingly, the 1901 Alabama Constitution offers the illusory protection against the superseding power of the Constitution of the United States. Section 256 of the Alabama Constitution still reads, "Separate schools shall be provided for white and colored children, and no child of either race shall be permitted to attend a school of the other race." The *Brown* decision, with its overarching interpretation of the Equal Protection Clause of the Fourteenth Amendment, essentially nullified this language, making it obsolete.

The Alabama constitution's segregation ban was brought to a ballot in 2004 in the hopes of overturning the onerous and overtly racist provision, but the measure failed by less than 2,000 votes. In 2012, another attempt was made, but this one was peppered with language denying Alabamans the right to an education, leading segregationists and desegregationists, alike, to oppose the measure. Amendment 4, as it was called, failed miserably at the poles, 39% to 61%. The segregationist language, although rendered legally meaningless, still haunts the Alabama Constitution.

Supreme Court of Appeals to nullify the law. The schools in Norfolk, Charlottesville, and Front Royal subsequently reopened.[371]

One Virginia jurisdiction however, Prince Edward County, took a decidedly different tack. Under court order to integrate its schools, Prince Edward County decided to completely close its public school system. White families, with their economic and political advantages, created organizations like the Prince Edward Foundation with the purpose educating white children. Black families resorted to organizing makeshift schools in their churches, sending their children to other communities to be educated by family members, and taking their children to other states to be educated by the Society of Friends.[372]

On March 30, 1964, the Supreme Court of the United States ruled that ". . . closing the Prince Edward County schools while public schools in all the other counties of Virginia were being maintained denied the petitioners and the class of Negro students they represent the Equal Protection of the laws guaranteed by the Fourteenth Amendment."[373] The Court's decision put an end to the Prince Edward County school closures and snuffed out the final stand of Massive Resistance.[374]

But Massive Resistance was not the last racist obstruction implemented by Democrats. Other interventions were designed to prevent the integration of the students in segregated districts. Pupil Placement Boards were created and empowered with broad authorities to assign students to the various schools using criteria other than race, but which operated to maintain school segregation.[375] Such techniques included reassigning children already attending schools to their same schools while preferentially assigning newly enrolled students elsewhere in a manner that would separate the children by race.[376] The result was that the preponderance of black children remained in black schools while virtually no white child was assigned to those same schools.

With the passage of the Civil Rights Act and its Title VI provision that withheld money from those schools that remained segregated, compliance marginally improved, but in many areas, local authorities searched for innovative ways to maintain segregation while still remaining eligible for federal moneys. Despite the efforts of the Courts and Congress, it appeared, 10 years after *Brown II*, that the country was little closer at enacting the Supreme Court's directive of desegregation, and it is here where the role of the courts began changing from decidedly judicial, to decidedly interventionist in nature.

In 1968, a complaint was filed in Kent County, Virginia, charging that the local school board had been employing Pupil Placement Boards, effectively maintaining segregation. In March of that year, motivated by the desire to keep federal funds, the school board elected to create a freedom of choice plan.[377] Under the plan, pupils, except first and eighth graders attending each school, were given the opportunity to go to the only other public school in Kent County.[378] Predictably, no white children chose to attend an all-black school and only 115 black students were sent to the white schools.[379] When a complaint was filed regarding the persistence of segregation in Kent County schools, the plan fell under judicial scrutiny. Seeing the continued separate educational system within the state of Virginia, the Court held that the freedom of choice plan was "intolerable" due to its inability to ". . . provide meaningful assurance of prompt and effective disestablishment of a dual system."[380] The Court then called for ". . . meaningful and immediate progress toward disestablishment of state-imposed segregation."[381] In fashioning its description of what it would consider a desegregated school the Court laid out six markers eventually known as the *Green* factors. They were: 1) student assignment; 2) faculty assignment; 3) staff assignment; 4) transportation; 5) extracurricular activities; and 6) facilities. Each of these factors needed to be desegregated in order for the school to be considered "unitary."[382]

In some areas, the Court's bold call for an aggressive resolution to state-sponsored school segregation prompted more innovative, good-faith solutions to the problem. The natural inclination was to simply open enrollment to all members of a community, which would lead to the natural and immediate desegregation of a local public school. However, that approach was deemed insufficient due to the racially and economically segregated nature of many of the nation's communities. As a result, the mere opening of local schools to members of all races was not acceptable to the courts.

As an alternative approach, school boards redrew district maps to capture a more varied segment of the area's population. Legal complaints subsequently arose, claiming the efforts were still insufficient under the criteria required in *Green*. One such situation arose in Charlotte, North Carolina, that reflected the growing pattern of direct judicial intervention in the matter. The school board implemented changes to improve the racial make-up of its schools. Soon after, a suit was brought in the federal court. The district court agreed that the measures were insufficient to comply with the standards mandated in *Green* and ordered the school board to develop plans for faculty and student desegregation in order to present them to the court for review. This process of plan submission went back and forth at least twice before the district court decided the Charlotte-Mecklenburg efforts were "unacceptable" and moved forward with its own plan.[383]

Without any precedence or authority, the district court hired its own expert to devise a solution to the segregation problem. Clearly acting in both an extra-constitutional *legislative* and *executive* capacity, the court adopted a modified version of the school board's plan and required an additional 300 black students be transferred to one of the previously all-white schools.[384] As opposed to the school board's plan, the court's plan included the active desegregation of elementary schools as well.[385]

This court-initiated, forced busing scheme was appealed to the Supreme Court, which upheld the action in *Swann v. Charlotte-Mecklenburg Bd. of Education*.[386]

With the approval of court-ordered forced transfers of students as a solution for school segregation, federal courts implemented such programs across the country. Forced busing programs then appeared in major metropolitan centers throughout the United States, most notably in urban centers such as Boston, Kansas City, Richmond, Detroit, Cleveland, and San Francisco. But for many—including many black parents—the prospect of having their children sent to a school that was miles away when a perfectly appropriate option existed within blocks of their homes seemed nonsensical and oppressive. Although they were powerless to resist an unchecked judiciary, many responded with active resistance, with communities such as Louisville and Boston requiring police intervention to control the crowds.

Another Supreme Court dispute arose in the federal district court overseeing Detroit. Finding that it could not adequately address the issue of segregation within Detroit's school system while employing an intra-city approach, the Court decided it would force transfer children from surrounding districts in order to reach racial balance. But the concept of transferring children between districts was too much for the Court, forcing it to put a stop to the program. In short, the Supreme Court concluded, "[n]o single tradition in public education is more deeply rooted than local control over the operation of schools . . . "[387]

Seeing a limitation in the scope of the courts' authorities to order the forced transfer of students to only single jurisdictions and not *across* jurisdictions, whites seeking to avoid busing began moving from the affected metropolitan areas to the surrounding suburbs, a phenomenon known as "white flight."[388] The ironic effect of this migration was to leave many metro areas more segregated than ever. Further, major municipalities inhabited by minority and poorer populations dominated many cities, sending central city governments into fiscal crisis.[389]

Today, urban centers continue to suffer from the devastating effects of the exodus of its economic base to suburban areas creating islands of poverty and minimal economic mobility. In retrospect, the question must be asked whether these court initiated actions actually served the best interests of the communities, or as is argued by many, whether they overstepped their bounds with devastating effects.

Affirmative Action and Governmental Corrections to Discrimination

Like in the nation's schools, the issue of violence and inequality among the races continued to riddle the country during the 1960s. Believing the disruptions resulted from a broad ranging conspiracy,[390] President Johnson resolved to address the problem by creating the National Advisory Commission on Civil Disorders, or the Kerner Commission. The Commission, named after Illinois Governor Otto Kerner, was to investigate the causes of race riots within the United States and to make recommendations for the improvement of socio-ethnic conditions within the country.

The result was one of the most ineffective efforts at improving race relations of the 1960s. In contradiction to the suspicions of President Johnson, the Commission failed to confirm conspiratorial elements. Instead, the essence of the Report warned that the country was moving into two societies, a black one and a white one—separate and unequal—with the main culprit being white racism.[391]

Johnson took the Commission's conclusions as a rebuke of his social programs and recognized the prohibitive expense of the Commission's recommendations.[392] With the election of Richard Nixon who had taken an unapologetic tone for America's history, the Kerner Commission's findings never took hold and faded into the pages of American history.

Despite its non-implementation, the Kerner Commission Report demonstrated the flawed reasoning of modern liberalism. First, it placed the cause of the episodes of civil unrest squarely on the backs of white racism without considering other issues that may have been at play. Second, it biasedly pointed to the development of two Americas, a white one and a black one, even though the reality in the latter half of the twentieth century was much more complicated. Third, it suggested the problems resulting in civil unrest throughout the nation were rooted in racism despite the fact that the riots discussed by the Commission did not take place in the nation's hotbeds of racism. And finally, the solutions envisioned by the Commission were based on the assumption that direct government intervention was required to rectify the situation. The role of government according to the Kerner Commission was not to help secure safety and security for the individual, but to arrange favorable outcomes for a subgroup of America's population.

In sum, the Kerner Report was emblematic of twentieth-century liberal thought and the tenets that drove it. In advocating for solutions, it could have based them on a legally level playing field. Instead, it abandoned any emphasis on the individual as the driver of reform and placed its emphasis on government interventions designed to respond to grievances. It was a philosophy that was adopted not just by liberals within the political spectrum. Having achieved the necessary legislative and judicial corrections to achieve equality before the law with the passage of the Civil Rights Act of 1964 and the Voting Rights Act of 1965, the call for Civil Rights for racial minorities shifted to a more unconstitutional goal: a guarantee for equality in *outcomes*. This was a role for which American governance was never designed and ran counter to every precept of the foundation of the American Republic.

The adoption of this interventionist philosophy preceded a rapid decline in the entrepreneurial activity within the black community.[393] Within a decade of its adoption, there developed a growing dependence on state-administered corrections, grievance advocacy, and reliance on welfare programs. Rapidly, the incentive for the individual to escape poverty and socioeconomic disadvantages dissipated and was replaced by a demand for the support and assistance from another; in this case government, be it local, state, or federal.[394]

One of the products of this philosophy was affirmative action, the policy of preferentially hiring and promoting members of a disadvantaged group, ostensibly with the goal of atoning for, or neutralizing, historical patterns of repression, exploitation, and discrimination. These policies can be traced to President John F. Kennedy's Executive Order 10925 issued on March 6, 1961, establishing the President's Committee on Equal Opportunity. In Subpart III, Section 301(a) dealing with requirements for agreements between contractors and the federal government, the President wrote:

> *The contractor will not discriminate against any employee or applicant for employment because of race, creed, color, or national origin. The contractor will take affirmative action to ensure that applicants are employed, and that employees are treated during employment, without regard to their race, creed, color, or national origin. Such action shall include, but not be limited to, the following: employment, upgrading, demotion or transfer; recruitment or recruitment advertising; layoff or termination; rates of pay or other forms of compensation; and selection*

> *for training, including apprenticeship. The contractor agrees to post in conspicuous places, available to employees and applicants for employment, notices to be provided by the contracting officer setting forth the provisions of this nondiscrimination clause.*
>
> (John F. Kennedy, Executive Order 10925, March 6, 1961)

It is striking that this Order did *not* call for the preferential hiring of minorities, but rather, the discontinuation of discriminatory hiring and promoting practices. This language was repeated in President Lyndon B. Johnson's later Executive Order regarding Equal Employment Opportunity.[395]

At some point during the Lyndon B. Johnson administration, the goal of the policy no longer was equal opportunities among races, but rather to ensure even distribution among classes. As Johnson pointed out in his commencement speech before Howard University, "We seek. . . not just equality as a right and a theory, but equality as a fact and equality as a result."[396]

The implications of a President calling for "equality as a result" in a country founded on equality of opportunity was not fully appreciated, but is nonetheless startling. No longer would the ideal be maximizing opportunities for individual pursuits defined by a person's aspirations. Instead, government was to guarantee that all achieve an equal result in social, political, and economic standing. This evolving vision for the role of the American federal government was interventionist in nature and a radical departure from what previously existed. It was a view shared by a large portion of the day's youths who faced the challenges of a rapidly changing society.

Clearly, the solutions for which Johnson espoused were inconsistent with the societal premises that gave rise to the Constitution and of the nation's exceptional nature. They were restrictive, repressive in their applications, and dehumanizing in their ultimate results.

Interestingly, and despite their allegiances to different parties, Johnson's equality guarantee was to be strengthened through the actions of President Nixon. In 1969, Philadelphia was ripe for a correction in the distribution of its racial hierarchy. The city saw massive rioting in 1964 and was home to about 2 million blacks that were underemployed, particularly in the construction fields.[397] The reason, according to the Department of Labor, was the high reliance by local contracting companies on craft unions as a source of labor coupled with the exclusionary practices of the unions with regards to minorities.[398] As a result, only about 5% of the area's construction workers were black.[399]

To remedy this situation, the Nixon Administration ordered that contractors bidding for work in federally funded construction projects include specific goals for using minorities.[400] The plan included a grid of the percentage of minority workers that would be hired in the contracted projects, spanning from a 4%-8% minority participation rate before 1970 to a 19% -23% minority participation rate in 1973.

The Philadelphia Plan and its progeny ushered in a tidal wave of preferential treatment of minorities. Throughout the country, people were provided opportunities, not because they were better qualified or possessed superior experiences or training, but merely because they would fill a slot devoted to persons of a particular skin color or background.

Over time, new and innovative ways of applying the concept of preferential treatment to minority groups developed. One such example dealt with medical school admission practices.

Allan Bakke was a white, 35-year-old National Merit Scholar from the University of Minnesota with a 3.51 GPA. He had served in Vietnam as a commanding officer of an anti-aircraft battery unit with the United States Marine Corps and worked at NASA as an engineer. In 1973, he applied to twelve medical schools, including the University of California-Davis Medical School, in an effort to become a doctor. He was rejected in all twelve despite having been favorably interviewed at UC-Davis. He applied again to UC-Davis in 1973 and was again rejected despite his superior scores and evaluations compared to those of some of the minority students that gained admission.

After his second rejection, Bakke sued in state court asking it to compel the university to grant him admission to the medical school. He based his plea on the allegation that he had been rejected because he was white, in violation of the Fourteenth Amendment's Equal Protection Clause.[401]

The case made its way to the Supreme Court, which agreed that in 1978 the strict quota system applied by UC-Davis was unconstitutional, but it upheld the use of race as one of many factors a university could consider in selecting students. Additionally, because UC-Davis was unable to prove that it would *not* have admitted Bakke if there had been no affirmative action program in place, the Court ordered the university to admit Bakke to its medical school class.

Bakke attended UC-Davis and sued the institution again for his legal fees, which he won. He graduated in 1982 and eventually worked for the Mayo Clinic as an anesthesiologist.

The manner in which race affected the allocation of federal funds also came under judicial scrutiny following the enactment of the Public Works Employment Act of 1977. This law required municipalities receiving federal funds for public works to spend 10% of those funds on minority businesses. The Act defined minority businesses as those where Negroes, Spanish-speaking, Orientals, Indians, Eskimos, and Aleuts owned at least 50% of the business. A group of contractors sued claiming the congressional action, in preferentially selecting minority groups, violated the Equal Protection Clause of the Fourteenth Amendment.

The Court disagreed, citing the small impact that 10% of the funds would have on the industry and the reasonableness of Congress's actions in its determination to correct past discriminatory practices.[402] But Justice John Paul Stevens dissented, stating the allocation ". . . creat[ed] monopoly privileges in a $400 million market for a class of investors defined solely by racial characteristics."[403] He also shared his concern about the consequences of the governmental actions, observing, "History teaches us that the costs associated with a sovereign's grant of exclusive privileges often encompasses more that the high prices and shoddy workmanship that are familiar handmaidens of monopoly; they engender animosity and discontent as well."[404] Justice Stevens ended his dissent by noting the particular inappropriateness of the congressional action when no evidence was provided that the preferred class of the legislation was ". . . less able to compete in the future."[405]

Justice Stevens' position would migrate to the majority as the Court, in later cases, expressed its discomfort with unconstrained affirmative action programs. In 1989, when a school board decided it would shrink down the number of its employees by preferentially discharging non-minority workers, the Court held the policy offensive to the Constitution.[406] In *City of Richmond v. J.A. Croson Company*, the Court struck down a program that required companies receiving city construction contracts to award at least 30% if its subcontracts to companies designated as minority businesses.[407] Perhaps even more importantly, the *Croson* Court directed that the constitutional appropriateness of any race-based action by government be reviewed using strict scrutiny.[408] This is important because the instruction speaks directly to the level of difficulty the government would have in defending an affirmative action program. In reviewing constitutional questions, the care or suspicion with which the Court reviews the merits of governmental action is referred to as scrutiny and is classified as minimum, moderate, or strict. Strict scrutiny is the highest level of judicial review and the most difficult for the government to defend against. It is applied, for example, to cases involving national origin, religion, voting rights, interstate travel, and the right to access the courts among other highly protected rights. In *Croson*, the Supreme Court essentially informed the lower courts that they need to employ strict scrutiny in cases dealing with race as well. Under strict scrutiny, the burden of proof falls on the government to show that its actions address a compelling state interest and are narrowly tailored to the goal. Strict scrutiny is such a difficult standard that an action subject to it is generally not upheld.[xxvi]

In response to the increasing hostility of the courts to government-initiated affirmative corrections, President Clinton provided a directive to

[xxvi] For cases involving quasi-suspected classifications, such as gender, the courts apply middle scrutiny, where the government must demonstrate its actions are related to an important state interest and is substantially related to that interest.

The lowest level of scrutiny is minimum, or rational basis scrutiny, and is applied to all other classes of plaintiffs (or complainants). Here, the burden of proof falls upon the plaintiff (not the government) to show that the governmental action is not rationally related to a legitimate state interest. In these cases, the government more often prevails.

executive agencies ordering them to eliminate or reform any program that created quotas, established preferences for unqualified individuals, or engaged in reverse discrimination practices. He also directed the discontinuation of any program that completed its purpose of equal opportunity.[409]

Although the Clinton memorandum chilled federal affirmative action programs, many states continued to employ methods of preferential treatment in selecting those with whom they contracted and those admitted into their schools. For example, the University of Texas School of Law continued to employ a review method of its middle-tier applicants that would allow for admission of applicants with lower numerical scores if they were black, or of Mexican descent. The Fifth Circuit Court, in applying its strict scrutiny standard, found the program was inadmissible because, according to the court, the promotion of a diverse student body was not a compelling state interest under the Fourteenth Amendment.[410]

However, the Ninth Circuit saw the matter differently in a similar case, finding that maintaining the ethnic and racial diversity of a university's incoming class was indeed a compelling state interest.[411]

In the face of such disagreement, the Supreme Court took up the question in *Gratz v. Bollinger*,[412] agreeing with the Ninth Circuit that the promotion of student diversity was indeed a compelling state interest.

The challenges against affirmative action programs would continue, and in 2003, the Court would have another opportunity to comment on the matter; this time regarding the admission policies at the University of Michigan College of Literature, Science, and the Arts. Here, the College allocated 20 points to underrepresented minority applicants for its freshman class to allow them an advantage over other ethnic groups. The Supreme Court struck the system down because, in the Court's opinion, the school's solution was not the most narrowly tailored intervention it could have devised.[413] In doing so, the Court reaffirmed its position that diversity promotion was a valid consideration for secondary schools in designing the composition of their classes, but the program would be offensive to the Constitution if the effort at achieving such diversity was not narrowly tailored.

So what does an appropriate affirmative action program look like according to the Court? In *Grutter v. Bollinger et al.*,[414] decided on the same day as *Gratz*, the Supreme Court upheld one run by the University of Michigan Law School. Specifically, the Court liked that the law school did not define diversity ". . . solely in terms of race or ethnicity."[415] The Court acknowledged the appropriateness of the Law School's commitment to diversity and its special attention to the inclusion of African-American, Hispanic, and Native-American students who otherwise might not be adequately represented in the student body. According to the Court, the University of Michigan Law School aimed to enroll a 'critical mass' of underrepresented minority students to ensure those members' abilities to contribute to the Law School's character and to the legal profession. In doing so, the law school escaped the prohibitions of the Equal Protection Clause.

But the courts have not been the only governmental bodies struggling with the issue of affirmative action programs. Since the 1990s, states have also been active in either restricting or prohibiting them. In California, Proposition 209 was placed on the general ballot as a state constitutional amendment on November 5, 1996, the crux of which stated, "The state shall not discriminate against, or grant preferential treatment to, any individual or group on the basis of race, sex, color, ethnicity, or national origin in the operation of public employment, public education, or public contracting."[416] The proposition passed 65.6% to 45.4%, essentially prohibiting any new affirmative action programs from being employed.

In Washington, Initiative 200, a referendum similar to that of California passed on November 3, 1998. And in Florida, Governor Jeb Bush invoked a prohibition upon the use of race as a consideration in government contracting or school admissions within the state.

Predictably, the legal attacks upon such state-based measures soon followed. In 2006, Michigan voters passed Proposal 2 by 58% to 42%. The Proposal, like those in California and Washington, amended the state's constitution to prohibit the state from ". . .discriminat[ing] against, or grant[ing] preferential treatment to, any individual or group on the basis of race, sex, color, ethnicity, or national origin in the operation of public employment, public education, or public contracting."[417] The Coalition to Defend Affirmative Action and others sued the state to overturn the measure on a constitutional basis. The Supreme Court of the United States ultimately upheld the Proposal.

The issue of race relations and civil rights predates the nation's founding. Admittedly, it has been one marred by injustice, bigotry, and hatred. As we have seen, their corrections have sometimes been as misguided as the problems they aimed to correct.

In reviewing the nation's approach to this complex problem, it is apparent that government's intrusions into the relations of men can be more obtrusive than helpful, more restrictive than liberating, and more confusing than enlightening. Perhaps the time has come to abandon the misguided and historically counterproductive beliefs that government officials are best suited to solve societal problems and return to the time-honored principles that guided the nation's Founders and Framers. It is the people, armed with a strong and reverential belief in a kind and benevolent Creator, that are in the best position to manage problems of such complexity and personal impact.

Perhaps, after all we have learned, all we have toiled, and all we have accomplished (and sometimes worsened), we are finally in a position to understand that the concept of natural law that gave rise to this nation is indeed the most appropriate model to inform the relations of men; assuming, of course, that the citizenry is ingrained with a strong regard for the rights of man, and with a strong faith in the appropriateness of its purpose.

Chapter 5

Consequences and Corrections

Today's Constitution is a different document than it was at the time of its ratification. Over two centuries of history, some significant additions, and the influence of activist courts have made the Constitution operate far differently from the product the Framers created. The changing of the legislative environment also had significant effects upon the nation and society. Some of these changes have been resoundingly positive, but others have had effects much more deleterious than helpful.

Throughout the pages of this book, we identified those areas where the most harmful deviations from the nation's initial visions took place. We explored the indelible stain of slavery and the harm it caused upon countless people and to the character of an otherwise great nation. We also saw that even after the shedding of massive quantities of blood for the permanent eradication of that vile institution, the nation was left to deal with a deep-rooted level of hatred and animus against a group of Americans based only on the color of their skin.

We saw the ill effects of a centralized government unleashed upon matters it was never meant to manipulate or control. We saw the zeal with which the federal government craves fiscal fuels to expand its powers and promote its growth. We also saw the government's proclivity to extricate God from the public forum and how the abandonment of religion and faith resulted in the deterioration of the family and morality in American culture. And we saw how the promotion of an excessive dependence on government robbed people of their liberties, their drive for success, and for some, their dignity.

A historical review of the nation's young history makes these findings irrefutable. The only question left for us to answer is how to restore those principles and mechanisms to our governing structure so that the nation may once again shine as the beacon of liberty, hope, and opportunity.

In the following pages, we will explore steps that should be taken to restore the engine that runs a great nation. We begin with measures to restore the proper size of government. We then follow by evaluating race relations and propose a bold new vision through which the peaceful coexistence of the various racial and ethnic groups may be enhanced. We then look at the office of the presidency and the recently identified threats to its integrity. We develop corrections to the judiciary with the aim of restoring its proper place in American jurisprudence and in policy development. And most importantly, we explore the necessary changes that will allow a restoration of God and religious worship to its central position within society and government.

1. Taxation Policy and the Nation's Financial Health

Without question, the federal government has become much larger and more intrusive than the Framers of the Constitution ever intended. Its growth is the clear result of a philosophy promoting centralized governance and one inconsistent with the principles of separation of powers inspiring America's founding. Key to the support of this growth is the federal government's expanded tax collecting authority. Indeed, a cursory evaluation of America's taxation history proves the government's unquenchable lust for the people's money.

Between 1789 and 1850, the federal government collected approximately $1.16 billion in taxes, for a collection rate of just under $20 million per year.[418] Similarly, between 1850 and 1900, despite the devastating effects of a colossally destructive and massively expensive Civil War, the federal government only collected $14.5 billion for an average of about $289 million per year. Even in 1915, the year of the passage of the Sixteenth Amendment, the United States showed $716 million in revenues.[419] But by 1916, the year immediately following the ratification of the Sixteenth Amendment, collections shot up to $1.1 billion, an increase of 144%, and by 1920, a mere three years later, federal revenue reached a temporary peak of $6.6 billion for an increase of 1,856% over a mere five years.[420] Federal revenue would continue to rise over the ensuing century to a total of *$3 trillion* in 2014.[421]

Separate from the federal government's taxing powers are its powers to spend, which, as we saw in decisions such as *Butler* and *Steward Machine Co.*, have loosened almost to the point that only Congress's imagination limits where it can spend the people's money. During the eighteenth and nineteenth centuries, federal spending and associated debt was essentially limited to funding the nation's military conflicts and to addressing the inherent costs of running government. This trend continued into the twentieth century with the national experience in funding World War I. Things changed with World War II and the nation's run up to it. The period of the Great Depression spelled the first time in American history where the federal government's spending, collecting, and borrowing powers coalesced to a size where it could manipulate the nation's economy through its expenditures.

In 1935, Congress passed the Social Security Act, creating the program to provide economic security for the elderly. As originally intended, benefits would be paid to the primary workers who turned 65 based on the payroll tax contributions they made during their lives. In order to obtain the authority to collect and keep workers' "contributions," Congress passed the Federal Insurance Contributions Act. The money collected from the nation's employees and the matching contributions from their employers would be placed in a Social Security Trust Fund created by Congress for that purpose.[422]

In 1937, the first year of Social Security collection, the program took in $265 million dollars and distributed nothing. By 2014, the program collected over $628 billion and distributed about $706 billion. In total, Social Security has collected $15.5 trillion and distributed $12.8 trillion.[423] Ominously, and perhaps predictably, the White House estimates that Social Security will become insolvent by 2030.[424]

Similarly, in 1965, Congress created Medicare and Medicaid.[i] Just like Social Security, the Medicare and Medicaid programs have grown precipitously, taking in $915 million in 1966, its first year of collections, compared to $603.7 billion in 2014. In parallel fashion, in 1966, the government spent $64 million in Medicare and Medicaid compared to $606.1 billion in 2014.[425] Although the expectation has been that Medicare and Medicaid would become insolvent at some point during the 2020s, changes resulting from the 2009 Affordable Care Act have indefinitely delayed the projected insolvency date for non-hospital services while extending the projected insolvency date for the Hospital Insurance Trust Fund to 2030.[426]

Butler and *Steward Machine Company* also cleared the road for the federal government to gobble up the autonomies of the various state governments through its budgetary allocations. There are various measures that demonstrate just how big the federal government's influence on state budgets and their activities really is. One measure is the ratio of moneys received by the state from the federal government compared to the state's total expenditures. In 2005, this ratio stood at 42.5%, meaning that for every dollar states spent, 42.5 cents were provided to them by the federal government.[427] The size of the federal government's funding of the states' economies is another measure and stands at 20% of the states' gross state product.[428] Additionally, federal contributions to state retirement and non-retirement benefits stood at 62%.[429]

---

[i] Medicare is a medical insurance program for seniors and disabled Americans. Medicaid is federal assistance program for states, for among other purposes, to assist in paying hospital and medical bills for low-income persons.

These numbers tell a compelling story of the explosion of federal intrusion into states' policies and economies that is made even greater by the myriad of requirements for participation in order for the states to *earn* federal funding. Clearly, such a dependence on the federal government runs counter to maintaining state sovereignty as a check against limitless federal power. If the original intent of the Constitution is to be restored, this overwhelming influence upon state governments and policies by the federal government must be countered.

No single solution for this growing imbalance of power is capable of rectifying the situation. Instead, a multi-faceted approach must be undertaken, the most important of which is passage of a balanced-budget amendment. Requiring Congress to spend an amount commensurate with its revenue will bring fiscal responsibility to governance. It will shrink government's footprint, both regulatory and economic. Perhaps most importantly, it will force lawmakers to make more sound decisions regarding the programs worthy of public finding.

One argument against a balanced-budget amendment maintains that the legislature must be given as much discretion as possible with which to address the economic and financial stressors of the day. This is a valid consideration. However, for the 103 years since the ratification of the Sixteenth Amendment, Congress's consistent actions have been relentless fiscal and regulatory expansion. The only correction is to curb government spending, and in an environment where government has proven unable to curb its own habits, it falls upon the people to intervene. Indeed, it is the *only* option.

In 2013, Congress presented a balanced budget amendment through House Resolution 1. This constitutional proposal capped total outlays while providing Congress with a supermajority override provision. It also allowed exceptions for times of war, or when Congress, through joint resolution, declares the United States to be engaged in military conflict that poses an imminent and serious threat to national security. The bill is reproduced, in its entirety, below:

113th CONGRESS
1st Session

H. J. RES. 1

Proposing a balanced budget amendment to the Constitution of the United States.

IN THE HOUSE OF REPRESENTATIVES

January 3, 2013

Mr. Goodlatte (for himself, Mr. Bachus, Mr. Bilirakis, Mrs. Blackburn, Mr. Boustany, Mr. Buchanan, Mr. Chabot, Mr. Chaffetz, Mr. Coffman, Mr. Collins of Georgia, Mr. Conaway, Mr. Crawford, Mr. Culberson, Mr. Duncan of South Carolina, Mr. Duncan of Tennessee, Mr. Franks of Arizona, Mr. Garrett, Mr. Gerlach, Mr. Griffith of Virginia, Mr. Huizenga of Michigan, Mr. Hultgren, Mr. Hurt, Mr. King of Iowa, Mr. Labrador, Mr. Lamborn, Mr. Lance, Mr. Luetkemeyer, Mr. Marino, Mrs. Miller of Michigan, Mr. Miller of Florida, Mr. Mulvaney, Mr. Nugent, Mr. Olson, Mr. Poe of Texas, Mr. Posey, Mrs. McMorris Rodgers, Mr. Roe of Tennessee, Mr. Roskam, Mr. Smith of Texas, Mr. Sensenbrenner, Mr. Walberg, Mr. Westmoreland, Mr. Wilson of South Carolina, Mr. Dent, Mr. Palazzo, Mr. McKinley, Mr. Pearce, Mr. Gibbs, and Mr. Broun of Georgia) introduced the following joint resolution; which was referred to the Committee on the Judiciary

JOINT RESOLUTION

Proposing a balanced budget amendment to the Constitution of the United States.

Resolved by the Senate and House of Representatives of the United States of America in Congress assembled (two-thirds of each House concurring therein), That the following article is proposed as an amendment to the Constitution of the United States, which shall be valid to all intents and purposes as part of the Constitution when ratified by the legislatures of three-fourths of the several States within seven years after the date of its submission for ratification:

Article —

Section 1. Total outlays for any fiscal year shall not exceed total receipts for that fiscal year, unless three-fifths of the whole number of each House of Congress shall provide by law for a specific excess of outlays over receipts by a rollcall vote.

Section 2. Total outlays for any fiscal year shall not exceed one-fifth of economic output of the United States, unless two-thirds of each House of Congress shall provide for a specific increase of outlays above this amount.

Section 3. The limit on the debt of the United States held by the public shall not be increased unless three-fifths of the whole number of each House shall provide by law for such an increase by a rollcall vote.

Section 4. Prior to each fiscal year, the President shall transmit to the Congress a proposed budget for the United States Government for that fiscal year in which total outlays do not exceed total receipts.

Section 5. A bill to increase revenue shall not become law unless three-fifths of the whole number of each House shall provide by law for such an increase by a rollcall vote.

Section 6. The Congress may waive the provisions of this article for any fiscal year in which a declaration of war is in effect. The provisions of this article may be waived for any fiscal year in which the United States is engaged in military conflict which causes an imminent and serious military threat to national security and is so declared by a joint resolution, adopted by a majority of the whole number of each House, which becomes law. Any such waiver must identify and be limited to the specific excess or increase for that fiscal year made necessary by the identified military conflict.

Section 7. The Congress shall enforce and implement this article by appropriate legislation, which may rely on estimates of outlays and receipts.

Section 8. Total receipts shall include all receipts of the United States Government except those derived from borrowing. Total outlays shall include all outlays of the United States Government except for those for repayment of debt principal.

Section 9. This article shall take effect beginning with the fifth fiscal year beginning after its ratification.

A second reform centers around the method by which the federal government amasses revenue. As we saw, the direct taxation of the people by the federal government is inconsistent with the Framers' vision. For one, the Sixteenth Amendment did not provide any check on the amount the federal government set out to collect from the American people. In the original model, the federal government's reliance on the various state governments for revenue collection served as an inherent check to the zeal with which the federal government could pursue its revenues.

Multiple solutions have been proffered as federal taxation alternatives. The flat tax, with its predefined income tax percentage, would carry with it the advantage of essentially eliminating the pernicious social engineering component in current tax policy. But since a flat tax on income could be placed at whatever level policymakers desire, it may well have little effect on the total revenues collected by the federal government. Nor would it, by itself, have any control on the amount the federal government spends.[ii] And the counter-argument is that the flat tax unduly burdens the poor, as a 20% tax, for example, would represent a much greater burden on those with limited means than it would on wealthier taxpayers.

Another recommendation is to get rid of the income tax altogether and implement a sales tax model. A sales tax would generate revenue through taxes assessed on the sales of goods and services. Although argued to be much more simplistic than the present tax plan, there are at least four conceivable dangers to the sales taxation scheme. First, if not properly implement it could provide the federal government with yet another taxing tool to the present income tax. Second, a sales tax tends to inhibit productivity, as the cost of purchasing goods and services predictably would rise. Third, although sales taxation is ostensibly billed as leveling the playing field, there is nothing

[ii] Additionally, a flat tax could offer significant savings in its administration as it would be much cheaper to implement and administer than the greater than $12 billion presently budgeted to the Internal Revenue Center each year. (Budget in Brief; Internal Revenue Service; FY 2015, U.S. Department of Treasury) Moreover, the administrative costs to the general public of complying with the present tax scheme has been estimated at $431 billion. (The Laffer Center. *http://www.laffer-center.com/wp-content/uploads/2011/06/2011-Laffer-TaxCodeComplexity.pdf.*)

in the mere concept of a sales tax to prohibit the unequal taxation of goods or services, nor is there any guarantee that Congress would not unevenly implement the tax to favor or disfavor certain groups of people or industries. Essentially, under a sales tax model, Congress would remain in the business of social engineering and of enabling favored activities. Finally, as would be the case with a flat income tax, the even application of a sales tax would excessively burden the poor over the rich.

In reality, the question of which taxation scheme the nation ought to be using, and in what manner, is a policy decision fraught with endless implications to the nation's economy and to the government's power. It would ultimately and continuously fall upon the American people to decide which they find preferable.

But there is a greater problem that evolved over the span of America's taxation and fiscal history that also needs to be addressed. As we discussed, the passage of the Sixteenth Amendment opened a massive source of revenue for the federal government, and the Seventeenth Amendment weakened the national legislature's loyalty to the states. The cumulative effects of adopting the two amendments is the equivalent of supplying an alcoholic with an unlimited supply of bourbon while telling him that he no longer has to answer to those close to him about his drinking habits. Although arguably, the voters serve as the natural limiting factor to an overactive taxing authority, their objections have been historically stymied. Clearly, the method by which the government's taxation authority is checked must be revamped.

In this regard, once again, the insight displayed by the Framers of the Constitution is startling. It truly appears that their model, which required the dependence of the federal government upon the states for revenue generation, is the most balanced method of providing federal revenue. We must recall, however, that the downfall of the nation's original taxation model was the disparate pressure it placed upon the various states because it was based purely on their populations. This can be corrected.

Specifically, a more appropriate taxation plan would be based on each state's productivity and the size of its industrial base. Consequently,

Congress would not be able to apply any direct tax unless in proportion, not to the state's population, but to the results of a formula evaluating each state's GDP and productivity potential. Properly balanced, such a formula could be construed so that the financial burden of funding the federal government could be felt equitably throughout the nation and avoid the population shifts likely to ensue as citizens of some states migrate to other states to avoid the greater economic burdens placed upon them. If done properly, a modern incarnation of the proportionate burden placed upon the states would decentralize the power presently vested in the federal government, prevent the implementation of unfunded mandates upon the states, and just as importantly, diminish the amount of money available for the federal government to irresponsibly spend.

2. The Onslaught of the Bureaucratic State

The zealous expansion of the executive branch of government and its relatively unchecked and obscure activities is the source of significant intrusions on the separation of powers—the key element in the model of federalism upon which America was built. Controlling and even repealing many of the regulatory authorities and agencies is integral to the continued existence of the nation as a republic and to the protection of the liberties of its citizens.

Beyond what the people can do through reform initiatives, there is one vital premise upon which the continued success of American constitutional government may be guaranteed: the jealously guarding of power by the people and by the various branches of government. Madison summarized this concept best in *Federalist 51* when he wrote, "But the great security against a gradual concentration of the several powers in the same department, consists in giving to those who administer each department the necessary constitutional means and personal motives to resist encroachments of the others."

Unfortunately, during the twentieth-century and into the twenty-first, a Congress that increasingly allowed the executive branch to act in legislative and quasi-judicial manners has eroded this precept. This submission of power to another department represents conduct Madison and the Framers assumed would not take place; conduct that, if routinely undertaken, would erode the very checks upon which the Constitution relied.

Ultimately, the chances of having those intrusions thwarted are dependent upon the character and resolve of the people elected to public office and the people who elect them. So, although it is nice to discuss the necessities of controlling government spending and implementing procedural safeguards that would protect the people from the unfettered growth of government, no check will exist unless the people elect men and women to office instilled with those goals and anxieties.

Despite the ultimate dependence on the members of the branches to preserve the role of each branch, the Achilles heel of regulatory overreach is money. Without funding, no agency can promote its agenda. Table 1 demonstrates the budget allocations of 2014 to a select number of federal agencies. It is reasonable to conclude that the size, power, and scope of these agencies would be more limited, and likely more appropriate to their essential tasks, if the federal government did not have such a wide access to revenue and spending. It follows that any intervention forcing government to control its spending and the money available to it will result in decreased regulatory oversight and the streamlining of government.

Earlier, we spoke about the unfettered march of the agencies. Clearly, without the financial fuel they need to inappropriately overrun the people and their businesses, these agencies could be subdued, a pleasant byproduct of the fiscal recommendations made in the previous section.

Table 1—OUTLAYS BY AGENCY: 2014
(in millions of dollars)

Department or other unit	2014
Legislative Branch	4,164
Judicial Branch	6,893
Department of Agriculture	141,808
Department of Commerce	7,895
Department of Defense--Military Programs	577,898
Department of Education	59,610
Department of Energy	23,638
Department of Health and Human Services	936,012
Department of Homeland Security	43,263
Department of Housing and Urban Development	38,527
Department of the Interior	11,279
Department of Justice	28,620
Department of Labor	56,774
Department of State	27,483
Department of Transportation	76,174
Department of the Treasury	446,897
Department of Veterans Affairs	149,074
Corps of Engineers--Civil Works	6,535
Other Defense Civil Programs	57,370
Environmental Protection Agency	9,399
Executive Office of the President	375
General Services Administration	-767
International Assistance Programs	18,740
National Aeronautics and Space Administration	17,095
National Science Foundation	7,053
Office of Personnel Management	87,917
Small Business Administration	194
Social Security Administration (On-Budget)	81,184
Social Security Administration (Off-Budget)	824,587
Other Independent Agencies (On-Budget)	9,087
Other Independent Agencies (Off-Budget)	-2,531
Allowances	....
Undistributed Offsetting Receipts	-246,158
(On-budget)	-130,155
(Off-budget)	-116,003
Total outlays	**3,506,089**

Source: Table 4.1- Outlay by Agency: 1962-2020, accessed May 6, 2016, *https://www.gpo.gov/fdsys/browse/collection.action?collectionCode=BUDGET&browsePath=Fiscal+Year+2016&searchPath=Fiscal+Year+2016&leafLevelBrowse=false&isCollapsed=-false&isOpen=true&packageid=BUDGET-2016-TAB&ycord=822.*

3. Restoring the Judiciary to Its Proper Place

As we saw, in *Brown I, Brown II,* and its progeny cases, the courts were instrumental in ending segregation within the United States. However, subsequent to that time, they became increasingly emboldened. Acting on John Marshall's premise that the courts decide whether a law is constitutional, the judiciary began shaping American policy based on declarations regarding the constitutionality of existing laws and practices within the United States.

Through this posture, the courts struck down numerous traditions and customs in a manner they were never intended to do. In *Alleghany*, the Supreme Court diminished the discretion governments had in crafting or allowing public displays of religion and faith. In *Engel*, the Court struck down prayer in schools, and in *Wallace*, it prohibited even a moment of silence. As demonstrated in earlier sections of this volume, these were cases that could have produced radically different outcomes using equally valid historical precedent and considerations. Instead, the road chosen has resulted in the growing politicization of the judiciary—the one branch intended to be the least political.

Today, the courts have continued the practice of ruling in seemingly politically biased manners on such constitutionally important issues as same-sex marriage, abortion, the rights of whales in the Pacific Ocean, electoral districts, freedom of speech, campaign funding, commercial practices conducted within a state, gun rights, and public displays of worship.

With every such constitutional ruling, whether it be a small, mundane nuance, or a massive overhaul of constitutional interpretation, the consequences are that the judges edit the Constitution of the United States with language Congress is powerless to reverse. Indeed, the only method by which a comment made by a Supreme Court justice in a majority opinion regarding a constitutional issue can be reversed is through an amendment to the Constitution, or through a subsequent Supreme Court majority opinion reversing the original opinion.

Unlike any other governmental structure, the power of the courts to strike down laws is performed by a very small group of people not answerable to the people or to the other branches of government. The concentration of such unbridled power within one small group of individuals who have recurrently demonstrated themselves to be as politically motivated as any other group within government, stands as arguably the single most ominous threat to the continuation of a democratic republic. With a stroke of a pen, the appointed inhabitants of these few elite chairs can decide that a citizen no longer has the right to refuse to perform an abortion, to refuse to participate in a gay wedding even though such a matrimony is contrary to his or her religious beliefs, to force a citizen to buy health insurance (or any other product for that matter), or to pray openly prior at the beginning of a city commission meeting.

Clearly, such widespread and unbridled authority was not what the Framers intended for a government created to endure through checks and balances. This conclusion stands especially true when one considers that the courts' authorities to rule on the constitutionality of laws stemmed not from Constitutional text, but rather from the opinion of John Marshall in *Marbury v. Madison*. In other words, the unchecked power of the Supreme Court as the final arbiter of constitutional questions was one singlehandedly amassed by the Court through its own design with ne'er a legislative review or executive oversight.

This act certainly caught the attention of Thomas Jefferson who wrote William Charles Jarvis, an author writing on the issue of the courts and judicial powers,

> *You seem, in pages 84 and 148, to consider the judges as the ultimate arbiters of all constitutional questions; a very dangerous doctrine indeed, and one which would place us under the despotism of an oligarchy. Our judges are as honest as other men, and not more so. They have, with others, the same passions for party, for power, and the privilege of their corps. Their maxim is "boni judicis est ampliare jurisdictionem," and their power the more dangerous as they are in office for life, and not responsible, as the other functionaries are, to the elective control.*
>
> (Thomas Jefferson to William Charles Jarvis, Sept. 28, 1820)

And if Jefferson's view is insufficient to generate an unshakeable unease, the courts' demonstrated willingness to work in an executive and legislative capacity that is equally unconstrained and dictatorial certainly should. One need only recall our discussion regarding *Swann* and its forced busing program for an example of a court commandeering the entirety of the governmental process and applying it to the people under its jurisdiction.

Unbridled legislative oversight by the courts was dangerous enough when the states stood on much stronger footing with the federal government. But following the implementation of the Fourteenth Amendment to the Constitution, the Court's comfort in redrafting the content and meaning of the Constitution has made it clear that the time has come to revisit and reverse the not-so-subtle power grab executed by the Supreme Court of the United States. For this we can learn from the experiences of other republican forms of government.

A design where the land's highest court serves as the final arbiter of the constitutionality of a statute is by no means the standard throughout the world's democratic republics. As a matter of fact, the United States' system of strong judicial review seems to be the exception rather than the rule.[430] Countries such as Canada, New Zealand, Britain, Australia, and Israel each have some form of provision imposing some kind of limitation upon their courts regarding constitutionality rulings.[431] In Canada, for example, section 33 of the Charter of Rights, known as the "Notwithstanding Clause," allows Parliament to declare a law operational notwithstanding the ruling of the court.[432]

Although never adopted in any of the states, discussions have begun within the state of Florida to craft legislation implementing some form of oversight of the Supreme Court.[433] Additionally, in South Carolina, legislation has been introduced suggesting that a consensus of the various states would allow for the discontinuation of the tradition of allowing the Supreme Court to serve as the final authority on the constitutionality of a law.[434]

Clearly, the courts have acted with increasing comfort and brazenness to write personal views upon the Constitution and upon the nation's statutes.

The power they have wielded has increased in intensity and influence, all while possessing the knowledge that they ultimately cannot be overruled, at least under America's present political system of governance.

As a result, we must entertain a correction to the finality of judicial authority in matters dealing with constitutional interpretation. Many variations on this theme exist. One possible constitutional amendment would allow a super-majority of Congress to override a Supreme Court opinion. It could read is as follows:

> *Any law, resolution, or other legislative act declared void by the Supreme Court of the United States or any District Court of Appeal may be deemed active and operational, notwithstanding the court's ruling, if agreed to by the legislature pursuant to a joint resolution adopted by a sixty percent vote of each chamber within five years after the date that the ruling becomes final. Such a joint resolution shall take effect immediately upon passage.*

Regardless of the method used, whether it is based on the opinion of multiple states, or of a large portion of the legislatures, some method must be implemented to provide a check on the actions of the judiciary. Without such a provision, the nation will be subject to the authority of a judiciary so vast it would operate exactly like the tyrannical oligarchy described by Jefferson.[iii]

[iii] Detractors of such a constitutional change would argue that without such overarching authorities over the legislatures, the courts would not have been able to reverse the centuries of racism and discrimination plaguing the United States. For this reason, they would aver the necessity of guaranteeing the courts retain such powers in the future. Although the observation about the courts and segregation may be valid, the reality is that there is no other issue in American governance that has, or will ever, produce the level of injustice as slavery and segregation did. Consequently, there will never again exist another issue of such gravity and of such massive scope as to require the courts retain such irreversible authority over the people and of their legislatures. By submitting to this argument, we would be accepting that America's independence in governance is illusory, and subject to the oversight of a small class of men and women who decide, without question, the acceptability of the opinions and actions of the electorate. In other words, we would accept America as not being a true Republic, but rather an oligocracy where the people make suggestions to the masters of how they wish to run their affairs and the masters would then decide whether the people's suggestion is acceptable.

4. Decentralizing Power

Few actions weakened the standing of the states before the authority of the federal government than the passage of the Seventeenth Amendment. Because of the Seventeenth Amendment, the state legislatures ceased to be the primary overseeing agency of the higher chamber. Although there were problems with the original design for selecting the nation's senators, few corrections could have been more corrosive than taking the selection out of the hands of the state legislative bodies. If the federal government is to be subdued in its authorities, then this error must be corrected; the Seventeenth Amendment must be repealed.

It is true that there were problems with the operation of the senatorial election process prior to the passage of the Seventeenth Amendment. Chief amongst these was the possibility of a state's lack of representation due to a political stalemate within a state. Although an argument can be made that this is as it should be, if the American people find such a possibility sufficiently repulsive, the defect can be corrected by a provision allowing the governor of a state to singlehandedly appoint the state's senator if the legislature has not acted within a certain period of time.

Another concern centered around the propensity for senators to control the state elections sufficiently to predetermine their election to the upper chamber, but this can similarly be corrected through campaign finance restrictions.

5. Selecting the President

The Office of the President of the United States is the highest office of the land and the most powerful position on earth. As the Framers correctly identified, the selection of the President must be geared toward the selection of an individual mature in the ways of governance and intensely allegiant to the people of the United States. What's more, the President must understand the principles that resulted in the nation's birth and in its later development and growth. He or she is the representative of the American people on the world stage and is the face by which our society is judged. Perhaps most importantly, the President is the Commander in Chief of the nation's armed forces. More than any other, his or her decisions in this capacity will determine the fates of many. For these reasons, the selection of the inhabitant of the Oval Office is perhaps the most important decision the people of the United States routinely make, not only for the United States, but for the world's inhabitants.

As we saw in Chapter 3, the Framers designed a system that was to be governed by the states and based on each candidate's individual qualities and accomplishments. Very quickly, the harsh realities of politics and political wrangling swept the nation, demonstrating the flawed system the Framers had initially envisioned. Appropriately, Congress and the American people responded by passing the Twelfth Amendment requiring that each state specify who was being selected for President and Vice President. But they kept the Electoral College, a decision vital to the observance of each state's sovereignty. By requiring that the states select their presidential candidates, the President's allegiance to the various states is ensured, separate from his subservience to the American people.

Over the past few decades, there have been discussions suggesting changes from a state-based system to one based purely on the popular vote. However, dismissing the Electoral College would serve as yet another step in the degradation of state autonomy. The President's efforts at seeking votes would shift to merely pursuing the approval of the most populous areas of the nation. In campaigning, the presidential candidate would astutely direct his or her efforts at visiting and pandering to the denser population centers, as these would be the areas where he or she would most efficiently garner votes. The power structure would consequently shift to the Northeast and to the more urban areas of the nation at the expense of the South and the Midwest. Additionally, the removal of the state as the central voting block would be yet another step in the march toward the centralization of power to the bureaucratic offices in Washington.

Yes, there is the argument that the results of the Electoral College may not reflect the outcomes of the popular vote. On at least two occasions, the candidate elected President did not garner the majority of the popular vote.

But this observation ignores a basic tenet of the nation's foundational structure, namely that the President of the United States is to be elected by the states, and not directly by the people. This not so subtle difference in organization is paramount to guaranteeing the allegiance of the President to the states and to ensuring that the balance of power continues to be decentralized and not excessively concentrated on the nation's Chief Executive. The continuation of this model is as integral to the survival of a federalist system of government as is any other of the suggestions made in this volume.

Equally important is the citizenship requirement of the Commander in Chief. Although the Framers made natural born citizenship a prerequisite to being President, as we saw, they never defined what constitutes a "natural born citizen." The propensity of conflicts arising out of the ambiguous language provided by the Framers has increased dramatically, thus placing the integrity of the Presidency, and the nation's security, at risk. It is therefore vitally important that the term "natural born citizen" be specifically defined.

One possible definition is as follows:

> *for the purposes of seeking the Presidency of the United States, a natural born citizen is any individual born within the United States of America, its territories and possessions, any American embassy or military outpost, except if he or she is born in any of the above named areas to persons inhabiting those areas in an undocumented status, or lives within those areas illegally or without permission from the United States of America. Additionally, any person born on foreign soil to American citizens who are temporarily on foreign soil because of employment, foreign service to the nation's military or an American agency, or pursuit of an education is a natural born citizen. But in such cases, except for those where a person's parents are serving in the nation's military or government service, that person must have returned to the United States or her territories by the age of five years old and resided continuously within the United States throughout the remainder of his or her childhood. A person born of parents who are on foreign soil shall not be considered a natural born citizen for the purpose of seeking the*

Office of the Presidency of the United States if those parents left the country with the intent of escaping the laws of the United States, avoid the draft, or had no intention of returning to the United States.[iv]

Not considered by the Framers, but equally important to the discussion, is the issue of dual citizenship. Increasingly, Americans are allegiant to more than one country through their citizenship status.[v] The concept of an unbridled allegiance to the United States of America was of resounding importance to the Framers. It is for this reason that they imposed the fourteen-year continuous residency requirement upon those seeking the Presidency.

But if continuous residency is important to guaranteeing one's loyalty to the nation, even more important is renouncing one's citizenship to any other nation.

Consequently, any person seeking election to the Office of the Presidency of the United States must have renounced his or her citizenship to any other nation obtained purely from his or her birth at least fourteen years previously. Additionally, anyone who affirmatively sought and obtained citizenship in another nation ought to be permanently ineligible to serve as President.

6. The Persistence of Racial Tensions

The issue of race relations stands among the most important challenges in America today. As we have seen, the nation has not yet eliminated race and ethnicity as factors in determining an individual's ability to succeed. Recent events in Ferguson, Missouri, Dallas, and Baltimore, among others, are clear

iv Here, I am specifically referring to the case of George Romney. Mr. Romney should not have been eligible to run for President of the United States by virtue of his foreign birth under circumstances hostile to American law.

v The question of whether dual citizenship should be recognized by the United States is definitely worthy of discussion. It is preferable that American citizens only have loyalty to the United States. Prudence would favor having foreign residents seeking American citizenship to renounce their citizenship in another country at the time they obtain their American citizenship.

indicators of the persistent frustrations existing within the country despite the great legal strides aimed at overcoming racial inequality.

From our review of the legal corpus, it is apparent that equality in one's standing before the law, regardless of race or ethnicity, has essentially been achieved. There are no Jim Crow laws still standing, no poll taxes, and no laws implementing plans for segregation. As a matter of fact, with the recognition of minorities as protected classes subject to safeguards to combat discrimination, it appears that in certain regards, members of these groups are given certain advantages in litigation and in job procurement.

But if we have succeeded in equalizing the legal standing of all racial groups in the eyes of the law, why does the racial divide still exist?

Traditionally, the default answer has been to blame the persistence of ethnic discrepancies in wealth and social standing on some form of racism and animus deeply ingrained within American culture. Prior to the Civil Rights Movement, there was no question that the principal reason for disparities in America was due to racism. As we previously saw, blacks, Hispanics, and Jews were actively kept from accessing America's greatest universities and industrial establishments.

But the inception of the Civil Rights Movement changed that. Blacks successfully fought for their rights such that today, overtly racist laws have been effectively eliminated. Schools have been largely desegregated, and any attempt at racially promoting one individual over another, if identified, is unacceptable in American society.

But if we accept that the laws designed to suppress blacks and other minorities have either been stricken from the legal corpus or are subject to immediate nullification by the courts, then why do racial and ethnic disparities continue to exist? Is it really because of the persistence of an all-pervasive culture of racism, or is there another factor at play? Any attempt at answering this question must begin by defining the disparities.

In 2013, blacks made up the largest portion of the American prison population at 498,100 prisoners, compared to 221,700 for Hispanics, and 462,600 for whites.[435] Out of every 100,000 black men, 2,805 are serving felony prison sentences. This number compares to 1,134 for Hispanic males and 466 for white males. For women, although the figure is lower, the pattern remains.[436] The reality is that blacks are incarcerated five times more frequently than whites, while for Hispanics, the number is double that of whites. And whereas 13% of the general American population is made up of blacks and 16% of Hispanics, 19% of the nation's prison population is Hispanic and an amazing 40% is black.[437]

The racial disparities in prison populations and incarceration rates are paralleled in disparities in the workforce and in socioeconomic status. Studies evaluating candidate successes at securing employment suggest a persistent bias against those seeking employment who possess African-American names.[438] These findings suggest the persistence of racial biases in hiring. Moreover, according to the United States Bureau of Labor Statistics, blacks and Hispanics earn considerably less, on the average, than whites and Asians.

According to a 2013 report, the median earnings for full-time weekly wages and salaries were $578 and $629 for Hispanics and blacks respectively, compared to $802 and $942 for whites and Asians.[439] Additionally, the jobless rate for blacks stood at 13.1% while Asians and whites were at 5.2% and 6.5% respectively.[440] Also in 2013, teenaged blacks had the highest unemployment rates at 38.8% compared to 27.5% for teenaged Hispanics, 20.3% for teenaged whites, and 10.7% for teenaged Asians.[441]

Although these numbers are telling, they are probably under-representative of the actual unemployment reality since the statistics consider only those persons still in the labor force—those who are still trying to find employment four weeks prior to the survey being conducted.[vi]

[vi] According to the Bureau of Labor Statistics, people are counted as unemployed if they do not have a job, are willing to work, and have looked for a job during the four weeks preceding the survey. People who want a job, have not looked for a job over the four weeks prior to the survey, but have sought employment during the prior twelve months are not considered unemployed, but are considered "marginally connected to the labor force." There is also a subgroup that is considered to be outside of the labor force. These include those who are in school, living in institutions, active duty military, and those who are 16 years of age or younger. [Labor Force Statistics from the Current Population Survey, How the Government Measures Unemployment, *http://www.bls.gov/cps/cps_htgm.htm#unemployed* (Nov. 3, 2015)]

The inevitable conclusion is that racial and ethnic disparities abound. But these facts alone do not answer the question of whether this is due to racism. To answer this question, we should begin by exploring those markers indicative of America's racial attitudes. A 2013 Gallup poll indicated that the approval rate of marriages between blacks and whites had increased from a 4% favorable rating in 1959 to 87% in 2013. If one stratifies out whites who were polled, the approval rate still remains at 84%.[442] Even more promising, those approval rates are much higher among younger adults relative to older ones (96% among 18-29 year-olds compared to 70% among those that are 65 year-old or older).[443] Moreover, the multiracial population (people who identify themselves as being of mixed races or multiple races) is growing at three times the rate of the general population with 60% of these mixed race people being proud of their background.[444] Also, the incidence of integrated metropolitan neighborhoods is increasing. One study by the Department of Housing and Urban Development found a 50% increase in integrated neighborhoods between 1990 and 2010 (up from 20% of neighborhoods overall to 30%), and the integration of these neighborhoods has been more permanent.[445]

So, with the favorable attitudes towards minorities and other races in America, is it possible that other explanations may exist for the persistence of racial disparities? The answer is yes.

One possible explanation is the correlation between intact marriages and life accomplishments among ethnicities. Consider that in America more than 67% of women who gave birth in 2011 identifying themselves as black were unmarried. For Hispanics, that number was 43%, and for Asians and whites,

---

Because of the exclusionary criteria in defining the unemployed, it is likely that the actual number of people who want a job, particularly during times of economic slowdown such as the Great Recession of 2008 is much higher than those officially reported to be unemployed. The U-6 unemployment rate, capturing those who are officially counted as unemployed plus those marginally attached to the work force as a percent of the sum of the labor force and the marginally attached population is aimed at providing a truer representation of the nation's unemployment figures. (Table A-15 Economic New Release, Alternative Measures of Labor Underutilization, U.S. Bureau of Labor Statistics, accessed Nov. 3, 2015, *http://www.bls.gov/news.release/empsit.t15.htm*) In October, 2009, during the height of the Great Recession, for example, while the official unemployment rate reached 10.1%, the U-6 unemployment rate stood at 17.4%. (U-6 Unemployment Rate, Macrotrends, accessed Nov. 3, 2015, *http://www.macrotrends.net/1377/u6-unemployment-rate*)

the numbers were 11.3% and 23% respectively.[446] What's more, blacks who were married remarry at a lower rate than non-blacks.[447]

These correlations between single parents and economic outcomes remain consistent for each ethnic group—even when factoring in racism. Asians have fewer children out of wedlock than whites and outperform whites *despite* a history of prejudice against them.

The statistical consequences of these trends have been stark, particularly on the data regarding broken homes and children in poverty. Thirty-seven percent of single-parent families live in poverty compared to 8.8% of married couples[448] while 49% of children in single-mother households grow up in poverty compared to 11.6% in households headed by married couples.[449]

Predictably, the distribution of childhood poverty mirrors the incidence of broken families among racial groups with 32% of Asians living in poverty compared to 32.3% of whites, 42.9% of blacks, and 51.4% of Hispanics. This is the same pattern encountered when measuring the prevalence of intact families throughout the various racial and ethnic groups.[450]

Similarly, the national imprisonment rates show associations between criminal and drug related activities and broken homes and families. In 2013, those incarcerated for drug-related offenses made up the largest subgroup of prisoners.[451] In the meantime, the lowest incidence of drug abuse among adolescents exists in families headed by the biological mother and the biological father.[452] Additionally, adolescents living in a single-parent home are significantly more prone to engage in delinquent behavior than those living in a family headed by the biological mother and the biological father.[453]

Of greater significance, children of disrupted families are at greater risk of engaging in drug use and illicit activities *despite the racial make up of the family.*[454] And finally, data from the National Longitudinal Survey of Youth show a higher incidence of incarceration in adolescents proceeding from fatherless families.[455]

So, perhaps the incidence of economic disparities is less a result of persistent racism than the effects of the relative frequencies in family breakdown.

If this is the case, then government's efforts today should be geared at creating an environment supportive of *families* rather than providing an environment supporting entitlement or outcomes equality.

And what promotes marital unity and cohesiveness?

Faith.

Many argue that religion does not play a role in maintaining intact families. In support of their argument they point out the similarities in divorce rates between religious denominations, even citing studies finding a lower divorce rate among individuals describing themselves as atheists.

They are missing the point.

The stabilizing influence in a marriage, a family, and even a person's life, generally, is not the denomination from which the person proceeds, but from the active presence of God and faith within the life of the individual and his or her family. This association is much more difficult to scientifically tease out because of the absence of a single source of data on such measures. Added to this is the difficulty in measuring faithfulness. But there are some indications that support an association between the intactness of the family and faith.

The Survey of U.S. Catholics performed by the Center for Applied Research in the Apostolate at Georgetown University found that the majority of Catholics who are divorced were not married in the Church.[vii] And although the divorce rates amongst Catholics were similar to the national average, those who attended church regularly had a substantially lower divorce rate of 28% compared to 47% for those who did not.[456]

From these statistics, it is reasonable to conclude that discrimination and racial prejudice is playing a progressively smaller role in racial disparities.

Other factors, such as the prevalence of drug use, the absence of positive role models for young people, and the integrity of the family unit are of great

[vii] Sixty five percent of Catholics reporting that they were divorced were not married within the church. [Mark M. Gray, Paul M. Perl, et al., "Marriage in the Catholic Church: A Survey of U.S. Catholics," Center for Applied Research in the Apostolate Wash. D.C.: Georgetown University, Oct. 2007) 4.]

importance in defining an individual's odds of success in life. These factors are at least partially influenced by the strength of the person's faith and the strength of the faith of those closest to him or her.

Consequently, if the nation truly wishes to unravel the influences propagating intergenerational poverty and incarceration, it needs to stop ignoring the positive influence of religion and faith. If advocates truly want people in poverty and members of racial and ethnic minorities to have a chance at breaking out of the seemingly endless cycle of poverty, drug use, and criminal behavior, then they should be advocating the promotion of those intangible factors that provide families with a better chance of survival and instill discipline, pride, and a sense of purpose in the individual.

These factors are not found in affirmative action measures or in the illusory crutches provided by government. Rather, the tools so desperately needed to survive and withstand the trials and tribulations confronting an individual come from an intact family with firm values and a belief in something greater than oneself. They proceed from an unyielding faith in a loving and benevolent Creator who demands from that individual service to those around him and an acknowledgment that his personal gains come second to the wellbeing of those around him. Strikingly, all these concepts and priorities are ones whose persistence have been hampered by a government increasingly hostile to religion and public worship.

7. Restoring Worship in the Public Square

Irrefutably, the removal of God from the public square has led to a significant decline in the nation's sense of moral clarity and ethics. The disruption of the family, the growing sense of moral apathy, the selfishness and disregard for others on display by a growing number of Americans, the somewhat astonishing disrespect for the nation and her greatness by her citizenry, and the senseless search for meaning in materials that can never substitute for the comfort found in God are all products of this extrication. The fact that a large driver of these changes has been judicial intervention rather than sociopolitical debate is particular troubling. For these reasons, and so many others, the single most important intervention that can be undertaken to guarantee the long-term survival of the American Republic is her restoration as a God-honoring nation where worship is welcomed and charity is encouraged. Consequently, urgent efforts need be taken to reverse these court-induced changes.

With the supremacy of the judiciary in matters of religion and religious worship, there are two ways in which a correction can take place. One approach calls for the courts to repair their mistakes. Indeed, there may come a day when the people of the United States, motivated by a strong desire to restore faith and prayer within the country, may elect a series of executives able to place a new majority of judges and justices in America's courts to persistently chip away at the great wall of legal precedents serving to separate God from the public square and America's schools. However, the chances of such a protracted and deliberate judicial correction are extremely remote—and will simply take too long.

If appointing judges capable of reversing past decisions is an unrealistic solution, then the only other method available for correcting these judicial blunders is amending the Constitution. Such an amendment would have to address a few key issues and questions. The first is whether the United States is a Christian nation built on Judeo-Christian traditions and Judeo-Christian morality.

As we have seen, the answer is a resolute yes. Only under Judeo-Christian ethics is the Constitution able to function. Only under Judeo-Christian ethics can the right to vote be preserved. Only under Judeo-Christian ethics can all races and cultures exist on equal footing. And only under Judeo-Christian ethics can women be seen equally to men under the law.

Recall that Madison and Jefferson, in their zeal to prevent intrusions by government into the beliefs of men, never considered whether the Constitution was even functional under assumptions of non-Judeo-Christian religions. Had they considered the question, the answer would have been a resounding no. The Founders and the Framers had the luxury of not being forced to answer the question of the nation's religious foundation, as it was a presumed fact of the time. But it is a question that *must* be answered today, and the answer *must* be Judeo-Christian in regards to the nation's morality and Christian in regards to its faith.

But this does not mandate Christianity upon the nation's people. The assertion above does not intrude or affect the separate and distinct question of whether the government ought to be intruding into the rights of conscience or the religious liberties of the individual. Regardless of the nation's philosophical and religious underpinnings, a government of free peoples still does not possess the authority to coerce into submission one's thoughts and beliefs. Doing so would make such a government as tyrannical as the one that overtly aims a gun at its dissenters. The government of the United States of America, regardless of its religious precepts, cannot ever be allowed to dictate a person's beliefs or thoughts.

It follows then, that despite acknowledging that the country has a common religious and ethical foundation, it cannot be allowed to have or impose a uniform, national church, denomination, or sect, but it must allow for the open reverence of God within the public square and for the passing of the traditions and beliefs that have served us so well.

So, if we were to change the First Amendment to allow for these goals, the proposed amendment might look something like this:

> *1. Whereas the United States is founded on the Christian faith and informed by Judeo-Christian ethics and morality, no conflicting moral, ethical, or religious code shall be upheld by any government of the United States in fashioning or applying its laws. However, the right of any person to practice any non-Christian faith in his or her private capacity shall not be infringed, nor shall Congress uphold any specific sect or religious denomination over another.*
>
> *2. Congress shall not infringe upon the right of the people to publicly worship in the Judeo-Christian tradition; erect symbols supporting Christianity or Judaism; or invoke the guidance of God, unless such actions or symbols interfere with the safety of the people. No court shall consider a person's objection or proclaimed offense to the worship of God in the Judeo-Christian tradition, or to the invocation of His guidance*

or intercession, as forming the basis for the restriction of another's right to publicly worship or to publicly invoke such guidance or intercession.

3. Congress shall make no law interfering with a state's authority to teach Judeo-Christian traditions nor a state's ability to establish an environment conducive to Christian forbearance and worship, but no state-sponsored religious program shall promote ethics or traditions contrary to the Judeo-Christian faith.

Whether this particular proposed amendment is the one adopted is of little relevance. The greater importance lies in the goals of allowing generations of Americans to once again acknowledge the presence of a Judeo-Christian God in the public square, to reinforce the moral and ethical foundations that strengthen society, and to empower the courts with the rules they need to ward off legal attacks from secularists and advocates for religious principles contrary to those espoused by Judeo-Christian ethic.

Chapter 6

Forging a Better Future

In 1789, Alexander Hamilton, James Madison, and John Jay brought their vision for a better tomorrow to the people of New York and explained the necessity of the ratification of the United States Constitution. Theirs was a treatise calling for a change to meet the foreseeable challenges that lay ahead.

For them, the Constitution represented the ticket to the country's continued existence. The document the men of the Constitutional Convention pieced together, although flawed, represented the single greatest possibility for the country's survival. It avoided the fragmentation of a precariously assembled union and prevented a cataclysmic war sure to turn the North American continent into a cesspool of regional conflicts and European-styled nation states. In short, the Constitution was the document that would grant stability to a tenuous coalition that was quickly destabilizing.

The significance of the United States Constitution to the wellbeing of the American citizenry, and by extension, to the stability of the neighborhood of nations is no less great today. Today, the Constitution stands as the oldest living document of its kind. Its foundation on power emanating from the consent of the governed is as critical today as it was 227 years ago. Back then, it was important for the men who helped create the Constitution to stand up and explain the necessity of her existence to the young nation. Similarly, today, it is necessary for those who understand this magnificent document and identify with its hallowed principles and religious foundations to boldly proclaim the necessity of reestablishing her proper existence in today's world.

Within the pages of this book we reviewed the unique circumstances leading to the establishment of the one truly exceptional nation on earth. We identified the philosophical brilliance resulting in her creation and acknowledged the horrible blunders that stained her birth. We looked at the consequences of the decisions made at the Constitutional Convention and studied how the nation evolved, abandoning many of the principles she adopted at her inception. And we explored the legislative changes required to restore the legal environment to one more consistent with that originally envisioned by the Framers.

The reason to engage in this grueling exercise is not merely to marvel at the Constitution. Rather, the purpose is to more insightfully identify the way forward for our noble nation and to recognize the repairs necessary for America to continue to serve as the shining beacon of inspiration for the rest of humanity. It is with these insights in mind that a blueprint for America's continued success is submitted.

Here are the goals for which we must aim.

America must be the home of a societal order respectful of the greatness of God. It must be a place where all citizens may interact without malice and hatred, free to pursue their passions with minimal interference from government. America must be a place where people not only dream, but dare to pursue those dreams and strive to make them a reality. It must be a place where parents have the confidence of investing in their posterity by knowing that they have given their children a place rich in opportunities and promise, just like the one they had during their lifetime. It must be a place where people are free to pursue opportunities, regardless of their skin color, gender, ethnicity, or status. And it must be one that understands the importance of respecting one's right to pursue opportunities and not the destructive guarantee of success.

And why not guarantee success? Because if government attempts to guarantee one's success, it will by necessity predetermine the state of each individual. And if the fate of the individual is predetermined, then gone will be the individual's will to fight, to dream, and to achieve. When it comes down to it, in robbing the person of his opportunity to struggle and to achieve, one is robbing the person of his humanity.

It is because the United States Constitution is founded on a philosophy embracing these principles that she is so important to the continuation of a dignified human existence.

Consequently, having seen the causes of her corruption, we are called to rectify her status and restore the principles that made her great.

We do this first by inviting our Judeo-Christian God back into our public lives, allowing the public to acknowledge the debt we owe Him for the blessings afforded to our nation—blessings that include not only the many bounties we gain from our fertile soils and fruitful waters, but from the many freedoms that ultimately spring from Him. Only in doing so can we re-instill our sense of obligation to neighbor and stranger alike. Indeed, only in embracing the concepts of Christian forbearance will the citizens of our nation once again be challenged with the question of what they can do for their country, instead of what their country can do for them. With the reinstatement of the nation's proper moral compass, we can restore the family's central position in society and promote the stability of our homes, our neighborhoods, our cities, and our society.

America's racial disparities must also disappear. But they will not disappear through government interference or artificially contrived corrections aimed at equal outcomes. A person's pride and sense of worth can never be achieved through handouts. Self-worth comes from achievement, and achievement can only materialize through struggle and perseverance. Consequently, the only possible way for racial and ethnic disparities to dissipate is if all Americans are seen equally under the law, if opportunity is accessible to all, and if each person is solely responsible for the heights he or she sets out to climb. If a community is disadvantaged, then it falls upon the members of that community to identify how the shortcomings will be rectified. Only then will there be a true sense of pride and achievement amongst all the races that may serve to neutralize their present disparities.

Finally, every building, every bureaucratic seat, every employee in excess of the minimum necessary to execute those functions essential to the running of the state is an affront to our economic freedoms, to our chances of individual success, and to our free and unfettered relationship with God. For these reasons, the American people *must* take all necessary actions to whittle government's footprint to its smallest possible size. No steps can be more effective at achieving this end than controlling government's access to our moneys and government's propensity to spend it.

The United States is truly the greatest nation on earth. But it holds this title not because it has the strongest military or because it has the largest economic engine on the planet. Instead, America's greatness stems from the uniqueness of her birth. It is due to the principle that the governed hold the fountain of the nation's power, and it is the government that serves the people—and not the other way around.

Now, more than ever, as we head into an increasingly complicated, uncertain, and hostile future, the time has come for Americans to restore the principles that gave rise to her birth and her historic world impact. It is time to rectify the errors that have not yet been corrected. But successfully achieving these goals will not take place through the solitary efforts of one writer, a single visionary politician, or even through the efforts of an amazingly heroic soldier. Rather, these goals will be achieved in the same manner by which America won her independence: through endless hours of work and resolute efforts informed by an absolute confidence in God and the respect for others he requires from each of his human creations.

I can only hope these *Federalist Pages* will serve as a small step in the Herculean effort to eventually salvage the greatest nation man has ever conceived and rekindle mankind's hope in a peaceful and glorious future through the magnanimous example set by the Shining City on the Hill.

Endnotes

1 William E. Gladstone, "Kin Beyond the Sea," *The North American Review*, 127, no. 264 (Sep.-Oct.): 185.

2 Report of Proceedings in Cong. *Journals of the Continental Cong*. vol. 38 (Feb. 21, 1787).

3 Paul Johnson, *A History of the American People* (New York: Harper Collins Publishers, 1997), 185.

4 Ibid., 185.

5 Ibid,, 184-186.

6 "America's Founding Fathers, Delegates to the Constitutional Convention," *The Charters of Freedom, National Archives*, accessed October 25, 2014, http://www.archives.gov/exhibits/charters/constitution_founding_fathers_overview.html.

7 Ibid.

8 James Madison, *The Federalist Papers*, No. 40, 2001 Modern Library Paperback Edition (New York: Random House, 2000), 253-254.

9 John Jay. *The Federalist Papers*, No. 2-5, 7-26; Madison. *The Federalist Papers*, No. 6, 27-33; Alexander Hamilton. *The Federalist Papers*, No. 7-8. 34-47.

10 U.S. Const. art. II, § 2.

11 Hamilton, *The Federalist Papers*, No. 69, 440.

12 Ibid.

13 U.S. Const. art. I, § 7.

14 U.S. Const. art. II, § 1, cl. 2.

15 U.S. Const. art. II, § 4.

16 U.S. Cont. art. II, § 1.

17 U.S. Cont. art. II, § 1.

18 U.S. Const. art. II, § 1.

19 Hamilton, *The Federalist Papers*, No. 78, 440.

20 U.S. Const. art. III, § 1.

21 U.S. Const. art. III, § 1.

22 U.S. Const. art. II, § 2

23 U.S. Const. art. III, § 3.

24 U.S. Const. art. III, § 2.

25 U.S. Const. art. III, § 2.

26 U.S. Const. art. III, § 2.

27 Hamilton, *The Federalist Papers*, No. 82, 527.

28 U.S. Const. art. IV, § 4.

29 U.S. Const. art. IV, § 3.

30 U.S. Const. art. I, § 9.

31 U.S. Const. art. I, § 9.

32 U.S. Const. art. III, § 3.

33 U.S. Const. art. I, § 9.

34 U.S. Const. art. I, § 9.

35 U.S. Const. art. I, § 9.

36 U.S. Const. art. I, § 10.

37 U.S. Const. art. I, § 10.

38 U.S. Const. art. I, § 10.

39 U.S. Const. art. I, § 10.

40 U.S. Const. art. VI.

41 U.S. Const. art. VI.

42 U.S. Const. art. IV, § 1.

43 U.S. Const. art. IV, § 2.

44 Willem Kieft, "The Charter, October 10, 1645" in *The Flushing Remonstrance*, draft edition, accessed Jul. 29, 2015, http://schools.nycenet.edu/offices/teachlearn/ela/Flushing_Remon.pdf.

45 Ibid., 6.

46 Ibid., .

47 A History of Flushing, accessed Jul. 31, 2015, http://www.nyym.org/flushing/history.html.

48 Kenneth Jackson, "A Colony with a Conscience," *The New York Times*, Dec. 27, 2007, accessed on July 31, 2015, http://www.nytimes.com/2007/12/27/opinion/27jackson.html.

49 Johnson, *A History of the American People*, 109.

50 John Adams to Abigail Adams, Sept. 16, 1774.

51 Ibid.

52 Resolution for a National Day of Humiliation, Fasting, and Prayer, Mar. 16, 1776.

53 The Declaration of Independence, July 4, 1776.

54 Greg Bailey . "Blackstone in America, Lectures by an English Lawyer Become the Blueprint for a New Nation's Laws and Leaders." *Early America*. accessed on Jul. 14, 2015, http://www.earlyamerica.com/early-america-review/volume-2/sir-william-blackstone-in-america/.

55 Ibid.

56 Justin P. Nichols. "The Hidden Dichotomy in the Law of Morality," *Campbell Law Review* (Spring 2009): 643.

57 Ibid.

58 An Ordinance for the Government of the Territory of the United States Northwest of the River Ohio, art. 3, July 13, 1787.

59 Rodney K. Smith, "Getting Off On the Wrong Foot and Back On Again: A Reexamination of the History of the Framing of the Religion Clauses of the First Amendment And a Critique of the *Reynolds* And *Everson* Decisions." *Wake Forest Law Review*, vol 20 (1984): 569-643.

60 James Madison in Smith, "Getting Off On the Wrong Foot and Back On Again," 579-584.

61 Ibid., 596-599.

62 An Act for Establishing Religious Freedom, Va. Assembly, Jan. 16, 1786.

63 Smith, "Getting Off On the Wrong Foot and Back On Again," 585 .

64 A Bill Establishing a Provision for Teachers of Christian Religion, Va. State Assembly, 1784.

65 Smith, "Getting Off On the Wrong Foot and Back On Again," 581-582.

66 Ibid., 590-593.

67 James Madison, "Memorial and Remonstrance Against Religious Assessments," June 20, 1785, ¶1.

68 Ibid.

69 Ibid., ¶4.

70 Ibid., ¶3.

71 James R. Rodgers, "Patrick Henry's Very Modern Proposal," *First Things*, (Aug. 20, 2013) accessed Aug. 12, 2015, http://www.firstthings.com/web-exclusives/2013/08/patrick-henrys-very-modern-proposal.

72 A Bill Establishing a Provision for Teachers of Christian Religion, Va. State Assembly, 1784.

73 Rodgers, "Patrick Henry's Very Modern Proposal."

74 A Bill Establishing a Provision for Teachers of Christian Religion, Va. State Assembly, 1784.

75 Rodgers, "Patrick Henry's Very Modern Proposal."

76 Article 22, Del. Const. art. 22 (adopted Sept. 10, 1776).

77 Article 22, Del. Const. art. 22 (adopted Sept. 10, 1776).

78 Ga. Const. art. VI (adopted Feb. 5, 1777).

79 Pa. Const. § 10 (adopted Sept. 28, 1776).

80 S.C. Const. art XIII (adopted Mar. 19, 1778).

81 S.C. Const. art XXXVIII (adopted March 19, 1778).

82 Vt. Const. ch.1, art. III (adopted July 4, 1786).

83 Ky. Const. art. VIII, § 5 (adopted 1792).

84 , Ky. Const. art. XII, § III (adopted 1792).

85 , Tn. Const. art. 8; § 1 (adopted 1796).

86 Tn. Const. art. 8, §2(adopted 1796).

87 La. Const. art. VI (adopted 1812).

88 *American Heritage Dictionary of the English Language*, 5th Ed. (Houghton Mifflin Harcourt Publishing Company).

89 Ibid.

90 *West's Encyclopedia of American Law*, 2nd ed.. (The Gale Group, Inc.: 2008),

91 Steve Sheppard, "What Oaths Meant to the Framers' Generation: A Preliminary Sketch," *Cardozo Law Review*, de Novo 27, (2009): 279.

92 Alexander Hamilton, Jun. 28, 1787, in James Madison, "Notes of Debates in the Federal Convention of 1787.

93 Hugh Williamson Jun. 28, 1787, in James Madison, "Notes of Debates in the Federal Convention of 1787.

94 J. Clarence Thomas Concurrence, *Rosenberger v. Rector and Visitors of Univ. of Va.*, 515 U.S. 819, 858 (1995).

95 "History of the Chaplaincy," (Office of the Chaplain, United States House of Representatives), accessed Aug. 16, 2015, http://chaplain.house.gov/chaplaincy/history.html; Smith, "Getting Off On the Wrong Foot and Back On Again," 603.

96 U.S. Const. amend. I.

97 1 Annals of Congress, 451, (1789).

98 Ibid., 759.

99 Ibid., 758.

100 Ibid.

101 Ibid., 760.

102 Ibid., 796.

103 Ibid.,, 77-78.

104 Conference Committee Report, Sept. 24, 1789.

105 Smith, "Getting Off On the Wrong Foot and Back On Again."

106 Ibid., 622-623.

107 Ibid., 622.

108 James Hutson, "'A Wall of Separation' FBI Helps Restore Jefferson's Obliterated Draft," (Library of Congress: June 1998) accessed Aug. 21, 2015, http://www.loc.gov/loc/lcib/9806/danbury.html.

109 Ibid.

110 Ibid.

111 Alexander Hamilton, "The First Report on Public Credit," Jan. 9, 1790.

112 Ibid.

113 U.S. Cont. art. I, § 8, cl. 1.

114 U.S. Cont. art. I, § 10, cl.18.

115 James Madison, 1 Annals of Cong, 1945 (Feb. 2, 1791) (Joseph Gales ed., 1793).

116 Ibid.

117 Ibid., 1946.

118 Ibid., 1947.

119 Ibid., 1947-48.

120 Thomas Jefferson, "Opinion on the Constitutionality of a National Bank," 1791.

121 Ibid.

122 Alexander Hamilton to George Washington, 23 February 1791.

123 Ibid.

124 *United States v. Butler*, 297 U.S. 1 (1936).

125 Ryan C. Squire, "Effectuating Principles of Federalism: Reevaluating the Federal Spending Power as the Great Tenth Amendment Loophole." *Pepperdine Law Review*, vol. 25, issue. 4 (May 15, 1998): 896-898.

126 *Steward Machine Co. v. Davis*, 301 U.S. 548 (1937).

127 Squire, "Effectuating the Principles of Federalism," 870.

128 Ibid., 908-909.

129 Hamilton, No, 84. *The Federalist Papers*, 550.

130 U.S. Const. art. III, § 3.

131 U.S. Const. art. III, § 2.

132 U.S. Const. art. I, § 9.

133 U.S. Const. art. I, § 9.

134 U.S. Const. art. I, § 9.

135 U.S. Const. art. III, § 3.

136 U.S. Const. art. IV, § 4.

137 Hamilton, *The Federalist Papers*, No. 84, 550.

138 Hamilton, *The Federalist Papers*, No. 84.

139 Ibid., 549.

140 Ibid., 550.

141 Madison at the Va. Convention, June 25, 1788, 5:231.

142 Dan T. Coenen, "Chisholm v. Georgia (1793), The New Georgia Encyclopedia." (Oct. 4, 2004), accessed Nov. 9, 2014, http://www.georgiaencyclopedia.org/articles/government-politics/chisholm-v-georgia-1793.

143 *Chisholm*, 2 U.S. 419.

144 Charles A. Shanor. *American Constitutional Law: Structure and Reconstruction Cases, Notes And Problems*, 4th ed. (West Academic Publishing, 2009), 305.

145 *Seminole Tribe of Florida v. Florida*, 517 U.S. 44 (1996).

146 Larson . "The Revolution of 1800," *American History*, (Dec. 2007), 32.

147 Ibid., 26.

148 Ibid.

149 Ibid., 31.

150 Ibid., 33.

151 Ibid..

152 U.S. Cont. art. I, §4, cl 2.

153 Statutes at Large, 28th Congress, 2nd Session, 721 .

154 Hamilton, *The Federalist Papers*, No. 72, 463.

155 Thomas E. Dewey in Thomas E. Cronin, "Term limits are a check against an American cult of personality." *The Washington Post*. January 3, 2014, accessed November 20, 2014, http://www.washingtonpost.com/opinions/term-limits-are-a-check-against-an-american-cult-of-personality/2014/01/03/270d3034-6374-11e3-aa81-e1dab1360323_story.html.

156 Margaret Mikyung Lee, "U.S. Citizenship of Persons Born in the United States to Alien Parents," CRS Report For Congress, September 13, 2005, 1-2, accessed Jan. 9, 2016, http://www.factcheck.org/UploadedFiles/CRS-Citizenship-Re-

port.pdf.

157 Ibid., 2.

158 William Blackstone, *Commentaries on the Laws of England; in Four Books*, 2nd ed., vol 1, bk. 1 (Chicago: Callaghan and Co., 1876), 373.

159 Ibid., 366.

160 John Jay to George Washington, July 25, 1787.

161 Madison, Aug. 22, 1787 in "James Madison's Notes of Debates in the Federal Convention of 1787".

162 Ibid., Sept. 7, 1787.

163 Act of Mar. 26, 1790, 1 Stat. 103.

164 Act of Jan. 29, 1795, 1 Stat. 414.

165 Johnson, *A History of the American People*, 4 .

166 The American Heritage Dictionary of the English Language, 4th Ed. (Houghton Mifflin Company, 2009), accessed Nov. 29, 2014, http://www.thefreedictionary.com/slave.

167 Johnson, *A History of the American People*, 4.

168 Johnson, *A History of the American People*, 27; John Rolfe to Sir Edward Sandys, January 1619, accessed Nov. 30, 2014, /20 . http://memory.loc.gov/cgi-bin/ampage?collId=mtj8&fileName=mtj8pagevc03.db&recNum=266.

169 John Rolfe to Sir Edward Sandys, Jan. 1619.

170 Johnson, *A History of the American People*, 27.

171 George H. Smith, "John Locke's *Two Treatises of Government*", (audio, The Cato Institute) accessed Dec. 1, 2014, http://cdn.cato.org/libertarianismdotorg/mod-2.mp3; George H. Smith, "'The Declaration of Independence' by Thomas Jefferson", (audio, The Cato Institute: 1987) accessed Dec. 1, 2014, http://cdn.cato.org/libertarianismdotorg/mod-3a.mp3.

172 June 11, 1776, *Journals of the Cont. Congress,* 431.

173 Richard J. Behn, "Treaty of Paris" in *History Essays* (The Lehman Institute) accessed Jan. 27, 2016, http://www.lehrmaninstitute.org/history/treaty-of-paris.html; "The Treaty of Paris" in Black Loyalist (University of Sidney) accessed Jan. 28, 2016, http://www.blackloyalist.info/treaty-of-paris.

174 Madison, *The Federalist Papers*, No. 7, 35-36

175 Madison, *The Federalist Papers*, No. 8, 43.

176 William Bennett, *America: The Last Great Hope*, vol. I. (Nashville, TN: Thomas Nelson, Inc. 2006), 122.

177 Madison, Jun. 6, 1787, "Notes on the Debates in the Federal Convention" accessed Dec. 9, 2014, http://avalon.law.yale.edu/18th_century/debates_606.asp (December 9, 2014).

178 John Jay to R. Lushington, Mar. 15, 1786 in *The Correspondence and Public Papers of John Jay,* vol. 3 (1782-1793), (New York, N.Y.: G.P. Putnam's Sons, 1890-1893) accessed Dec. 9, 2014, 173 http://lf-oll.s3.amazonaws.com/titles/2329/Jay_1530-03_EBk_v6.0.pdf.

179 Bennett, *America: The Last Great Hope*, 122.

180 George Washington to Robert Morris, April 12, 1786, in *Founders Online,* accessed Dec. 9, 2014, http://www.pbs.org/georgewashington/collection/other_1786apr12.html.

181 Madison in the Virginia Convention, in Wendell Phillips, *The Constitution a pro-slavery compact*" 3d ed (New York, NY: American Anti-Slavery Society, 1856) accessed Dec. 9, 2014, http://books.google.com/books?id=yhu09hOUdOYC&pg=PA93&lpg=PA93&dq=madison+unhappy+species+of+population&source=bl&ots=pzjuazsT5Q&sig=pqVnXaPkYvLUhNfWId4neYBIuj8&hl=en&sa=X&ei=6AgeVN39HMaBsQTUtoKQBg&ved=0CCgQ6AEwAQ#v=onepage&q=madison%20unhappy%20species%20of%20population&f=false.

182 Charles Cotesworth Pinckney, Aug. 21, 1787, in James Madison, "Notes on the Debates in the Federal Convention," accessed Dec. 10, 2014, http://avalon.law.yale.edu/18th_century/debates_821.asp.

183 Charles Pinckney, August 21, 1787, in Madison, "Notes on the Debates in the Federal Convention." accessed Dec. 10, 2014.

184 George Mason, Aug. 21, 1787, in Madison, "Notes on the Debates in the Federal Convention" accessed Dec. 10, 2014).

185 U.S. Const. art. I, § 2.

186 U.S. Const. art. IV, § 2.

187 James Madison Aug. 25, 1787, in James Madison, "Notes on the Debates in the Federal Convention" accessed Dec. 10, 2014).

188 Gary M. Walton and Hugh Rockoff, *History of the American Economy*; 11th ed. (Mason, OH: Cengage Learning, 2010), 138.

189 Ibid.

190 Ibid.

191 Johnson, *A History of the American People*, 313.

192 Ibid., 448-449.

193 *Dred Scott v. Sanford*, 60 US 393, 404 (1857).

194 Ibid*.,* at 404-405.

195 Ibid., at 405

196 Bennett, *America: The Last Great Hope*, 301-303.

197 "Civil War Casualties" *Historynet* accessed Jan. 7, 2014, http://www.historynet.com/civil-war-casualties.

198 Bruce A Ragdale, "*Ex parte Merryman* and Debates on Civil Liberties During the Civil War" (Federal Judicial History Office: 2007), 1, accessed Dec. 10, 2014, http://www.fjc.gov/history/docs/merryman.pdf.

199 Ibid.

200 Ibid., 2.

201 Roger Brooke Taney in Ragdale "*Ex parte Merryman* and Debates on Civil Liberties During the Civil War,", 4 accessed Dec. 10, 2014.

202 Ragdale "*Ex parte Merryman* and Debates on Civil Liberties During the Civil War," 7, accessed Dec. 10, 2014)

203 "The Preliminary Emancipation Proclamation, February 4, 2016, accessed Feb. 4, 2016, http://www.archives.gov/exhibits/american_originals_iv/sections/preliminary_emancipation_proclamation.html#.

204 Abraham Lincoln "The Emancipation Proclamation, A Transcription," January 1, 1863.

205 Johnson, *A History of the American People*, 473

206 "Emancipation Proclamation," Abraham Lincoln Online, Speeches & Writings accessed Jan. 7, 2014, http://www.abrahamlincolnonline.org/lincoln/speeches/emancipate.htm.

207 "Civil War Casualties" *Historynet*, accessed Jan. 7, 2014.

208 U.S. Cont. art. I, §2, cl. 1.

209 U.S. Const. amend. XIV, §1.

210 Johnson, *A History of the American People*, 656 .

211 Johnson, *A History of the American People*, 657.

212 *Leser v, Garnett*, 258 U.S. 130 (1922),

213 *Oregon v. Mitchell*, 400 U.S. 112 (1970).

214 "Amendment XXVII," in *The Charters of Freedom Constitution of the United States* accessed Mar. 10, 2015, http://www.archives.gov/exhibits/charters/constitution_amendment_27.html.

215 Richard B. Bernstein, "The Sleeper Wake: The History an Legacy of the Twenty-Seventh Amendment." *Fordham Law Review* . vol 6, issue 3, (1992), 535.

216 Ibid., 539-540.

217 Walton and Rockoff, *History of the American Economy*, 166.

218 Ibid., 171.

219 Ibid.

220 Ibid., 247.

221 Ibid., 250.

222 Ibid., 298.

223 Ibid., 306.

224 Ibid., 319.

225 Larry Schweikart and Michael Allen Larry, *A Patriot's History of the United States*. (NY: Sentinel, 2004), 254.

226 Ibid.

227 Ibid., 255.

228 Ibid.

229 Walton and Rockoff, *History of the American Economy*, 322.

230 Ibid., 299.

231 Ibid., 328.

232 Johnson, *A History of the American People*, 608.

233 Madison, *The Federalist Papers*, No. 22, 128.

234 *McCulloch v. Maryland*, 17 U.S. 316, 431 (1819).

235 U.S. Const. art. I, sec. 10, cl 2

236 "The Revolutionary War to the War of 1812, *Tax History Museum: 1777-1785*, (Tax Analyst, 2014), accessed Nov. 27, 2014, http://www.taxhistory.org/www/website.nsf/Web/THM1777?OpenDocument.

237 "The Civil War," *Tax History Museum: 1861-1865*, (Tax Analyst, 2014), accessed Nov. 27, 2014, http://www.taxhistory.org/www/website.nsf/Web/THM1777?OpenDocument.

238 Ibid.

239 "Reconstruction to the Spanish-American War," *Tax History Museum: 1866-1900*, (Tax Analyst, 2014), accessed Npv. 28, 2014, http://www.taxhistory.org/www/website.nsf/Web/THM1866?OpenDocument.

240 *Springer v. U.S.*, 102 U.S. 586 (1880)

241 Alexander Hamilton in *Springer v. U.S.*, 102 U.S. 586, 597-598 (1880); original source Alexander Hamilton, *Carriage Tax*, Feb. 24, 1795.

242 *Springer*, 102 U.S. at 599.

243 Ibid,, 600.

244 Ibid., 602.

245 Ibid.

246 "Reconstruction to the Spanish-American War," accessed Nov. 28, 2014.

247 *Pollock v. Farmers Loan Trust Co I*, 157 U.S. 429 (1895); *Pollock v. Farmers Loan Trust Co II*, 158 U.S. 601 (1895).

248 *Pollock, II.*, 158 U.S. 601, 618 (1895) .

249 Ibid., 618.

250 Sheldon D. Pollack, "Origins of the Modern Income Tax, 1894-1913," *The Tax Lawyer*, vol 66. no. 2. (2013), 301-302.

251 "The Income Tax Archives," *Tax History Museum: 1901-1932*, (Tax Analyst, 2014) accessed Nov. 28, 2014; "Reconstruction to the Spanish-American War," *Tax History Museum: 1866-1900*, (Tax Analyst, 2014) accessed Nov. 28, 2014.

252 "The Income Tax Archives," *Tax History Museum: 1901-1932*, (Tax Analyst, 2014) accessed Nov. 28, 2014; "Reconstruction to the Spanish-American War," *Tax History Museum: 1866-1900*, (Tax Analyst, 2014) accessed Nov. 28, 2014.

253 William H. Riker, "The Senate and American Federalism," *The American Political Science Review*, vol 49, No. 2, 457 (Jun. 1955).

254 Ibid., 456.

255 Ibid., 458.

256 Ibid., 456.

257 Ibid., 461.

258 Ibid., 468.

259 Perrin. "Popular Election of United States Senators," 800.

260 Ibid., at 803.

261 "Oregon Legislature Continues in Deadlock." *Sacramento Daily Union*, vol 92 no. 167, Feb. 5, 1897.

262 "The Election Case of William A. Clark of Monatana (1900)," *United States Senate* . accessed Feb. 16, 2015, https://www.senate.gov/artandhistory/history/common/contested_elections/089William_Clark.htm.

263 Jay S. Bybee, "Ulysses at the Mast: Democracy, Federalism, and the Sirens' Song of the Seventeenth Amendment." *Northwestern Law Review*, vol 91., no. 2, 553 (1997).

264 Ibid., 552.

265 Ibid.

266 Ibid., 554.

267 Schweikart and Larry, *A Patriot's History of the United States*, 528.

268 Ibid., 530.

269 Johnson, *A History of the American People*, 678.

270 Ibid, 683.

271 Marshall J. Breger and Gary J. Edies, "Established by Practice: The Theory and Operation of Independent Federal Agencies," *Administrative Law Review*, vol 52, no. 4, 1117 (Fall 2000).

272 Ibid., 1128-1129.

273 Ibid., 1130.

274 Ibid., 1131.

275 Jonathan Turley, "The Rise of the Fourth Branch of Government," *The Washington Post*, May 24, 2013, accessed Oct. 19, 2015, *https://www.washingtonpost.com/opinions/the-rise-of-the-fourth-branch-of-government/2013/05/24/c7faaad0-c2ed-11e2-9fe2-6ee52d0eb7c1_story.html.*

276 Breger and Edies, "Established by Practice: The Theory and Operation of Independent Federal Agencies," 1137.

277 William G. Howell and David E. Lewis, "Agencies by Presidential Design," *The Journal of Politics*, vol 64, no. 4, 1096 (Nov. 2002), accessed Oct. 20, 2015, *http://home.uchicago.edu/~whowell/papers/Agencies.pdf on October 20, 2015.*

278 Ibid.

279 Ibid., 1099.

280 Ibid.

281 *Gibbons v. Ogden*, 22 U.S. 1 (1824).

282 Ibid., 194.

283 Ibid., 195.

284 Ibid.

285 William E. Leuchtenburg, "When Franklin Roosevelt Clashed with the Supreme Court – and Lost; Buoyed by his reelection but dismayed by rulings of the U.S. Supreme Court, a president overreaches," *Smithsonian Magazine*, May, 2005, accessed Jun. 3, 2015, *http://www.smithsonianmag.com/history/when-franklin-roosevelt-clashed-with-the-supreme-court-and-lost-78497994/?no-ist=&page=2.*

286 Ibid.

287 Ibid.

288 *Wickard v. Filburn* 317 U.S. 111, 114 (1942).

289 Ibid., 114-115.

290 *Ogden*, 22 U.S. 1, at 195.

291 *Filburn* 317 U.S. 111, at 125.

292 *United States v. Lopez*, 514 U.S. 549, 561 (1995).

293 *United States v. Morrison*, 529 U.S. 598, 613 (2000).

294 *Nat'l Fed'n of Indep. Bus. v. Sebelius*, 567 U.S. ___ (2012).

295 *Slaughterhouse Cases*, 83 U.S. 36, 79 (1872).

296 *Adamson v. Cal.*, 332 U.S. 46 (1947).

297 *Hebert v. Louisiana*, 272 U.S. 312, 316 (1926).

298 *Palko v. Connecticut*, 302 U.S. 319 (1937).

299 *McDonald, et al. v. City of Chicago*, No 08-1521 U.S., at fn13 (2010).

300 Nathan A. Adams, IV, "Florida's Blaine Amendment: Goldilocks and the Separate Buy Equal Doctrine," *St. Thomas Law Review*, vol 24, no 1, 1-31 (2011).

301 Ibid., 4.

302 Ibid., 7.

303 *Reynolds v. United States*, 98 U.S. 145 (1878).

304 *Cantwell*, 310 U.S. 296.

305 Ibid., 302-303.

306 Ibid., 303.

307 *Everson v. Board of Education*, 330 U.S. 1 (1947).

308 *McCollum v. Board of Education*, 333 U.S. 203 (1948).

309 *Engel v. Vitale*, 370 U.S. 421 (1962).

310 *Lee v. Weisman*, 505 U.S. 577 (1992).

311 *Santa Fe Independent School District v. Doe*, 530 U.S. 290 (2000).

312 *Wallace v. Jaffree*, 472 U.S. 38 (1985).

313 *Lynch v. Donnelly*, 465 U.S. 668 (1984).

314 *Alleghany v. ACLU*, 492 U.S. 573 (1989).

315 *Stone v. Graham*, 449 U.S. 39 (1980).

316 *Van Orden v. Perry*, 545 U.S. 677 (2004).

317 *McCreary County v. ACLU*, 545 U.S. ____ (2005).

318 *Committee for Public Education v. Nyquist*, 413 U.S. 756 (1973).

319 J. Kingston Pierce, "Scopes Trial," *American History Magazine*, (Aug. 2000) accessed Mar. 16, 2016, http://www.historynet.com/scopes-trial.htm/3.

320 *Kitzmiller v. Dover Area School Dist*, 400 F. Supp. 2d 707 (USDC MD Penn 2005)

321 Smith, "Getting Off On the Wrong Foot and Back On Again: A Reexamination of the History of the Framing of the Religion Clauses of the First Amendment and a Critique of the *Reynolds* And *Everson* Decisions," 682.

322 Ibid., 633.

323 John Marshall in Rodney K. Smith, "Getting Off On the Wrong Foot and Back On Again: A Reexamination of the History of the Framing of the Religion Clauses of the First Amendment And a Critique of the *Reynolds* And *Everson* Decisions," 633.

324 Joseph Story in Rodney K. Smith, "Getting Off On the Wrong Foot and Back On Again: A Reexamination of the History of the Framing of the Religion Clauses of the First Amendment And a Critique of the *Reynolds* And *Everson* Decisions," 633.

325 *Plessy v. Ferguson*, 163 U.S. 537 (1896).

326 Ibid., 559.

327 "Teaching With Documents: Photographs of the 369th Infantry and African American during World War I," *National Archives*, accessed Mar. 1, 2015, http://www.archives.gov/education/lessons/369th-infantry/.

328 Ibid.

329 Jami Bryan, "Fighting for Respect: African-American Soldiers in WWI," *Military History on Line.com* accessed Mar. 18, 2015, http://www.militaryhistoryonline.com/wwi/articles/fightingforrespect.aspx.

330 "African Americans in World War II Fighting for a Double Victory," *Nationalww2museum.org* accessed Mar. 26, 2015, http://www.nationalww2museum.org/assets/pdfs/african-americans-in-world.pdf.

331 "Lynchings, by Year and Race, 1882-1968," *The Charles Chestnut Digital Archive* accessed Mar. 29, 2015, http://www.chesnuttarchive.org/classroom/lynching_table_year.html.

332 *Murray v. Pearson*, 169 Md. 478 (1936).

333 "Montgomery Bus Boycott (1955-1956) Martin Luther King and the Global Freedom Struggle" *King Encyclopedia* accessed Apr. 4, 2015.

334 *Browder v. Gayle*, 142 F Supp. 707 (AL ND June 5, 1956).

335 Chris Austin "On Violence and Nonviolence: The Civil Rights Movement in Mississippi," *Mississippi History Now*. accessed Apr. 20, 2015, http://mshistorynow.mdah.state.ms.us/articles/62/the-civil-rights-movement-in-mississippi-on-violence-and-nonviolence.

336 Civil Rights Memorial, (Southern Poverty Law Center) accessed Apr. 23, 2015, http://www.splcenter.org/civil-rights-memorial/civil-rights-martyrs; "John Earl Reese," The Civil Rights and Restorative Justice Project (Northeastern University College of Law) accessed Apr. 23, 2015, http://nuweb9.neu.edu/civilrights/john-earl-reese/.

337 Civil Rights Memorial accessed Apr. 23, 2015; Adam Nossiter, "Murder, Memory and the Klan: A special report; Widow Inherits a Confession To a 36-Year-Old Hate Crime." The *New York Times*, Sept. 4, 1993, accessed Apr. 24, 2015, http://www.nytimes.com/1993/09/04/us/murder-memory-klan-special-report-widow-inherits-confession-36-year-old-hate.html.

338 Austin "On Violence and Nonviolence: The Civil Rights Movement in Mississippi," accessed Apr. 20, 2015.

339 Austin, "On Violence and Nonviolence: The Civil Rights Movement in Mississippi," Apr. 20, 2015.

340 "1963 Birmingham Bombing Fast Facts," *CNN Library*, accessed Apr. 24, 2015, http://www.cnn.com/2013/06/13/us/1963-birmingham-church-bombing-fast-facts/.

341 Ibid.

342 Ibid.

343 Robert F. Williams, *Negros with Guns*, (NY: Marzani & Munsell, Inc., 1962, reprinted Wayne State University Press, 1998), 14-17.

344 "Negroes with Guns: Rob Williams and Black Power," *Independent Lens WEDU*, accessed Apr. 26, 2015, http://www.pbs.org/independentlens/negroeswith-guns/rob.html.

345 Malcolm X, in Nam Nguyen, *The United States Presidents and Government* (Nam Nguyen, 2015).

346 *Heart of Atlanta Motel v. United States*, 379 U.S. 241 (1964).

347 *Katzenbach v. McClung*, 379 U.S. 294 (1964).

348 Walter C. Rucker and James N. Upton, *Encyclopedia of American Race Riots*, vol 2, (Westport, CT: G.eewood Press, 2007) 478-480, accessed Apr. 29, 2015.

349 Rucker and Upton, *Encyclopedia of American Race Riots*, 478-480, accessed Apr. 29, 2015.

350 Charles A. Gallagher and Cameron D. Lippard, *Race and Racism in the United States: An Encyclopedia of the American Mosaic*, (Santa Barbara, CA: ABC-CLIO, LLC, 2014), 703-707.

351 Hubert G. Locke, *The Detroit Riot of 1967*, Wayne State University Press, 1969, 45.

352 "Selma to Montgomery March (1965)," Martin Luther King and the Global Freedom Struggle, accessed May 2, 2015, http://mlk-kpp01.stanford.edu/index.php/encyclopedia/encyclopedia/enc_selma_to_montgomery_march.

353 "Jackson, Jimmie Lee (1938-1965)," Martin Luther King and the Global Freedom Struggle, accessed on May 2, 2015, http://mlk-kpp01.stanford.edu/index.php/encyclopedia/encyclopedia/enc_selma_to_montgomery_march.

354 "Selma to Montgomery March (1965)," accessed May 2, 2015.

355 "1,300 Members Participate in Memphis Garbage Strike (February 1968) Wurf Heads Union Negotiating Team Seeking Pay Hike" American Federation of State, County, and Municipal Employees, accessed Apr. 26, 2016, https://web.archive.org/web/20061102004632/http://www.afscme.org/about/1529.cfm.

356 "This Day in History, April 4," *History*, accessed Apr. 26, 2016, http://www.history.com/this-day-in-history/dr-king-is-assassinated.

357 Gerard Posner, "The Truth About Memphis, Washingtonpost.com, (1998), accessed Apr. 26, 2016, http://www.washingtonpost.com/wp-srv/national/longterm/mlk/memphis/memphis.htm.

358 Robert W Kweit and Mary G. Kweit, *People and Politics in Urban America*, 2d ed. (New York: Garland Publishing, 1999), 81 .

359 *Brown v. Board of Education of Topeka*, 349 U.S. 294.

360 Ibid., 349.

361 "History of the Federal Judiciary, *Bush v. Orleans Parish School Board and the Desegregation of New Orleans Schools*," Historical Documents; The Southern Manifesto, accessed May 23, 2015, http://www.fjc.gov/history/home.nsf/page/tu_bush_doc_6.html on May 23, 2015.

362 Ibid.

363 Ibid.

364 Anthony Lewis, "President Sends Troops to Little Rock, Federalizes Arkansas National Guard; Tells Nation He Acted to Avoid An Anarchy," The *New York Times*, Sept. 25, 195,) 1.

365 "Autherine Lucy," *Encyclopedia of Alabama*, accessed May 28, 2015, http://www.encyclopediaofalabama.org/article/h-2489.

366 "Stand in the Schoolhouse Door," *Encyclopedia of Alabama*, accessed May 28, 2015, http://www.encyclopediaofalabama.org/article/h-2489.

367 "Autherine Lucy," accessed May 28, 2015.

368 "Thomas B. Stanley," *Encyclopedia of Virginia* (Virginia Foundation for the Humanities) accessed May 24, 2015, http://www.encyclopediavirginia.org/Stanley_Thomas_Bahnson_1890-1970#start_entry.

369 "Virginia's 'Massive Resistance to School Desegregation," *The University of Virginia's Digital Resources for United States History*, accessed May 24, 2015, http://www2.vcdh.virginia.edu/xslt/servlet/XSLTServlet?xml=/xml_docs/solguide/Essays/essay13a.xml&xsl=/xml_docs/solguide/sol_new.xsl§ion=essay.

370 Ibid.

371 Ibid.

372 "The Closing of Prince Edward County's Schools," Virginia Historical Society, accessed May 24, 2015, http://www.vahistorical.org/collections-and-resources/virginia-history-explorer/civil-rights-movement-virginia/closing-prince.

373 *Griffin v. School Board*, 377 U.S. 218, 225 (1964).

374 "Virginia's 'Massive Resistance' to School Desegregation," accessed May 24, 2015.

375 Ibid.

376 *Green v. School Board of Kent County*, 391 U.S. 430, 432-433 (1968).

377 Ibid., 434-435.

378 Ibid.

379 Ibid., 441.

380 Ibid., 438.

381 Ibid., 439.

382 Ibid., 430.

383 Swann v. Charlotte-Mecklenburg Bd. of Educ. 402 U.S. 1, 8 (1971).

384 Ibid., 9.

385 Ibid., 10.

386 Swann v. Charlotte-Mecklenburg Bd. of Educ. 402 U.S. 1 (1971).

387 *Milliken v. Bradley*, 418 U.S. 717, at 741 (1974).

388 William H. Frey, "Central City White Flight: Racial and Nonracial Causes," *American Sociological Review*, vol. 44, no. 3 (Jun., 1979), 425-448.

389 Frey, "Central City White Flight: Racial and Nonracial Causes"; "School Busing," (Virginia Historical Society) accessed May 31, 2015, http://www.vahistorical.org/collections-and-resources/virginia-history-explorer/civil-rights-movement-virginia/massive.

390 Gene Schlickman, "The Kerner Commission and the Search for Answers," *The Chicago Tribune*, March 11, 1992.

391 Report of the National Advisory Commission on Civil Disorders, Summary of Report, March 1, 1968, accessed May 2, 2015, http://www.eisenhowerfoundation.org/docs/kerner.pdf (May 2, 2015); Vernon N. Briggs, Jr, "Report of the National Advisory Commission on Civil Disorders: Review Article," DigitalCommons@ILR, (Cornell University ILR School, from Journal of Economic Issues, 2, 200-201, 1968) accessed May 2, 2015, http://digitalcommons.ilr.cornell.edu/cgi/viewcontent.cgi?article=1047&-context=hrpubs.

392 Briggs, "Report of the National Advisory Commission on Civil Disorders: Review Article," accessed May 2, 2015.

393 Robert Woodson, Sr, "DIFFERENT CAUSES OF POVERTY REQUIRE DIFFERENT SOLUTIONS" in The Kerner Commission Report, Stephan Thernstrom, Fred Siegel and Robert Woodson, Heritage Lecture Series Lecture #619 on Poverty and Inequality, Jun. 24, 1998, accessed May 5, 2015, http://www.heritage.org/research/lecture/the-kerner-commission-report.

394 Ibid.

395 Lyndon B. Johnson, Executive Order Number 11246, Sept. 28, 1965.

396 Lyndon B. Johnson, Commencement Address, Howard University, Jun. 4, 1965.

397 Kevin L. Yuill, *Richard Nixon and the Rise of Affirmative Action: The Pursuit of Racial Equality in an Era of Limits*, (Lanham, Maryland: Rowman & Littlefield Publishers, Inc., 2006), 135.

398 *Contractors Association of Eastern PA v. Secretary of Labor*, 442 F.2d 159 (1971).

399 Ibid.

400 Ibid.

401 *Regents of Univ. of California v. Bakke*, 438 U.S. 265 (1978).

402 *Fullilove et al. v. Klutznick, Secretary of Commerce et al.*, 448 US 448 (1980).

403 Ibid., 532.

404 Ibid., 552-553.

405 Ibid., 553.

406 *Wygant v. Jackson Board of Education*, 468 U.S. 267 (1986).

407 *City of Richmond v. Croson*, 488 U.S. 469 (1989).

408 Ibid.

409 William J. Clinton, Memorandum of Affirmative Action, Jul. 19, 1995.

410 *Hopwood, et al. v. State of Texas, et al.*, 78 F.3d 932, 944 (5th Cir. 1996).

411 *Smith v. University of Wash. Law School*, 233 F.3d 1188 (CA9 2000).

412 *Gratz v. Bollinger*, 539 U.S. 244 (2003).

413 Ibid.

414 *Grutter v. Bollinger et al.*, 539 U.S. 306 (2003).

415 Ibid.

416 Proposition 209: Text of Proposed Law, 1996.

417 *Schuette v. Coalition to Defend Affirmative Action*, 547 US __ (2014).

418 Table 1.1 Summary of Receipts, Outlays, and Surpluses or Deficits 1789-2020 , Office of Management and Budget, The White House, accessed Sept. 2, 2015, https://www.whitehouse.gov/omb/budget/Historicals (September 2, 2015).

419 Ibid.

420 Ibid.

421 Ibid.

422 "Historical Background and Development of Social Security," Social security Administration, accessed Oct. 4, 2015, http://www.ssa.gov/history/briefhistory3.html.

423 Table 13.1- Cash Income, Outgo, and Balances of the Social Security and Medicare Trust Funds: 1936-2020, Office of Management and Budget, The White House accessed Oct. 4, 2015, https://www.whitehouse.gov/omb/budget/Historicals.

424 CBO's 2014 Long-Term Projections for Social Security: Additional Information,, CBO, Dec., 2014, 2, accessed Oct. 14, 2015, https://www.cbo.gov/sites/default/files/113th-congress-2013-2014/reports/49795-Social_Security_Update.pdf.

425 Table 13.1- Cash Income, Outgo, and Balances of the Social Security and

Medicare Trust Funds: 1936-2020, accessed Oct. 4, 2015.

426 Paul N. Van De Water, "Medicare is not 'Bankrupt.' Health Reform Has Improved Program's Financing ," Center on Budget and Policy Priorities: Jul. 30, 2015, accessed Oct. 4, 2015, http://www.cbpp.org/research/health/medicare-is-not-bankrupt.

427 Sven Larson, "Federal Funds and State Independence," (The Heritage Foundation, May 15, 2008) accessed Oct. 6, 2015, http://www.heritage.org/research/reports/2008/05/federal-funds-and-state-fiscal-independence.

428 Federal Spending in the States 2004-2013, The Pew Charitable Trusts: Dec. 2, 2014) accessed Oct. 6, 2015, http://www.pewtrusts.org/en/research-and-analysis/issue-briefs/2014/12/federal-spending-in-the-states.

429 Ibid.

430 Mark V. Tushet, "New Forms of Judicial Review and the Persistence of Rights-And Democracy-Based Worries," *Wake Forest Law Review* no. 38, (2003), 813-814.

431 Ibid., 818-819.

432 Ibisd., 819.

433 Personal experience, 2015.

434 South Carolina Senate Resolution S. 787, 2015.

435 E. Ann Carson, "Prisoners in 2013" Table 14," Bureau of Justice Statistics, U.S. Department of Justice: Sept. 2014, accessed Nov. 10, 2015, http://www.bjs.gov/content/pub/pdf/p13.pdf.

436 Ibid.

437 Leah Sakala, "Breaking Down Mass Incarceration in the 2010 Census: State-by-State Incarceration Rates by Race/Ethnicity," Prison Policy Initiative. accessed Nov. 5, 2015, http://www.prisonpolicy.org/reports/rates.html.

438 John Nunley, Adam Pugh, et al, "An Examination of Racial Discrimination in the Labor Market for Recent College Graduates: Estimates from the Field," (Auburn U. Dept. of Economics Working Paper Series: Mar 24, 2014), accessed Nov. 2, 2015, http://cla.auburn.edu/econwp/Archives/2014/2014-06.pdf.

439 "Labor Force Characteristics by Race and Ethnicity, 2013, Report 1050" BLS Reports (Wash. D.C.: U.S. Bureau of Labor Statistics, Aug. 2014). accessed Nov. 2, 2015, http://www.bls.gov/cps/cpsrace2013.pdf.

440 Ibid.

441 Ibid.

442 Frank Newport in "U.S., 87% Approve of Black-White Marriage, vs. 4% in 1958," (Gallup: Jul. 25, 2013) accessed Oct. 25, 2013, http://www.gallup.com/poll/163697/approve-marriage-blacks-whites.aspx.

443 Ibid.

444 "Multiracial in America; Proud, Diverse, and Growing in Numbers," (Pew Research Center Social & Demographic Trends: Jun. 11, 2015), accessed Oct. 25, 2015, http://www.pewsocialtrends.org/2015/06/11/multiracial-in-america/.

445 Ingrid Gould Ellen, Keren Horn and Katherine O'Regan, "Pathways to Integration: Examining Changes in the Prevalence of Racially Integrated Neighborhoods," *Cityscape: A Journal of Policy Development and Research*, vol. 14, no. (Wash., D.C.: Dept. of Housing and Urban Development, 2012), 33-53.

446 Rachel M. Sharruck, and Rose M. Kreider, "Social and Economic Characteristics of Unmarried Women With a Recent Birth," *American Community Survey Reports*, (Wash., D.C.,: United States Census Bureau: May 2013) 5. accessed Nov. 4, 2015, https://www.census.gov/prod/2013pubs/acs-21.pdf.

447 "Marriage and Divorce: Patterns by Gender, Race, and Educational Attainment . Monthly Labor Review, Table 3," (Wash., D.C.: United States Bureau of Labor Statistics, Oct. 2013), accessed Nov. 5, 2015, http://www.bls.gov/opub/mlr/2013/article/pdf/marriage-and-divorce-patterns-by-gender-race-and-educational-attainment.pdf.

448 Zakia Redd, Tachilin Sanchez Karver, et al., "Two Generations in Poverty: Status and Trends Among Parents and Children in the United States, 2000-2010." *Child Trends Research Brief*, 2, (Nov., 2011) accessed Nov. 4, 2015, http://www.childtrends.org/wp-content/uploads/2011/11/2011-25DUPGenerationsInPoverty.pdf.

449 Ibid.

450 Anderson Moore, Redd, et al., Children in Poverty: Trends, Consequences, and Policy Options. Child Trends Research Brief, Fig. 1, accessed Nov. 4, 2015.

451 E. Ann Carson, "Prisoners in 2013" Table 15, accessed Nov. 10, 2015.

452 John P Hoffman and Robert A. Johnson. 1998. "A National Portrait of Family Structure and Adolescent Drug Use." *Journal of Marriage and Family*, vol 60, no 3. (1998), 633-645.

453 Stephen Demuth and Susan L. Brown, "Family Structure, Family Processes, and Adolescent Delinquency: The Significance of Parental Absence vs. Parental Gender." *Journal of Research in Crime and Delinquency*, vol 41, no 1, 58-81 (2004).

454 Robert L Flewelling, and Karl E. Bauman, "Family Structure as a Predictor of Initial Substance Use and Sexual Intercourse in Early Adolescence," *Journal of Marriage and Family* vol 52, no. 1, (Feb. 1990), 171-181.

455 Cynthia C. Harper and Sara S. McLanahan, "Father Absence and Youth Incarceration," *J. of Research on Adolescence*, vol. 14, no. 3,(Sept. 2004), 369-397.

456 Gray, Perl, et al., "Marriage in the Catholic Church: A Survey of U.S. Catholics," accessed Nov. 5, 2015.

Appendix 1

The Declaration of Independence

IN CONGRESS, July 4, 1776.

The unanimous Declaration of the thirteen United States of America:

When in the Course of human events, it becomes necessary for one people to dissolve the political bands which have connected them with another, and to assume among the powers of the earth, the separate and equal station to which the Laws of Nature and of Nature's God entitle them, a decent respect to the opinions of mankind requires that they should declare the causes which impel them to the separation.

We hold these truths to be self-evident, that all men are created equal, that they are endowed by their Creator with certain unalienable Rights, that among these are Life, Liberty and the pursuit of Happiness.—That to secure these rights, Governments are instituted among Men, deriving their just powers from the consent of the governed, —That whenever any Form of Government becomes destructive of these ends, it is the Right of the People to alter or to abolish it, and to institute new Government, laying its foundation on such principles and organizing its powers in such form, as to them shall seem most likely to effect their Safety and Happiness. Prudence, indeed, will dictate that Governments long established should not be changed for light and transient causes; and accordingly all experience hath shewn, that mankind are more disposed to suffer, while evils are sufferable, than to right themselves by abolishing the forms to which they are accustomed. But when a long train of abuses and usurpations, pursuing invariably the same Object evinces a design to reduce them under absolute Despotism, it is their right, it is their duty, to throw off such Government, and to provide new Guards for their future security.--Such has been the patient sufferance of these Colonies; and such is now the necessity which constrains them to alter their former Systems of Government. The history of the present King of Great Britain is a history of repeated injuries and usurpations, all having in direct object the establishment of an absolute Tyranny over these States. To prove this, let Facts be submitted to a candid world.

He has refused his Assent to Laws, the most wholesome and necessary for the public good.

He has forbidden his Governors to pass Laws of immediate and pressing importance, unless suspended in their operation till his Assent should be obtained; and when so suspended, he has utterly neglected to attend to them.

He has refused to pass other Laws for the accommodation of large districts of people, unless those people would relinquish the right of Representation in the Legislature, a right inestimable to them and formidable to tyrants only.

He has called together legislative bodies at places unusual, uncomfortable, and distant from the depository of their public Records, for the sole purpose of fatiguing them into compliance with his measures.

He has dissolved Representative Houses repeatedly, for opposing with manly firmness his invasions on the rights of the people.

He has refused for a long time, after such dissolutions, to cause others to be elected; whereby the Legislative powers, incapable of Annihilation, have returned to the People at large for their exercise; the State remaining in the mean time exposed to all the dangers of invasion from without, and convulsions within.

He has endeavoured to prevent the population of these States; for that purpose obstructing the Laws for Naturalization of Foreigners; refusing to pass others to encourage their migrations hither, and raising the conditions of new Appropriations of Lands.

He has obstructed the Administration of Justice, by refusing his Assent to Laws for establishing Judiciary powers.

He has made Judges dependent on his Will alone, for the tenure of their offices, and the amount and payment of their salaries.

He has erected a multitude of New Offices, and sent hither swarms of Officers to harrass our people, and eat out their substance.

He has kept among us, in times of peace, Standing Armies without the Consent of our legislatures.

He has affected to render the Military independent of and superior to the Civil power.

He has combined with others to subject us to a jurisdiction foreign to our constitution, and unacknowledged by our laws; giving his Assent to their Acts of pretended Legislation:

For Quartering large bodies of armed troops among us:

For protecting them, by a mock Trial, from punishment for any Murders which they should commit on the Inhabitants of these States:

For cutting off our Trade with all parts of the world:

For imposing Taxes on us without our Consent:

For depriving us in many cases, of the benefits of Trial by Jury:

For transporting us beyond Seas to be tried for pretended offences.

For abolishing the free System of English Laws in a neighbouring Province, establishing therein an Arbitrary government, and enlarging its Boundaries so as to render it at once an example and fit instrument for introducing the same absolute rule into these Colonies:

For taking away our Charters, abolishing our most valuable Laws, and altering fundamentally the Forms of our Governments:

For suspending our own Legislatures, and declaring themselves invested with power to legislate for us in all cases whatsoever.

He has abdicated Government here, by declaring us out of his Protection and waging War against us.

He has plundered our seas, ravaged our Coasts, burnt our towns, and destroyed the lives of our people.

He is at this time transporting large Armies of foreign Mercenaries to compleat the works of death, desolation and tyranny, already begun with circumstances of Cruelty & perfidy scarcely paralleled in the most barbarous ages, and totally unworthy the Head of a civilized nation.

He has constrained our fellow Citizens taken Captive on the high Seas to bear Arms against their Country, to become the executioners of their friends and Brethren, or to fall themselves by their Hands.

He has excited domestic insurrections amongst us, and has endeavoured to bring on the inhabitants of our frontiers, the merciless Indian Savages, whose known rule of warfare, is an undistinguished destruction of all ages, sexes and conditions.

In every stage of these Oppressions We have Petitioned for Redress in the most humble terms: Our repeated Petitions have been answered only by repeated injury. A Prince whose character is thus marked by every act which may define a Tyrant, is unfit to be the ruler of a free people.

Nor have We been wanting in attentions to our Brittish brethren. We have warned them from time to time of attempts by their legislature to extend an unwarrantable jurisdiction over us. We have reminded them of the circumstances of our emigration and settlement here. We have appealed to their native justice and magnanimity, and we have conjured them by the ties of our common kindred to disavow these usurpations, which, would inevitably interrupt our connections and correspondence. They too have been deaf to the voice of justice and of consanguinity. We must, therefore, acquiesce in the necessity, which denounces our Separation, and hold them, as we hold the rest of mankind, Enemies in War, in Peace Friends.

We, therefore, the Representatives of the united States of America, in General Congress, Assembled, appealing to the Supreme Judge of the world for the rectitude of our intentions, do, in the Name, and by Authority of the good People of these Colonies, solemnly publish and declare, That these United Colonies are, and of Right ought to be Free and Independent States; that they are Absolved from all Allegiance to the British Crown, and that all political connection between them and the State of Great Britain, is and ought to be totally dissolved; and that as Free and Independent States, they have full Power to levy War, conclude Peace, contract Alliances, establish Commerce, and to do all other Acts and Things which Independent States may of right do. And for the support of this Declaration, with a firm reliance on the protection of divine Providence, we mutually pledge to each other our Lives, our Fortunes and our sacred Honor.

The 56 signatures on the Declaration appear in the positions indicated:

Column 1:
Georgia: Button Gwinnett, Lyman Hall, George Walton

Column 2:
North Carolina: William Hooper, Joseph Hewes, John Penn
South Carolina: Edward Rutledge, Thomas Heyward, Jr., Thomas Lynch, Jr., Arthur Middleton

Column 3:
Massachusetts: John Hancock
Maryland: Samuel Chase, William Paca, Thomas Stone, Charles Carroll of Carrollton
Virginia: George Wythe, Richard Henry Lee, Thomas Jefferson, Benjamin Harrison, Thomas Nelson, Jr., Francis Lightfoot Lee, Carter Braxton

Column 4

Pennsylvania: Robert Morris, Benjamin Rush,
Benjamin Franklin, John Morton, George Clymer
James Smith, George Taylor, James Wilson
George Ross

Delaware: Caesar Rodney, George Read, Thomas McKean

Column 5

New York: William Floyd, Philip Livingston, Francis Lewis
Lewis Morris

New Jersey: Richard Stockton, John Witherspoon
Francis Hopkinson, John Hart, Abraham Clark

Column 6

New Hampshire: Josiah Bartlett, William Whipple

Massachusetts: Samuel Adams, John Adams
Robert Treat Paine, Elbridge Gerry

Rhode Island: Stephen Hopkins, William Ellery

Connecticut: Roger Sherman, Samuel Huntington
William Williams, Oliver Wolcott

New Hampshire: Matthew Thornton

Appendix 2

The Articles of Confederation

To all to whom these presents shall come,

We, the undersigned Delegates of the States affixed to our Names send greeting:

Whereas the Delegates of the United States of America in Congress assembled did on the fifteenth day of November in the year of our Lord one thousand seven hundred and seventy seven, and in the second year of the Independence of America agree to certain articles of Confederation and perpetual Union between the States of Newhampshire, Massachusetts-bay, Rhodeisland and Providence Plantations, Connecticut, New York, New Jersey, Pennsylvania, Delaware, Maryland, Virginia, North Carolina, South Carolina, and Georgia in the Words following, viz.

ARTICLES OF CONFEDERATION AND PERPETUAL UNION,

between the States of Newhampshire, Massachusetts-bay, Rhode Island and Providence Plantations, Connecticut, New York, New Jersey, Pennsylvania, Delaware, Maryland, Virginia, North Carolina, South Carolina, and Georgia.

Article I. The style of this confederacy shall be, "THE UNITED STATES OF AMERICA."

Article II. Each state retains its sovereignty, freedom and independence, and every Power, Jurisdiction and right, which is not by this confederation expressly delegated to the United States, in Congress assembled.

Article III. The said States hereby severally enter into a firm league of friendship with each other, for their common defence, the security of their liberties, and their mutual and general welfare, binding themselves to assist each other, against all force offered to, or attacks made upon them, or any of them, on account of religion, sovereignty, trade, or any other pretence whatever.

Article IV. §1. The better to secure and perpetuate mutual friendship and intercourse among the people of the different States in this Union, the free inhabitants of each of these States, paupers, vagabonds and fugitives from Justice excepted, shall be entitled to all privileges and immunities of free citizens in the several States; and the people of each state shall have free ingress and regress to and from any other State, and shall enjoy therein all the privileges of trade and commerce, subject to the same duties, impositions and restrictions as the inhabitants thereof respectively, provided that such restrictions shall not extend so far as to prevent the removal of property imported into any state, to any other State of which the Owner is an inhabitant; provided also that no imposition, duties or restriction shall be laid by any State, on the property of the United States, or either of them.

§2. If any person guilty of, or charged with, treason, felony, or other high misdemeanor in any State, shall flee from justice, and be found in any of the United States, he shall upon demand of the Governor or executive power of the State from which he fled, be delivered up, and removed to the state having jurisdiction of his offence.

§3. Full faith and credit shall be given in each of these States to the records, acts and judicial proceedings of the courts and magistrates of every other State.

Article V. §1. For the more convenient management of the general interests of the United States, delegates shall be annually appointed in such manner as the legislature of each state shall direct, to meet in Congress on the first Monday in November, in every year, with a power reserved to each state to recall its delegates, or any of them, at any time within the year, and to send others in their stead, for the remainder of the year.

§2. No State shall be represented in Congress by less than two, nor by more than seven members; and no person shall be capable of being delegate for more than three years, in any term of six years; nor shall any person, being a delegate, be capable of holding any office under the United States, for which he, or another for his benefit receives any salary, fees or emolument of any kind.

§3. Each State shall maintain its own delegates in a meeting of the states, and while they act as members of the committee of the States.

§4. In determining questions in the United States, in Congress assembled, each State shall have one vote.

§5. Freedom of speech and debate in Congress shall not be impeached or questioned in any Court, or place out of Congress, and the members of congress shall be protected in their persons from arrests and imprisonments, during the time of their going to and from, and attendance on congress, except for treason, felony, or breach of the peace.

Article VI. §1. No State, without the consent of the United States, in congress assembled, shall send any embassy to, or receive any embassy from, or enter into any conference, agreement, alliance, or treaty, with any king, prince or State; nor shall any person holding any office of profit or trust under the United States, or any of them, accept of any present, emolument, office, or title of any kind whatever, from any king, prince, or foreign State; nor shall the United States, in congress assembled, or any of them, grant any title of nobility.

§2. No two or more States shall enter into any treaty, confederation, or alliance whatever between them, without the consent of the United States, in congress assembled, specifying accurately the purposes for which the same is to be entered into, and how long it shall continue.

§3. No State shall lay any imposts or duties, which may interfere with any stipulations in treaties, entered into by the United States in Congress assembled, with any king, prince, or State, in pursuance of any treaties already proposed by congress, to the courts of France and Spain.

§4. No vessels of war shall be kept up in time of peace, by any State, except such number only, as shall be deemed necessary by the United States, in Congress assembled, for the defence of such State, or its trade; nor shall any body of forces be kept up, by any State, in time of peace, except such number only as, in the judgment of the united states, in Congress assembled, shall be deemed requisite to garrison the forts necessary for the defence of such state; but every state shall always keep up a well regulated and disciplined militia, sufficiently armed and accounted, and shall provide and constantly have ready for use, in public stores, a due number of field pieces and tents, and a proper quantity of arms, ammunition, and camp equipage.

§5. No State shall engage in any war without the consent of the United States in congress assembled, unless such State be actually invaded by enemies, or shall have received certain advice of a resolution being formed by some nation of Indians to invade such State, and the danger is so imminent as not to admit of a delay till the united states in congress assembled, can be consulted: nor shall any state grant commissions to any ships or vessels of war, nor letters of marque or reprisal, except it be after a declaration of war by the United States in Congress assembled, and then only against the kingdom or State, and the subjects thereof, against which war has been so declared, and under such regulations as shall be established by the United States in Congress assembled, unless such State be infested by pirates, in which case vessels of war may be fitted out for that occasion, and kept so long as the danger shall continue, or until the United States in Ccongress assembled shall determine otherwise.

Article VII. When land forces are raised by any State, for the common defence, all officers of or under the rank of colonel, shall be appointed by the legislature of each State respectively by whom such forces shall be raised, or in such manner as such state shall direct, and all vacancies shall be filled up by the State which first made appointment.

Article VIII. All charges of war, and all other expenses that shall be incurred for the common defence or general welfare, and allowed by the United States in Congress assembled, shall be defrayed out of a common treasury, which shall be supplied by the several States, in proportion to the value of all land within each State, granted to or surveyed for any person, as such land and the buildings and improvements thereon shall be estimated, according to such mode as the United States, in Congress assembled, shall, from time to time, direct and appoint. The taxes for paying that proportion shall be laid and levied by the authority and direction of the legislatures of the several States within the time agreed upon by the United States in congress assembled.

Article IX. §1. The United States, in Congress assembled, shall have the sole and exclusive right and power of determining on peace and war, except in the cases mentioned in the sixth Article, of sending and receiving ambassadors, entering into treaties and alliances, provided that no treaty of commerce shall be made, whereby the legislative power of the respective States shall be restrained from imposing such imposts and duties on foreigners, as their own people are subjected to, or from prohibiting the exportation or importation of any species of goods or commodities whatsoever; of establishing rules for deciding, in all cases, what captures on land or water shall be legal, and in what manner prizes taken by land or naval forces in the service of the United States, shall be divided or appropriated; of granting letters of marque and reprisal in times of peace; appointing courts for the trial of piracies and felonies committed on the high seas; and establishing courts; for receiving and determining finally appeals in all cases of captures; provided that no member of Congress shall be appointed a judge of any of the said courts.

§2. The United States, in Congress assembled, shall also be the last resort on appeal, in all disputes and differences now subsisting, or that hereafter may arise between two or more states concerning boundary, jurisdiction, or any other cause whatever; which authority shall always be exercised in the manner following. Whenever the legislative or executive authority, or lawful agent of any State in controversy with another, shall present a petition to Congress, stating the matter in question, and praying for a hearing, notice thereof shall be given, by order of Congress, to the legislative or executive authority of the other State in controversy, and a day assigned for the appearance of the parties by their lawful agents, who shall then be directed to appoint, by joint consent, commissioners or judges to constitute a court for hearing and determining the matter in question; but if they cannot agree, Congress shall name three persons out of each of the United States, and from the list of such persons each party shall alternately strike out one, the petitioners beginning, until the number shall be reduced to thirteen; and from that number not less than seven, nor more than nine names, as Congress shall direct, shall, in the presence of Congress, be drawn out by lot, and the persons whose names shall be so drawn, or any five of them, shall be commissioners or judges, to hear and finally determine the controversy, so always as a major part of the judges, who shall hear the cause, shall agree in the determination; and if either party shall neglect to attend at the day appointed, without showing reasons which Congress shall judge sufficient, or being present, shall refuse to strike, the Congress shall proceed to nominate three persons out of each State, and the secretary of congress shall strike in behalf of such party absent or refusing; and the judgment and sentence of the court, to be appointed in the manner before prescribed, shall be final and conclusive; and if any of the parties shall refuse to submit to the authority of such court, or to appear or defend their claim or cause, the court shall nevertheless proceed to pronounce sentence, or judgment, which shall in like manner be final and decisive; the judgment or sentence and other proceedings being in either case transmitted to Congress, and lodged among the acts of Congress, for the security of the parties concerned: provided that every commissioner, before he sits in judgment, shall take an oath to be administered by one of the judges of the supreme or superior court of the State where the cause shall be tried, "well and truly to hear and determine the matter in question, according to the best of his judgment, without favour, affection, or hope of reward: "provided, also, that no State shall be deprived of territory for the benefit of the united states.

§3. All controversies concerning the private right of soil claimed under different grants of two or more States, whose jurisdictions as they may respect such lands, and the States which passed such grants are adjusted, the said grants or either of them being at the same time claimed to have originated antecedent to such settlement of jurisdiction, shall, on the petition of either party to the congress of the United States, be finally determined, as near as may be, in the same manner as is before prescribed for deciding disputes respecting territorial jurisdiction between different States.

§4. The United States, in Congress assembled, shall also have the sole and exclusive right and power of regulating the alloy and value of coin struck by their own authority, or by that of the respective States; fixing the standard of weights and measures throughout the United States; regulating the trade and managing all affairs with the Indians, not members of any of the States; provided that the legislative right of any State, within its own limits, be not infringed or violated; establishing and regulating post-offices from one State to another, throughout all the United States, and exacting such postage on the papers passing through the same, as may be requisite to defray the expenses of the said office; appointing all officers of the land forces in the service of the United States, excepting regimental officers; appointing all the officers of the naval forces, and commissioning all officers whatever in the service of the United States; making rules for the government and regulation of the said land and naval forces, and directing their operations.

§5. The United States, in Congress assembled, shall have authority to appoint a committee, to sit in the recess of Congress, to be denominated, "*A Committee of the States*," and to consist of one delegate from each State; and to appoint such other committees and civil officers as may be necessary for managing the general affairs of the united states under their direction; to appoint one of their number to preside; provided that no person be allowed to serve in the office of president more than one year in any term of three years; to ascertain the necessary sums of money to be raised for the service of the United States, and to appropriate and apply the same for defraying the public expenses; to borrow money or emit bills on the credit of the United States, transmitting every half year to the respective States an account of the sums of money so borrowed or emitted; to build and equip a navy; to agree upon the number of land forces, and to make requisitions from each state for its quota, in proportion to the number of white inhabitants in such State, which requisition shall be binding; and thereupon the legislature of each State shall appoint the regimental officers, raise the men, and clothe, arm, and equip them, in a soldier-like manner, at the expense of the United States; and the officers and men so clothed, armed, and equipped, shall march to the place appointed, and within the time agreed on by the United States, in Congress assembled; but if the United States, in Congress assembled, shall, on consideration of circumstances, judge proper that any state should not raise men, or should raise a smaller number than its quota, and that any other State should raise a greater number of men than the quota thereof, such extra number shall be raised, officered, clothed, armed, and equipped in the same manner as the quota of such State, unless the legislature of such State shall judge that such extra number cannot be safely spared out of the same, in which case they shall raise, officer, clothe, arm, and equip, as many of such extra number as they judge can be safely spared. And the officers and men so clothed, armed, and equipped, shall march to the place appointed, and within the time agreed on by the United States in Congress assembled.

§6. The United States, in Congress assembled, shall never engage in a war, nor grant letters of marque and reprisal in time of peace, nor enter into any treaties or alliances, nor coin money, nor regulate the value thereof nor ascertain the sums and expenses necessary for the defence and welfare of the United States, or any of them, nor emit bills, nor borrow money on the credit of the United States, nor appropriate money, nor agree upon the number of vessels of war to be built or purchased, or the number of land or sea forces to be raised, nor appoint a commander in chief of the army or navy, unless nine States assent to the same, nor shall a question on any other point, except for adjourning from day to day, be determined, unless by the votes of a majority of the United States in congress assembled.

§7. The Congress of the United States shall have power to adjourn to any time within the year, and to any place within the United States, so that no period of adjournment be for a longer duration than the space of six months, and shall publish the journal of their proceedings monthly, except such parts thereof relating to treaties, alliances, or military operations, as in their judgment require secrecy; and the yeas and nays of the delegates of each State, on any question, shall be entered on the journal, when it is desired by any delegate; and the delegates of a State, or any of them, at his or their request, shall be furnished with a transcript of the said journal, except such parts as are above excepted, to lay before the legislatures of the several States.

Article X. The committee of the States, or any nine of them, shall be authorized to execute, in the recess of Congress, such of the powers of Congress as the United States, in Congress assembled, by the consent of nine States, shall, from time to time, think expedient to vest them with; provided that no power be delegated to the said committee, for the exercise of which, by the Articles of Confederation, the voice of nine states, in the Congress of the United States assembled, is requisite.

Article XI. Canada acceding to this confederation, and joining in the measures of the United States, shall be admitted into, and entitled to all the advantages of this Union: but no other colony shall be admitted into the same, unless such admission be agreed to by nine States.

Article XII. All bills of credit emitted, monies borrowed, and debts contracted by or under the authority of Congress, before the assembling of the united states, in pursuance of the present confederation, shall be deemed and considered as a charge against the United States, for payment and satisfaction whereof the said United States and the public faith are hereby solemnly pledged.

Article XIII. Every State shall abide by the determinations of the United States, in Congress assembled, on all questions which by this confederation are submitted to them. And the Articles of this confederation shall be inviolably observed by every State, and the union shall be perpetual; nor shall any alteration at any time hereafter be made in any of them, unless such alteration be agreed to in a congress of the United States, and be afterwards confirmed by the legislatures of every State.

And whereas it hath pleased the great Governor of the world to incline the hearts of the legislatures we respectively represent in Congress, to approve of, and to authorize us to ratify the said articles of confederation and perpetual union, Know Ye, that we, the undersigned delegates, by virtue of the power and authority to us given for that purpose, do, by these presents, in the name and in behalf of our respective constituents, fully and entirely ratify and confirm each and every of the said Articles of Confederation and perpetual union, and all and singular the matters and things therein contained. And we do further solemnly plight and engage the faith of our respective constituents, that they shall abide by the determinations of the United States in congress assembled, on all questions, which by the said confederation are submitted to them. And that the articles thereof shall be inviolably observed by the States we respectively represent, and that the union shall be perpetual. In Witness whereof, we have hereunto set our hands, in Congress.

Done at Philadelphia, in the State of Pennsylvania, the 15th day of November, in the year of our Lord 1777, and in the third year of the Independence of America.

Index

Symbols

A

B

C

Q

R

S

T

U

V

W